MW00652481

THE KLEINMAN EDITION

A Torah theme for every day of every week,
blending profound perspectives
from all areas of Torah literature –
Scripture, Mishnah, Jewish Law, Mussar/Ethics,
Tefillah/Prayer, and Hashkafah/Jewish Thought –
collected for daily study.

ArtScroll Series®

THE KLEINMAN EDITION

A TORAH THEME FOR EVERY DAY OF EVERY WEEK FROM ALL AREAS OF TORAH LITERATURE — COLLECTED FOR DAILY STUDY.

Rabbi Yosaif Asher Weiss
General Editor

OF TORAH

VOLUME 4

DAILY STUDY FOR THE WEEKS OF
שמות-בשלח
SHEMOS–BESHALACH

Published by
ARTSCROLL ❖ Mesorah Publications, ltd

FIRST EDITION
First Impression ... December 2006

Published and Distributed by
MESORAH PUBLICATIONS, LTD.
4401 Second Avenue / Brooklyn, N.Y 11232

Distributed in Europe by
LEHMANNS
Unit E, Viking Business Park
Rolling Mill Road
Jarow, Tyne & Wear, NE32 3DP
England

Distributed in Israel by
SIFRIATI / A. GITLER — BOOKS
6 Hayarkon Street
Bnei Brak 51127

Distributed in Australia and New Zealand by
GOLDS WORLDS OF JUDAICA
3-13 William Street
Balaclava, Melbourne 3183
Victoria, Australia

Distributed in South Africa by
KOLLEL BOOKSHOP
Ivy Common
105 William Road
Norwood 2192, Johannesburg, South Africa

ARTSCROLL SERIES®
THE KLEINMAN EDITION — LIMUD YOMI / A DAILY DOSE OF TORAH
VOL. 4: SHEMOS–BESHALACH

ISBN:
ISBN 10: 1-4226-0142-0 (hard cover)
ISBN 13: 978-1-4226-0142-6 (hard cover)

Typography by CompuScribe at ArtScroll Studios, Ltd.

Printed in the United States of America by Noble Book Press Corp.
Bound by Sefercraft, Quality Bookbinders, Ltd., Brooklyn N.Y. 11232

Dedication of This Volume

כֹּה אָמַר ה׳ מָצָא חֵן בַּמִּדְבָּר,
עַם שְׂרִידֵי חָרֶב הָלוֹךְ לְהַרְגִּיעוֹ יִשְׂרָאֵל

So said Hashem: It has found favor in the wilderness,
this people that survived the sword,
as I lead Israel to its tranquility (Jeremiah 31:1).

Never has there been a spiritual wilderness more desolate and threatening than the Soviet Union. And never have there been greater heroes who fought and conquered that desolation than our parents

Rabbi Eliyahu and Anya Essas שליט״א

Our father was a brilliant mathematician with a bright future, but he chose the Creator over the commissars and made himself not only a *talmid chacham*, but an unparalleled leader whose Torah pierced the darkness of Communism and lit up countless lives.

Our mother spent endless hours organizing programs and summer camps for adults and children, while never letting KGB intimidation prevent her from being a magnificent wife and mother.

The KGB was all-powerful, but our parents' will was stronger. With incredible courage and matchless charisma, they blew the breath of life and hope and inspiration into Jews whom they reunited with the faith of their forebears.

Our beloved parents left the Soviet Union for Israel during the week of *Parashas Beshalach* 5746/1986. How fitting, therefore, that we dedicate this volume of the Daily Dose of Torah to them. During these weeks of *Shemos, Va'eira, Bo,* and *Beshalach,* we read of the back-breaking *galus* and the breathtaking miracles of Klal Yisrael's salvation. Our parents lived through the modern manifestation of *galus* and *geulah* — and wrote a glorious chapter in the book of *Am Yisrael Chai.*

Yossi and Bella Essas (Los Angeles)
and their children
Noam Zvi, Hillel Avraham,
Adina Batya, and Ashira Miriam

The Kleinman Edition

**To our fathers and grandfathers, daily Torah study was the first priority.
It is fitting, therefore, that we dedicate this Limud Yomi Series in their memory**

Avrohom Kleinman ז״ל

ר׳ אברהם אייזיק ב״ר אלכסנדר ז״ל

נפ׳ י״ב שבט תשנ״ט

After years of slave labor and concentration camps — years when he risked his life to put on *tefillin* every day! — he courageously rebuilt. Wherever he was — in DP camps, Poughkeepsie, Borough Park, or Forest Hills — he was a one-man *kiruv* movement, before "*kiruv rechokim*" was a familiar phrase. Everyone was drawn to his enthusiasm for Yiddishkeit.

His home was open to anyone in need, even when there was barely enough for family.

All his life he felt close to his Rebbe, the Nitra Rav, and to the father-in-law he never knew; their *sefarim*, *Naos Desheh* and *Lechem Abirim*, were part of our Shabbos table. He was a caring and gentle man whose life was defined by his love of learning Torah, *gemillas chasadim*, *kiruv* work, *hachnasas orchim*, *askanus*, and love for his family. He left a noble legacy that we are honored to perpetuate.

Mendel Indig ז״ל

ר׳ מנחם דוד ב״ר מרדכי שמואל ז״ל

נפ׳ ט׳ אדר ב׳ תשס״ג

"It was as if a *maloch* protected us," he used to say about the dark years of Churban Europa. He lost almost everything — even the *tefillin* that he put on every day until the very end — but he kept his spirit, his *emunah*, his dedication to Torah, and his resolve to rebuild.

He became a living legend of Torah, *chesed*, and service to his Bensonhurst community. His home was open to anyone in need, and there was always enough room for guests. His *succah* was the largest in the neighborhood, and he always found a way to bring endangered relatives to America and help them become established.

After he retired, he devoted himself to learning and bringing others close to Yiddishkeit, especially immigrants from the former Soviet Union, teaching them to put on *tefillin* and reuniting them with the Judaism of their ancestors. It is our privilege to carry on his glorious legacy.

We pay tribute to our mothers

Ethel Kleinman תחי׳

Rose Indig תחי׳

To us and our children and grandchildren — and to all who know them — they are role models of *emunah*, *chesed*, love and wisdom.

Our mothers שיחיו and our fathers ז״ל planted seeds of Torah in America and produced magnificent *doros* of children, grandchildren, and great-grandchildren following their example. May Hashem continue to bless our mothers with good health and many nachas-filled years.

Elly and Brochie Kleinman and their children

Deenie and Yitzy Schuss　Yossie Kleinman　Aliza and Lavey Freedman

and families

PATRONS OF LIMUD YOMI / A DAILY DOSE OF TORAH

With dedication to the principle that Torah study should always be available,
the following generous and visionary patrons
have dedicated volumes of this series:

VOL. 1: BEREISHIS-VAYEIRA / בראשית־וירא

Elly and Brochie Kleinman and family

In memory of their fathers

ר׳ אברהם אייזיק ב״ר אלכסנדר ז״ל – Avrohom Kleinman ז״ל

ר׳ מנחם דוד ב״ר מרדכי שמואל ז״ל – Mendel Indig ז״ל

and יבלח״ט in tribute to their mothers שתחי׳ לאוי״ט

Ethel Kleinman

Rose Indig

VOL. 2: CHAYEI SARAH-VAYISHLACH / חיי שרה־וישלח

Motty and Malka Klein

for the merit of their children שיחי׳

Esther and Chaim Baruch Fogel   Dovid and Chavie   Binyomin Zvi

Elana Leah and Natan Goldstein   Moshe Yosef   Yaakov Eliyahu

In honor of his mother שתחי׳

Mrs. Suri Klein לאוי״ט

In memory of his father

ר׳ יהודה ב״ר דוד הלוי ז״ל נפ׳ כ״ז אדר ב׳ תשס״ג – Yidel Klein

In memory of her parents

ר׳ אשר אנשיל ב״ר משה יוסף ז״ל נפ׳ ג׳ שבט תשנ״ט – Anchel Gross

שרה בת ר׳ חיים אליהו ע״ה נפ׳ כ״ד סיון תשס״א – Suri Gross

And in memory of their grandparents who perished על קידוש השם in the Holocaust

ר׳ דוד ב״ר יעקב הלוי ע״ה ופערל בת ר׳ צבי ע״ה הי״ד – Klein

ר׳ מרדכי ב״ר דוד הלוי ע״ה ולאה בת ר׳ יעקב הלוי ע״ה הי״ד – Klein

ר׳ משה יוסף ב״ר בנימין צבי ע״ה ומלכה בת ר׳ יחיאל מיכל ע״ה הי״ד – Gross

ר׳ חיים אליהו ב״ר מרדכי ע״ה ויוטא בת ר׳ שלמה אליעזר ע״ה הי״ד – Gartenberg

VOL. 3: VAYEISHEV-VAYECHI / וישב־ויחי

Leon and Agi Goldenberg

Mendy and Estie Blau – Efraim, Rivka, and Chava

Shiffie Grossman – Chanie, and Rikki

Abi and Shoshana Goldenberg – Yehudis

Tzvi and Leilie Fertig

and Yitzy Goldenberg

In memory of their fathers and uncle

ר׳ אברהם אבא ב״ר צבי ז״ל – Abba Goldenberg ז״ל

ר׳ יוסף אליעזר ב״ר יעקב יצחק ז״ל – Joseph Brieger ז״ל

ר׳ יעקב שלמה ב״ר משה הלוי ז״ל – Yaakov Shlomeh Lebovits ז״ל

and יבלח״ט in tribute to their mothers שתחי׳ לאוי״ט

Chaya (Sicherman) Goldenberg   Malka (Karfunkel) Brieger

and their aunt – Faiga (Sicherman) Lebovits

VOL. 4: SHEMOS-BESHALACH / שמות-בשלח
Yossi and Bella Essas (Los Angeles)
Noam Zvi Hillel Avraham Adina Batya Ashira Miriam
In honor of his parents
Rabbi Eliyahu and Anya Essas שליט״א

VOL. 5: YISRO-TETZAVEH / יתרו-תצוה
Edward J. and Rose F. Leventhal
in honor of their children,
Alison, Martin and Bonnie,
and in honor of their parents
Eddie and Irma Muller,
and Ruth Leventhal,
and in beloved memory of his father,
ברוך בן משה ז״ל – Bernard E. Leventhal ז״ל

VOL. 14: THE FESTIVALS / מועדי השנה
The Teichman Family (Los Angeles)
In memory of their parents and grandparents
שמואל ב״ר יששכר דוב ז״ל – Sam Teichman ז״ל
ליבה ברײנדל בת ר׳ יהושע הלוי ע״ה – Lujza Teichman ע״ה
רחל בת ר׳ אלכסנר סנדר ע״ה – Rose Teichman ע״ה
יצחק אייזיק ב״ר אברהם חיים ז״ל – Isaac Nae ז״ל

◈ Publisher's Preface

King David said: גַּל עֵינַי וְאַבִּיטָה נִפְלָאוֹת מִתּוֹרָתֶךָ, *Unveil my eyes that I may perceive wonders from your Torah* (*Psalms* 119:18).

Shammai said: עֲשֵׂה תוֹרָתְךָ קֶבַע, *Make your Torah study a fixed practice* (*Avos* 1:15).

Rav Saadiah Gaon said: The Jewish people is a nation only by virtue of the Torah.

The Torah is the essence of the Jewish people, and not a day should go by without Torah study. How much learning should there be? Just as the Torah itself is infinite, there is no limit to the effort to master its contents. The task does not end when one bids farewell to the academy and enters the world of work and business. All over the world, study halls are filled before dawn and after dark with men plumbing the depths of the Talmud and other works. Before and after their workdays, they overcome fatigue with a relentless desire to absorb more and more of God's word.

To such people, **The Kleinman Edition: Limud Yomi / A Daily Dose of Torah** will be a welcome supplement, an enrichment that offers glimpses of additional topics and a means of filling the day's spare minutes with nourishment for the mind and spirit.

To those who as yet have not been able to savor the beauty of immersion in the sea of study, this new series will be a vehicle to enrich their every day with an assortment of stimulating Torah content.

We are gratified that Volumes 1 through 3 of this new series has been phenomenally well received. Many people have told us how they are filling once-empty gaps in their day with these "daily doses," and how this work has stimulated them to do further research in these subjects. As King Solomon said, תֵּן לְחָכָם וְיֶחְכַּם־עוֹד הוֹדַע לְצַדִּיק וְיוֹסֶף לֶקַח, *Give the wise man and he will become wiser; make known to the righteous and he will add [to his] learning* (*Proverbs* 9:9).

Each "Daily Dose of Torah" includes selections from a broad spectrum of Torah sources (see below); in combination they provide a multi-dimensional study program. Each selection can stand on its own, or, ideally, serve as a vehicle for further research and enrichment. These components are as follows:

❏ ***A Torah Thought for the Day***, focusing on a verse in the weekly *parashah*. The discussion may revolve around various classic interpretations, or it may offer a selection of insights and lessons that are derived from the verse. This section will draw from a wide gamut of early and later commentators, and will enhance the reader's appreciation for the wealth of Torah interpretation and its lessons for life.

❏ ***The Mishnah of the Day,*** presenting a Mishnah selection every day, with text, translation, and concise commentary, adapted from the classic ArtScroll Mishnah Series and the Schottenstein Edition of the Talmud. This daily dose will begin with Tractate Shabbos, and continue through Seder Moed.

❏ ***Gems from the Gemara,*** presenting some of the Talmud's discussion of the daily Mishnah. Thus the reader will "join the academy" of the Talmud's question-and-answer clarification of the laws and underlying principles of the Mishnah.

❏ ***A Mussar Thought for the Day,*** building upon the theme of the *Torah Thought for the Day*, by presenting an ethical or moral lesson drawn from the masters of Mussar, Hashkafah, and Chassidus. This selection will stimulate thought and growth — and be a welcome source of uplifting ideas for times when the reader is called upon to speak at a *simchah*.

❏ ***The Halachah of the Day,*** presenting a practical, relevant halachic discussion, beginning with the thirty-nine forbidden categories of Shabbos labor. The selections are adapted from Rabbi Simcha Bunim Cohen's popular and authoritative works, which are part of the ArtScroll Series. [These brief discussions are not intended to be definitive. Questions should be directed to a qualified rav.]

❏ ***A Closer Look at the Siddur,*** broadening the reader's understanding of the rich tapestry of *tefillah*/prayer. The Shabbos Daily Dose will focus on the Shabbos prayers. And once a week, this section will discuss such universal themes as the Thirteen Principles of Faith or the Six Constant Commandments.

❑ ***A Taste of Lomdus,*** a special weekly feature that will present a brief but in-depth discussion of a Talmudic subject, in the tradition of the Torah giants whose reasoning and novellae are the basis of research and study in advanced yeshivas. Every day, there will be a challenging "Question of the Day," related to the theme of the day. The answers for the questions will come at the end of each week.

Each volume of the Daily Dose of Torah Series will present a capsule study program for twenty-eight days. The annual cycle will be comprised of thirteen four-week volumes, covering all fifty-two weeks of the year, and a fourteenth volume devoted to Rosh Hashanah, Yom Kippur, and the festivals. We are confident that the complete series will bring the excitement of Torah study to countless people, and that many of them will use it as a springboard to further learning, both independently and by joining *shiurim.*

The Kleinman Edition: Limud Yomi / A Daily Dose of Torah is dedicated by **ELLY AND BROCHIE KLEINMAN,** in memory of their fathers ז"ל and in honor of their mothers שיחיו. The Kleinmans have long distinguished themselves as generous and imaginative supporters of Torah and *chesed* causes. With warmth and kindness, they have opened their home countless times to help institutions and individuals. They have richly earned the respect and affection of all who know them, and we are honored to count them not only as major supporters of our work, but as personal friends. They and their family bring honor to the legacy of their parents.

This volume of the Daily Dose of Torah is dedicated by **YOSSI AND BELLA ESSAS** of Los Angeles. In doing so they pay tribute to his parents, **RABBI AND MRS. ELIYAHU ESSAS,** who are legendary heroes of the *baal teshuvah* movement in the Soviet Union. When teaching and spreading Torah was a crime and the next knock on the door could be the KGB, Reb Eliyahu and Anya showed incredible courage and inspired countless Jews to return to the Judaism of their forefathers. Yossi and Bella are relative newcomers to Los Angeles, but they are already making their mark, in the mold of his parents.

Mr. Essas is a Board member of Yeshivah Toras Emes, one of the founders of a new shul in the Beverly Wood neighborhood and, with his friends, is in the process of organizing a new *kollel* that will breathe Torah life into the area. Mrs. Essas is deeply involved in *chesed* activities, not only by making contributions but by personal involvement, such as preparing and delivering meals for the needy. Together, Yossi and Bella are a model couple who bring pride to their parents and are a role model to those who know them. We are proud to welcome them to the ArtScroll/ Mesorah family.

The editor of this new series is **RABBI YOSAIF ASHER WEISS**, Rosh Yeshivas Ohr Hadaas, Staten Island, who is also a distinguished editor of the Schottenstein Editions of the Talmud Bavli and Yerushalmi. Rabbi Weiss' reputation as a noted scholar and educator will be justly embellished by the Daily Dose Series.

We are grateful to **RABBI RAPHAEL BUTLER**, the dynamic and innovative founder and president of the Afikim Foundation, who conceived of this concept and had a significant role in its development. We are proud to enjoy his friendship.

We are grateful to the outstanding *talmidei chachamim* who are contributing to this series: **RABBI YOSEF GAVRIEL BECHHOFER, RABBI REUVEN BUTLER, RABBI ELIYAHU COHEN, RABBI ASHER DICKER, RABBI MAYER GOLDSTEIN, RABBI MOSHE YEHUDA GLUCK, RABBI BERYL SCHIFF, RABBI MORDECHAI SONNENSCHEIN, RABBI MOSHE UNGAR, AND RABBI YISROEL DOV WEISS.** The quality of their scholarship shines through every page. We thank **RABBI SIMCHA SHAFRAN** for allowing us to use his *sefer Maadanei Simchah* as a source for some of the Questions of the Day.

The beauty and clarity of the book's design is yet another tribute to the graphics genius of our friend and colleague **REB SHEAH BRANDER**. As someone once said in a different context, "I can't put it into words, but I know it when I see it." It is hard to define good taste and graphics beauty in words, but when one sees Reb Sheah's work, one knows it.

ELI KROEN, a master of graphics in his own right, designed the cover with his typical creativity and good taste. **MOSHE DEUTSCH** had an important hand in the typesetting and general design. **MRS. CHUMIE LIPSCHITZ**, a key member of our staff, paginated the book. **TOBY GOLDZWEIG, SURY REINHOLD, AND SARA RIFKA SPIRA** typed and corrected the manuscript. **MRS. ESTHER FEIERSTEIN** proofread the final copy.

MRS. MINDY STERN proofread and made many important suggestions. **AVROHOM BIDERMAN** was involved in virtually every aspect of the work from its inception, and **MENDY HERZBERG** assisted in shepherding the project to completion.

As this new series continues to take shape, we express our great appreciation to our long-time friend and colleague **SHMUEL BLITZ**, head of ArtScroll Jerusalem. His dedication and judgment have been indispensable components of virtually every ArtScroll/Mesorah project.

We are grateful to them all. The contributions of ArtScroll/Mesorah to the cause of Jewish life and Torah study are possible because of the skill and dedication of the above staff members and their colleagues.

It is an enormous privilege to have been instrumental in bringing Torah knowledge to the people of Torah. There are no words to express our gratitude to Hashem Yisbarach for permitting us to disseminate His Word to His children.

Rabbi Meir Zlotowitz / Rabbi Nosson Scherman

Kislev 5767 / December 2006

פרשת שמות

Parashas Shemos

פרשת שמות

SUNDAY

PARASHAS SHEMOS

A TORAH THOUGHT FOR THE DAY

וְאֵלֶּה שְׁמוֹת בְּנֵי יִשְׂרָאֵל הַבָּאִים מִצְרָיְמָה אֵת יַעֲקֹב אִישׁ וּבֵיתוֹ בָּאוּ. רְאוּבֵן שִׁמְעוֹן לֵוִי וִיהוּדָה וגו׳

And these are the names of the Children of Israel who were coming to Egypt; with Yaakov, each man and his household came. Reuven, Shimon, Levi and Yehudah, etc. (*Shemos* 1:1-2).

Rashi asks the obvious question: Why must the Torah repeat the names of Yaakov and his children, when they were all listed at length in *Sefer Bereishis*? *Rashi* answers: The Torah wants to make known how precious the Jews are to Hashem; they are compared to the stars which He brings out and brings in by number and by name, as the verse states (*Yeshayah* 40:26): הַמּוֹצִיא בְמִסְפָּר צְבָאָם לְכֻלָּם בְּשֵׁם יִקְרָא, *He takes out their hosts by number, He calls them all by name.*

The *Me'am Loez* explains the analogy between Bnei Yisrael and the stars: Hashem counts the stars twice daily, once at twilight when they first appear on the horizon, and once at daybreak when they retreat from the sky upon completion of their duties. So too, Hashem counted and listed the names of the *shevatim* twice — in their lifetime, and then again upon their death. This is a clear indication of *hashgachah pratis* (הַשְׁגָּחָה פְּרָטִית), individual Divine supervision of every single Jew. Only the Jews merit such supervision, while the other nations are under only a general watch — *hashgachah klalis* (הַשְׁגָּחָה כְּלָלִית).

What needs further explanation is: Why does the Torah stress that Hashem counts the Jews with numbers, and then gives them names? What is the purpose of this double display of love, and what lesson can we derive from it?

The answer may be as follows: We know that these verses speak of the beginning of the formation of Klal Yisrael, and their first encounter with *galus* in Mitzrayim (Egypt). The Torah is reminding us that we as Jews play a double role.

A name is an individual identity. שֵׁם, *name,* has the same letters as שָׁם, which means *over there,* and is a way of identifying something (*R' Hirsch*). A number, on the other hand, is connected to all numbers, both below and above it. For instance, the number seven tells us that it has an accumulation of six digits below it; it also immediately precedes the number eight that follows it.

Every Jew carries a dual responsibility. While he should recognize his individual role as a single person, he should also remember his role as a "team player" in Klal Yisrael.

This is the lesson to be learned from our comparison to the stars: Hashem gives each Jew his own name, but he is given a number as well. With this loving reminder, a Jew can enter *galus* and come out unharmed.

Chazal tell us that the Jews in *galus* were careful not to change their names and not to give up their mode of dress or language. Although Klal Yisrael did fall from their spiritual level during *Galus Mitzrayim,* their names — i.e., individual identities — and their clothing and language, which are descriptive of a nation, were not lost. These fundamentals remained. In their merit, the Jews were freed from Egypt, for they had demonstrated that the essence of Klal Yisrael was still intact.

MISHNAH OF THE DAY: SHABBOS 13:6

The following Mishnah continues to discuss the forbidden labor of *trapping* animals:

צְבִי שֶׁנִּכְנַס לַבַּיִת — If ***a deer entered a house*** by itself, **וְנָעַל אֶחָד בְּפָנָיו** — ***and one locked*** the door ***in front of it,*** **חַיָּיב** — ***he is liable*** *to a* ***chatas*** for trapping it.[1] **נָעֲלוּ שְׁנַיִם** — But if ***two*** people ***locked*** the door when it was possible for one to do it alone, **פְּטוּרִין** — ***they are*** both ***exempt.***[2] **לֹא יָכוֹל אֶחָד לִנְעוֹל** — However, ***if one*** person alone ***could not lock*** the door,[3] **וְנָעֲלוּ שְׁנַיִם** — ***and two locked*** it together, **חַיָּיבִין** — ***they are*** both ***liable.***[4] **וְרַבִּי שִׁמְעוֹן פּוֹטֵר** — ***But R' Shimon exempts*** them even in such a case.[5]

NOTES

1. Although the person did not put the deer inside the house, this makes no difference. Since by locking the door in front of the deer he prevents its escape, he is liable for having trapped it (*Rav; Rashi*).

2. This ruling follows the principle we have learned above (10:5), that when two people perform a forbidden labor together, and the labor is such that could have been performed by one person, both are exempt from punishment (*Rashi*).

3. Viz., if the door was too heavy for one person to close without assistance.

4. Since it is normal for two people to lock such a door together, it is considered as though each person performed the forbidden labor himself, since without him it could not have been accomplished (*Rav; Rashi*).

5. As we saw above (10:5), R' Shimon exempts from liability *any* labor done by two people together — even when that labor requires the participation of two people (*Rashi*).

פרשת שמות

SUNDAY

PARASHAS SHEMOS

GEMS FROM THE GEMARA

This Mishnah cites the dispute between the Sages and R' Shimon regarding whether two people who perform a forbidden labor in concert are liable. This dispute was also taught in the Mishnah earlier (10:5), regarding a case where two people carried a burden from a private domain to a public domain; the Sages hold both liable if both were needed to transfer the burden, and R' Shimon exempts them. The commentators offer several reasons as to why this dispute is repeated here.

Tos. Yom Tov explains that in truth nothing new is being taught in our Mishnah by citing this dispute; the Mishnah cites it only to introduce the next Mishnah, which teaches about cases where two people perform actions and only one is liable (because he alone performs the entire *melachah* — see Mishnah there). *Tiferes Yisrael,* however, explains that each of the two Mishnahs teaches a novelty. The first Mishnah teaches us that even in the case of a burden where each of the two people *could* have carried half the burden himself, R' Shimon nevertheless exempts them. And our Mishnah teaches that even in a case where two people bar a door together and trap a deer, where it is impossible for either one to accomplish the *melachah* himself, the Sages nevertheless hold that they are both liable. [It should be noted that this explanation of the above Mishnah (10:5) assumes that the case of the dispute discussed there involves the transfer of an item that could have been divided and carried out in halves. Now, the *first* case of the Mishnah there (which deals with a burden that could have been carried by a single person) speaks of a loaf of bread. Thus, *Tiferes Yisrael* will understand the second case of the Mishnah — the case of the dispute — as referring to something that can be divided, such as a sack of loaves. *Rambam (Hil. Shabbos* 1:16), however, understands the Mishnah's dispute there to be speaking of a case where the two people are carrying out a heavy beam, which *cannot* be divided; this understanding does not dovetail with *Tiferes Yisrael's* explanation here.]

For other explanations of the Mishnah, see *Meleches Shlomo* and *Shoshanim LeDavid.*

QUESTION OF THE DAY:

Why does the Torah speak of the Jews "who were coming" to Egypt, rather than the Jews "who had come" to Egypt?

For the answer, see page 54.

A MUSSAR THOUGHT FOR THE DAY

פרשת שמות

SUNDAY

PARASHAS SHEMOS

We discussed earlier (see *A Torah Thought for the Day*) the comparison of the Bnei Yisrael to the stars. *HaRav Aharon Bakst* offers a novel interpretation of this comparison. We know that there are an infinite number of stars in the heavens, as the verse states (*Bereishis* 15:5): הַבֶּט־נָא הַשָּׁמַיְמָה וּסְפֹר הַכּוֹכָבִים אִם־תּוּכַל לִסְפֹּר אֹתָם, *Look up at the sky, and count the stars, if you are able to count them.* Nevertheless, Hashem gives each star its own individual importance and loving care. Why, he asks, do the stars receive such a special level of love and affection, more than all the other heavenly bodies?

HaRav Bakst explains that the special affection Hashem has for the stars is a consequence of the reason for which they were created. The Gemara tells us that when the world was created, the sun and moon were of equal size. The moon then complained, saying, "How can two kings use the same crown?" Hashem concurred, and resolved the problem by diminishing the size of the moon. When the moon complained that it had in effect been punished for pointing out a problem that it had not caused, Hashem attempted to console it in various ways. In one of these attempts, Hashem created the stars, to placate the moon by adding many heavenly hosts (see *Bereishis* 1:16).

A creation whose very reason for coming into existence is to appease and conciliate is deserving of Hashem's unrestrained affection. Thus, Hashem counts the stars repeatedly, to let it be known how dear they are to Him.

The lesson that we must learn is that Hashem expects of us as Jews to act as do the stars — to care and be concerned, and to try always to appease our friends, neighbors and brothers. This will cause Hashem to shower us with love in turn.

Rav Yitzchak of Volozhin writes that his father *Rav Chaim of Volozhin* would tell his children on a steady basis, "A person is not created to worry about himself; rather, he must always reach out and help others." If we remember always to think about our fellow Jew first, and ourselves second, we will shine like the stars and enjoy Hashem's abundant love.

HALACHAH OF THE DAY

The next in the count of the thirty-nine labors forbidden on Shabbos is the *melachah* of מְלַבֵּן, *bleaching*. *Bleaching* was a necessary activity in the preparation of the Mishkan, since the wool used in weaving the various tapestries had to be bleached before it could be dyed and used. The *melachah* of *bleaching* is an *av melachah.* Since כִּבּוּס, *laundering*, is similar to bleaching, laundering is considered a *toladah,* or corollary, of the primary *melachah* of bleaching, and it is thus also Biblically prohibited on Shabbos.

The definition of *laundering* is removing dirt that is somewhat absorbed in a fabric. Thus, the prohibition applies only to laundering materials that are at least somewhat absorbent, but not to washing hard surfaces such as wood, glass, metal, stone or ceramic.

The prohibition of *laundering* applies equally to washing fabric through the use of water or other cleansing agents, and to the cleaning of fabrics without the use of *any* cleansing agents. Additionally, it is not necessary to remove *all* of the absorbed dirt; one transgresses this prohibition even through the removal of only a portion of the dirt or stain from the fabric.

The Biblical prohibition against laundering can be divided into three categories, comprising these different cleaning methods: washing the fabric with water or any cleansing agent; removing dust that is absorbed in the fabric; removing a stain from the fabric. We will now further clarify each of these methods of *laundering.*

Washing fabric with water or other cleansing agents involves three successive steps. It involves soaking the fabric in a solvent, scrubbing the wet fabric, and wringing out the fabric. It is Biblically prohibited to perform any one of these acts.

Soaking a dirty fabric in water or a cleansing agent is considered an act of *laundering*, since by merely soaking the fabric, some of the dirt will already be removed from it. Pouring water on a soiled fabric is considered soaking, and it is therefore likewise forbidden.

This prohibition of soaking (and pouring) applies only to absorbent materials, such as wool, cotton, or linen. With such materials, the rule is that "its soaking is the first step of its laundering." Leather, plastic, and rubber are exempt from this prohibition, since they are not truly absorbent materials; such materials cannot be substantially cleaned through soaking alone. [Many *poskim* rule that nylon has the same status as leather.] Soaking any non-absorbent material in water is permitted.

In keeping with the above rule, it is forbidden to pour water on a soiled linen tablecloth, for the water will begin to remove the absorbed stain. However, a dirty *plastic* tablecloth may be cleaned by pouring water on it, because the dirt is not absorbed into the fabric. One must be careful, however, not to wet any soiled cloth trim, if it is made from an absorbent fabric. Likewise, if the plastic tablecloth has soiled stitching around its perimeter, one must take care that the stitching will not get wet.

A CLOSER LOOK AT THE SIDDUR

וְלַלְּבָנָה אָמַר שֶׁתִּתְחַדֵּשׁ, עֲטֶרֶת תִּפְאֶרֶת לַעֲמוּסֵי בָטֶן,
שֶׁהֵם עֲתִידִים לְהִתְחַדֵּשׁ כְּמוֹתָהּ.

To the moon He said that it should renew itself as a crown of splendor for those borne [by Him] from the womb, those who are destined to renew themselves like it.

This sentence is part of the opening blessing of *Kiddush Levanah,* the prayer that is recited each month upon the new moon. *Rashi* in *Maseches Sanhedrin* (42a) explains that the moon was instructed to renew itself each month, as a sign and signal to Klal Yisrael in *galus,* reminding them that they, too, will one day regain their original glory. [Klal Yisrael arrange their calendar according to the lunar system, as opposed to the other nations, whose calendar is based upon the solar system.]

This message of hope and renewal is thus specifically targeting the Jews in *galus.* Do not despair or give up, as bleak as the darkness of *galus* may seem. Look at the moon! It is true that each month it starts getting smaller and smaller until it totally disappears and completely fades away. Suddenly, however, a shaft of light appears — a new moon, a new beginning, a new month has begun.

This special gift of renewal was bestowed upon Klal Yisrael as the first mitzvah they received as a nation, while they were still in Egypt. Hashem introduced this mitzvah to Moshe and Aharon with the words: הַחֹדֶשׁ הַזֶּה לָכֶם, *This month is for you* (*Shemos* 12:2). *Chazal* expound this verse as if it read: "*Hachidush hazeh lachem* — the power to renew and change is yours." No Jew is ever locked into a particular situation. The constant renewal of the moon is a signal to us that nothing is permanent, as a month is no longer than thirty days. The other nations, however, arrange their years by the sun, whose yearly orbit is hardly discernible. They lack the tool of change, the gift of renewal.

This message is intended not only to remind us to hope for the Ultimate Redemption for which we are all waiting; it is meant for every difficult situation or uncomfortable circumstance that may throw someone off balance. As dark as a situation may seem, as helpless as one feels, the moon is there to remind him that days of change are ahead — a light is about to shine on the horizon.

Rav Chaim Shmulevitz used to relate the following story with great emotion. A Holocaust survivor told him that during those bitter days, when the Nazis robbed him of everything, the one thing that kept him going was the moon. He used to look up and anticipate *Kiddush Levanah.* "They deprived us of any joy or mitzvah, but this one mitzvah was beyond their reach. Its clear message will outlive them: We will prevail and make it through this dark tunnel to see the light and renew our lives to shine forever."

A TORAH THOUGHT FOR THE DAY

וַיְמָרְרוּ אֶת־חַיֵּיהֶם בַּעֲבֹדָה קָשָׁה בְּחֹמֶר וּבִלְבֵנִים וּבְכָל־עֲבֹדָה בַּשָּׂדֶה אֵת כָּל־עֲבֹדָתָם אֲשֶׁר־עָבְדוּ בָהֶם בְּפָרֶךְ

And they embittered their lives with hard work, with mortar and with bricks, and with every labor of the field; all of their labors that they performed with them were crushing labors (*Shemos* 1:14).

This verse describes the harsh nature of the servitude to which the Jews were subjected during the period of their slavery in Egypt. The Midrash expands upon the description of the verse, explaining that Pharaoh made the lot of the Jews even more miserable by forcing the women to do work that was usually done by men, and vice versa. Moreover, as the earlier verse states, he drafted them for the task of building the storage cities of Pisom and Raamses. The Midrash tells us that these cities were built on foundations of sand, so that they crumbled as soon as they were built. Thus, the Jews were locked into a constant spiral of ever-increasing labor.

Although the terrible suffering of the Jews during this period would seem to be without any redeeming features, in truth this was not the case. For according to the decree that Hashem had revealed to Avraham many years earlier, the Jews were destined to be sojourners in a land not their own, and oppressed for 400 years (see *Bereishis* 15:13). Hashem, in His mercy, allowed the count of 400 years to begin from the birth of Yitzchak, and thus the Jews remained in the Egyptian exile for only 210 years.

However, a difficulty remained. Although, by counting from Yitzchak's birth, the decree of sojourning for 400 years could be fulfilled (for Yitzchak was merely a *sojourner* in Eretz Yisrael, as we have discussed earlier — see *A Torah Thought for the Day,* Sunday of *Parashas Vayeishev*), Hashem had decreed that the Jews would be *oppressed* for 400 years. How was that element of the decree to be achieved? To resolve this issue, Hashem increased the suffering of the Jews in Egypt, so that the suffering of 400 years was compacted into the years that the Jews were actually enslaved in Egypt. Thus, had the Jews *not* been subjected to this extra-harsh labor, they would have died as slaves, together with their children, grandchildren, and great-grandchildren; only future generations, those living 190 years later, would have been able to leave. Instead, they themselves were the ones who left Egypt and received the Torah. The increased suffering actually saved their lives and their futures.

This is hinted at in the words we find in the *Haggadah Shel Pesach* —

חִשַּׁב אֶת הַקֵּץ, *He calculated the end* (*keitz*) of the servitude. The numerical value of the Hebrew word קֵץ is 190; thus, Hashem calculated that 190 years could be removed from the requirement of exile and oppression.

Gra finds a remarkable allusion to this in our verse as well. He notes that the *trop* (the cantillation marks which tell one who reads the Torah which tune to use when reading each word) that appears on the words וַיְמָרְרוּ אֶת־חַיֵּיהֶם, *and they embittered their lives,* is called קַדְמָא וְאַזְלָא, which, literally translated, means, *get up and go out.* This, says *Gra,* is a clear indication that the Jews were permitted to "get up and go out" of Egypt early because they fulfilled the decree of oppression through the extra suffering. Moreover, says *Gra,* the numerical value of the words קַדְמָא וְאַזְלָא is also 190! Thus, the *trop* itself hints to the amount of time removed from the decree due to the intensity of the suffering.

MISHNAH OF THE DAY: SHABBOS 13:7

The following Mishnah considers other cases of possible trapping in situations where a deer came into a house by itself:

יָשַׁב הָאֶחָד עַל הַפֶּתַח — If ***one*** person ***sat in the doorway*** וְלֹא מִילְאָהוּ — ***but did not completely fill*** (i.e., block) ***it,***[1] יָשַׁב הַשֵּׁנִי וּמִילְאָהוּ — and then ***a second*** person ***sat down*** next to the first person, ***and*** thereby ***completely filled [the opening],*** thus preventing the deer from escaping, הַשֵּׁנִי חַיָּיב — ***the second*** person ***is liable*** to a ***chatas***.[2] יָשַׁב הָרִאשׁוֹן עַל הַפֶּתַח וּמִילְאָהוּ — But if ***the first*** person ***sat in the doorway and completely filled it,*** וּבָא הַשֵּׁנִי וְיָשַׁב בְּצִידּוֹ — ***and then the second*** person ***came and sat down alongside him***, completely filling it as well,[3]

NOTES

1. I.e., there was sufficient open room left for the deer to escape through the doorway (*Ran*).

2. Because, by completely blocking the opening, he effected the capture of the deer (*Rav; Rashi*). Were it not for him, the deer could still have escaped. Even though the first one assisted him in the trapping by remaining in place, he is, nevertheless, exempt, since at the moment the deer was actually trapped, his participation was completely passive (*Ran*).

3. I.e., the second person sat in the doorway in such a way that he too blocked the passageway completely — viz., the first person sat in the doorway facing the interior of the house, and then the second person sat down back to back with the first one, facing out. Thus, the second person is also completely blocking the doorway (*Tos. Yom Tov*).

אַף עַל פִּי שֶׁעָמַד הָרִאשׁוֹן וְהָלַךְ לוֹ — then *even though the first* person *stood up and went away,* הָרִאשׁוֹן חַיָּיב וְהַשֵּׁנִי פָּטוּר — *the first* person *is liable, and the second is exempt.*[4] הָא לְמָה זֶה דּוֹמֶה — *To what is this analogous?*[5] לְנוֹעֵל אֶת בֵּיתוֹ לְשׁוֹמְרוֹ — *To one who locks his house to safeguard it,*[6] וְנִמְצָא צְבִי שָׁמוּר בְּתוֹכוֹ — *and a deer is found to be guarded therein.*[7]

NOTES

4. The first one is liable because he effected the original trapping. The second one is not liable: His initial act of sitting down in the doorway incurs no liability, because by that time the deer had already been trapped by the first person; he merely added to the security of the trap. Even when the first person gets up and walks away, the second person is still passive, as he merely has to stay in place to prevent the deer from escaping. The second person is thus exempt from any liability (*Tos. Yom Tov,* as explained by *Chemed Moshe* 316:3; cf. *Magen Avraham* 316:11).

[The Gemara (107a) explains that the second person is not only exempt from liability, but is *permitted* to sit down there.]

5. I.e., to what is the function of the second person analogous? (*Rashi*).

6. I.e., to one who locks his house to safeguard it from thieves, not to trap animals (*Rav; Rashi*).

7. I.e., a deer that had already been trapped the day before is found guarded in the house (*Rav; Rashi*). This refers to a case where, for example, a deer is tied up inside a house, and someone then locks the door. Since the deer, at the time the person locks the door, was already tied up (and thus trapped), locking the door is not in itself an act of *trapping*. Therefore, even if the deer escapes the original trap (e.g., the deer tears free from its binding), and is now trapped only by virtue of the subsequently added lock, nevertheless, since at the moment of locking the door no act of trapping was performed, the person who locked the door is not liable. Similarly, in our case, when the second person sits down, the deer was already trapped. Hence, the second person does not effect the trapping, and is not required to leave the doorway to allow the deer to escape (*Ran; Tos. Yom Tov*).

GEMS FROM THE GEMARA

Throughout this tractate, the term "exempt" (פָּטוּר), when used in regard to Sabbath law, means "exempt but prohibited [by Rabbinic decree]." However, the Gemara (107a) teaches that the term "exempt," when it is used in our Mishnah with respect to a person who sat alongside another person who had already trapped a deer inside, is to be interpreted as "exempt and permitted"; as we explained in the Mishnah, the person is *permitted* to sit there even in the first place. The Gemara, citing Shmuel, states that there are three instances where we interpret the word "exempt" in the Mishnah to mean "exempt and permitted."

The first example is our case of sitting in the doorway of a house in which a deer is already trapped. How do we know that it means "exempt and permitted"? Because the end of the Mishnah draws an analogy between this case and the case of one who locks his house to safeguard it, and a deer is found to be guarded therein. This case is clearly totally permissible; thus, the meaning of "exempt" here also must mean "exempt and permissible."

The second case is found in another Mishnah (*Eduyos* 2:5), that teaches: "One who lances a boil on Shabbos, if he does so to make an opening for it, he is liable to a *chatas* (for performing the forbidden *melachah* of *building*); if his intent is only to remove the pus from the boil, he is exempt." We know that this case is "exempt and permitted," because we learn in another Mishnah (below, 17:2) that a hand needle may be used on the Sabbath to take out a thorn. The fact that the needle may be handled initially for this purpose shows that the Sages did not forbid this, because of the pain felt by the person with the thorn. In the case of the boil, as well, the Rabbis did not forbid a person to lance the boil and remove the pus.

The third case is in the same Mishnah (*Eduyos* ibid.): "One who traps a snake on the Sabbath, if he is involved with it so that it will not bite him, he is exempt; if for a cure, he is liable." Here we know that the Mishnah means "exempt and permitted," because it is analogous to a ruling in another Mishnah (below, 16:7), that it is permissible to invert a bowl over a scorpion so that it does not sting.

A MUSSAR THOUGHT FOR THE DAY

Rambam, in the fifth chapter of his *Hilchos Teshuvah,* discusses the axiomatic belief that Hashem does not create people as righteous or wicked — every person has בְּחִירָה (*bechirah*), *free choice,* to decide whether he will be righteous or evil. In the sixth chapter, *Rambam* deals with several instances in the Scriptures that appear to contradict this concept. One of his questions involves the Egyptians and the exile of Mitzrayim. Why, asks *Rambam,* were the Egyptians punished with the Ten Plagues, and later drowned in the *Yam Suf* (Reed Sea)? Hashem had decreed many years earlier that the Jews were to be subjugated in a foreign land. Thus, it would seem that the Egyptians were predestined to enslave the Jews. Why should they be punished for this?

Rambam answers this question by pointing out that when Hashem told Avraham that his children would be enslaved, He did *not* state that the enslavement would occur at the hands of the Egyptians; He said only that they would be "in a land not their own." [Indeed, it transpired that during a large part of the 400 years, they were actually in Eretz Yisrael, as we discussed above in *A Torah Thought for the Day.*] It was the *Egyptians,* in their freely chosen wickedness, who jumped at the chance to be the nation that would subjugate the Jews, and for this they were punished. Had the Egyptians chosen not to enslave the Jews, the decree would have been fulfilled by some other nation.

Raavad (ibid.) professes dissatisfaction with *Rambam's* approach, and offers two other answers for why the Egyptians deserved such punishment. In his first explanation, he posits that if Pharaoh would have agreed to release the Jews as soon as Moshe came to him, the punishment visited upon the Egyptians would indeed not have occurred; it was only Pharaoh's disdainful reply, "*Who is HASHEM that I should heed His voice?*" (*Shemos* 5:2), and his stubborn refusal to release the Jews, that led to these punishments.

In his second explanation *Raavad* points to our verse. Although it may be true, says *Raavad*, that the Egyptians were meant to oppress the Jews, our verse shows that their cruelty went far beyond that which was required. The oppression did not have to include backbreaking labor — nor did the Egyptians have to drown Jewish babies in the river, or suffocate them by placing them into buildings as human building material when impossible quotas of bricks were not met. These excesses revealed the Egyptians for the wicked people that they really were, and rendered them liable to the full extent of Hashem's wrath.

HALACHAH OF THE DAY

Yesterday, we discussed the first of the three methods of laundering, namely, washing fabric with water or a cleansing agent. We started by discussing the first step of washing a fabric, that of soaking. We also mentioned that pouring water on a fabric is tantamount to soaking, and is thus prohibited. We will now discuss a few additional points regarding soaking.

There are some *poskim* who rule that the prohibition against soaking applies even to soaking a *clean* fabric. Although there are other *poskim* who dispute this ruling, later authorities rule that we must follow the stringent view. Thus, one may not soak even a clean garment in water or in a cleansing agent.

The prohibition against soaking a fabric does not apply to soaking a fabric in dirty liquid, since the fabric does not get any cleaner in this way. It is therefore permissible to dry one's hands on a towel, although this action causes the towel to get wet. We discussed earlier that wetting a fabric — even a clean one — is prohibited on Shabbos. However, since one's hands generally have some dirt on them, by drying one's hands, the towel becomes wet and dirty rather than wet and clean, and it is therefore permitted. This is also why it is permissible to use a dishtowel to dry dishes on Shabbos.

The second step of washing a garment is to scrub it. This act is Biblically prohibited, and includes scrubbing with one's hands or a brush, as well as rubbing two parts of the fabric against each other. It even includes swishing the fabric back and forth in water.

The prohibition against scrubbing does not apply only to absorbent fabrics. Rather, it applies to any soft material, including leather, rubber and nylon. Scrubbing hard leather is also prohibited, but only by Rabbinic decree. Thus, while one would be permitted to pour water on leather shoes (being careful to avoid any stitching), one would not be allowed to scrub the dirt off the shoes while they are wet.

Although we have stated that it is forbidden to scrub all types of soft material, even non-absorbent ones, Rav Moshe Feinstein was in doubt as to whether this applies to plastic. He therefore ruled that plastic may be scrubbed gently, but not forcefully.

A CLOSER LOOK AT THE SIDDUR

This week, we will discuss the tenth of the Thirteen Fundamental Principles (י״ג עיקרים) enumerated by *Rambam*, which states:

> אֲנִי מַאֲמִין בֶּאֱמוּנָה שְׁלֵמָה שֶׁהַבּוֹרֵא יִתְבָּרַךְ שְׁמוֹ יוֹדֵעַ כָּל מַעֲשֵׂה בְנֵי אָדָם וְכָל מַחְשְׁבוֹתָם שֶׁנֶּאֱמַר ״הַיֹּצֵר יַחַד לִבָּם הַמֵּבִין אֶל־כָּל־מַעֲשֵׂיהֶם״.
> *I believe with complete faith that the Creator, Blessed be His Name, knows all the deeds of human beings, and all of their thoughts, as it is stated: "He Who fashions all their hearts together, Who comprehends all of their deeds."*

In this principle, we acknowledge that Hashem is always aware of our thoughts and actions. This serves to contradict the mistaken belief of some people that Hashem created the world, and then tossed it away into the cosmos, no longer caring or paying attention to what happens to the world and its inhabitants. We, of course, know that this is not the case. Hashem created this world for the purpose of enabling us to excel in serving Him, and He supervises us constantly, aware of all that we think and do.

We emphasize that Hashem understands each human being more completely than is even humanly possible. Even a person's close friend or spouse, who knows him extremely well, cannot plumb the depths of his mind, and be privy to all of his hidden thoughts and plans. Hashem, however, has no such limitation. Nothing can be hidden from Him; as the Creator, he is aware of man's every thought and wish. A clear realization of the fact that Hashem cannot be misled or fooled is a powerful motivational tool, which one can use to help himself remain on the path of proper behavior and service to Hashem.

Rambam cites the verse in *Tehillim* (33:15) as proof of this principle: *He Who fashions all their hearts together, Who comprehends all of their deeds*. According to *Radak* (*Tehillim* ibid.), this verse is explaining *why* Hashem has the power to see into men's hearts; because He alone fashioned them, He alone has the ability to truly understand them. *Alshich* (ibid.) finds another level of meaning in the verse. He explains that the phrase *all their hearts together* is a reference to the dual nature of the forces that battle within the human heart — *the yetzer tov* (Good Inclination) and the *yetzer hara* (Evil Inclination). A person is constantly beset by warring impulses. Sometimes, he will succeed and triumph over his evil impulses; other times he may fail and succumb to his baser urges. To the human observer, this behavior may seem random and inconsistent. But Hashem *fashions all their hearts together;* He alone knows of the many components that make up a person's mind and heart. Thus, it is possible for Him to *comprehend all of their deeds.*

QUESTION OF THE DAY:

What ritual performed during the Pesach Seder commemorates the harsh labor forced upon the Jews?

For the answer, see page 54.

A TORAH THOUGHT FOR THE DAY

וַתָּבֹאנָה אֶל־רְעוּאֵל אֲבִיהֶן וַיֹּאמֶר מַדּוּעַ מִהַרְתֶּן בֹּא הַיּוֹם.
וַתֹּאמַרְןָ אִישׁ מִצְרִי הִצִּילָנוּ מִיַּד הָרֹעִים . . .

And they came to Reuel, their father. He said: "How could you come so quickly today?" They replied: "An Egyptian man saved us from the shepherds . . ." (*Shemos* 2:18-19).

One wonders: How could the daughters of Reuel (Yisro) have mistaken Moshe for an Egyptian man? If they realized that he was a Jew, even if he was from Egypt, would it not have been more appropriate to refer to him as "a Jewish man"?

The Midrash (*Shemos* 1:32) explains that Moshe was wearing Egyptian clothing; therefore they referred to him as an Egyptian. But this gives rise to an even greater difficulty. If the Jews in Egypt were careful not to change their attire to the Egyptian style of dress, then why was Moshe — who was not even in Egypt and thus had no reason to dress in their manner — wearing Egyptian clothing?

Michtav Sofer suggests an answer, based upon the comments of *Chasam Sofer* regarding a verse found later in the *parashah*. The verse (3:22) states that Hashem told Moshe what was to occur shortly before the redemption: וְשָׁאֲלָה אִשָּׁה מִשְּׁכֶנְתָּהּ . . . כְּלֵי־כֶסֶף וּכְלֵי זָהָב וּשְׂמָלֹת, *Each woman shall request from her neighbor . . . silver vessels, golden vessels, and garments. Chasam Sofer* wonders: Why would they borrow garments from the Egyptians? Hadn't the Jews been careful all these years never to wear Egyptian clothing? He explains: Although while in Egypt throughout the exile they did not wear Egyptian clothing, upon their departure from Egypt they all put on Egyptian clothing, to commemorate the great miracle of the Exodus. [This is similar to *Ramban's* explanation (13:2) of why Ezra referred to the Jewish months by their Persian names; this was done to commemorate the miracle of the redemption from Bavel.]

Michtav Sofer explains that it was for the same reason that Moshe was wearing Egyptian clothing. He had miraculously escaped being killed by Pharaoh, and therefore wore Egyptian clothing to commemorate the miracle of that salvation.

In truth, though, another Midrash (*Devarim* 2:5) does seem to hold Moshe culpable for not declaring his Jewishness openly, for it states that when Moshe heard himself being referred to as an Egyptian and remained silent, he was punished by not being buried in Eretz Yisrael. On the other hand, Yosef announced that he was a Jew (as evidenced by the fact that the cupbearer of Pharaoh referred to Yosef as a נַעַר עִבְרִי, *a Jewish lad*), and he merited that his remains were brought to burial in Eretz Yisrael.

Not wearing the clothing of other nations was especially important during the period before the Torah was given, for until that time there were no mitzvos to show the difference between a Jew and a non-Jew. Therefore, if a Jew would dress like an Egyptian, it would indeed not be discernible that he was a Jew. Accordingly, Moshe was punished for dressing like an Egyptian (*Meshivas Nefesh*). After the Torah was given, however, we have quite a few mitzvos that make us different from the other nations; many commentators thus rule that not changing names and clothing in our times is only a *middas chassidus,* a pious trait, but not a halachic requirement [provided, of course, that Jewish standards of modesty are adhered to] (see *Igros Moshe*, *Orach Chaim* 4:66).

MISHNAH OF THE DAY: SHABBOS 14:3

Continuing the previous chapter's discussion of the forbidden labor of *trapping* animals, the following Mishnah contrasts this forbidden labor with the forbidden labor of *bruising* animals:

שְׁמֹנָה שְׁרָצִים הָאֲמוּרִים בַּתּוֹרָה — With respect to ***the eight sheratzim that are mentioned in the Torah,***[1] **הַצָּדָן וְהַחוֹבֵל בָּהֶן חַיָּיב** — the law is that ***one who traps them,***[2] ***or one who bruises them,***[3] ***is liable*** to a

NOTES

1. The Mishnah refers here to the eight creeping creatures listed in *Leviticus* 11:29-30 (*Rav*). [Although the identification of these *sheratzim* is by no means unanimously agreed upon, the following commonly used translations are offered as an indication of the types of creatures included in this classification: הַחֹלֶד, *the weasel;* הָעַכְבָּר, *the mouse;* הַצָּב, *the toad* or *the turtle;* הָאֲנָקָה, *the hedgehog;* הַכֹּחַ, *the chameleon*; הַלְּטָאָה, *the lizard;* הַחֹמֶט, *the snail;* הַתִּנְשֶׁמֶת, *the mole.* These are all small animals whose carcasses are a source of *tumah*. Since this group includes reptiles, rodents, amphibians, and mollusks, we have left the word שְׁרָצִים, *sheratzim,* untranslated.]

2. Since these species are customarily hunted (*Rav; Rashi*) for their hides (*Ran*), one who traps them is liable to a *chatas*.

3. Since the hides of these animals are tougher than the flesh beneath them, any bruise mark visible in them is of such severity that the blood of that bruise can no longer be reabsorbed by the body, and it is only the thickness of the hide that prevents the blood from flowing out (*Rambam Commentary*). Therefore, one who bruises them is liable *to a chatas* — even if he has not pierced their hides.

chatas.[4] וּשְׁאָר שְׁקָצִים וּרְמָשִׂים — ***But** with respect to **other vermin and crawling things,***[5] הַחוֹבֵל בָּהֶן פָּטוּר — the law is that ***one who bruises them is exempt;***[6] הַצָּדָן לְצוֹרֶךְ חַיָּיב — and ***one who traps them for a*** positive ***purpose is liable*** to a *chatas*,[7] שֶׁלֹּא לְצוֹרֶךְ פָּטוּר — while one who traps them ***not for a*** positive ***purpose is exempt.***[8] חַיָּה וָעוֹף שֶׁבִּרְשׁוּתוֹ — ***Beasts and birds that are under one's control,*** הַצָּדָן פָּטוּר — ***one who traps them is exempt,***[9] וְהַחוֹבֵל בָּהֶן חַיָּיב — ***but one who bruises them is liable.***[10]

NOTES

4. The exact forbidden labor for which one is liable for bruising one of the *sheratzim* is subject to dispute. Some rule that he is liable for מְפָרֵק, *unloading* — i.e., separating the blood from the flesh. This is a derivative (*toladah*) of the forbidden labor of *threshing*, which consists of separating the kernels of grain from the chaff (*Rav; Rambam*). Others maintain that since the hides of these creatures become colored by the blood coming to the surface, the perpetrator is liable for the forbidden labor of *dyeing* (*Rav; Rashi*).

5. Such as worms and scorpions (*Rav*), and snakes (*Rashi*).

6. Since their skin is soft, their blood rushes easily to the surface. Were the severity of the wound sufficient to prevent the blood from being reabsorbed by the body, the blood would have immediately flowed through the soft skin of these creatures (*Rambam Commentary.*). If the skin is only bruised, not pierced, the blood will eventually be reabsorbed by the body, and hence the person who bruises these creatures is exempt. This is true in any instance where the skin becomes only temporarily suffused with blood — e.g., when one slaps a human being (*Tiferes Yisrael; Mishnah Berurah* 316:32). [Of course, if one actually pierces the skin and causes a creature of any species to bleed, he is liable.]

7. The Mishnah specifies that one is liable only if he intends to use the creature for some purpose, because these other creatures are generally not needed, and are therefore usually captured only so that one will be rid of them. Nevertheless, if one captured one of them for some use, he is indeed liable. On the other hand, the eight *sheratzim* are usually trapped for their hides. Hence, one is liable for their capture, without any qualification (*Tos.* 107a).

8. This Mishnah follows the opinion of R' Shimon, who rules that one who performs *a labor not needed for its defined purpose* is exempt (Gemara 107b).

9. Since they are already trapped in his domain, the prohibition against catching them does not apply (*Rav; Rashi*). [See Mishnah 13:7 above for a full discussion of the details of this rule.]

10. Since they have hides, one is liable for bruising them, just as one is liable for bruising the eight *sheratzim* mentioned in the Torah. This is true only if the one who inflicts the wound is drawing the blood for some use. However, if he inflicts the wound in order to harm the beast, it is considered a destructive act and he is exempt — as are all those whose forbidden labor has a destructive purpose [see above, 13:3] (*Rav* from Gemara 106a).

GEMS FROM THE GEMARA

Apropos of our Mishnah's discussion of animals and their hides, the Gemara (108a) considers the subject of which hides are fit for *tefillin.* At the end of its discussion, it cites a Baraisa in which the Sages state that one may write *tefillin* on the hide of a kosher animal (בְּהֵמָה), or on the hide of a kosher beast (חַיָּה), or on the hides of the *neveilos* or *tereifos* of these species. [A *neveilah* is an animal that died without *shechitah.* A *tereifah* is an animal that has one of certain fatal injuries, and for which *shechitah* is of no benefit. The meat of such animals may not be eaten. However, *tefillin* written on their hides are valid.] Moreover, the individual parchments of the *tefillin* are to be wrapped in the hair of these species before they are inserted into their respective compartments in the *tefillin* casing, and any sewing in *tefillin* (e.g., to close the casings) must be performed with the sinews of these species. On the other hand, neither nonkosher animals nor nonkosher beasts may be used for these purposes.

The Baraisa concludes with a question posed by one Boethusian [a heretical sect named after Boethus, who was a disciple of Antigonos of Socho, and one of the two pupils of Antigonos who departed from the ways of the Torah and formed hedonistic groups — the Sadducees (Tzedokim), named after Tzadok, and the Boethusians, named after Boethus] to R' Yehoshua HaGarsi: From where is it derived that one may not write *tefillin* on the hide of an animal that is not kosher?

R' Yehoshua responded that the verse (*Shemos* 13:9): לְמַעַן תִּהְיֶה תּוֹרַת ה' בְּפִיךָ, *So that the Torah of HASHEM will be in your mouth*, is interpreted as teaching that the material on which *tefillin* are written must be from something that is permissible in your mouth — i.e., from an animal that may be eaten.

The Boethusian argued: If this is so, then it should not be permitted to write *tefillin* on hides manufactured from the *neveilos* or *tereifos* of kosher animals either, for they may not be eaten!

R' Yehoshua replied by drawing an analogy to two people who were sentenced to death by the government. One was executed by the king himself, while the other was executed by the king's chief executioner. Which one of them is superior? I would say that the one executed by the king is superior. This demonstrates that *neveilos* and *tereifos,* that died at the hand of Heaven, are superior to ritually slaughtered animals, that died at the hand of man. Therefore, since ritually slaughtered animals may be used for *tefillin, neveilos* and *tereifos* may definitely be used!

The Boethusian countered: But if *neveilos* and *tereifos* are superior to animals killed through *shechitah,* then why is it that *neveilos* and *tereifos* are forbidden? If we may eat animals after *shechitah,* it should certainly be permitted to eat *neveilos* and *tereifos*!

R' Yehoshua retorted: The Torah says *(Deuteronomy* 14:21): לֹא תֹאכְלוּ כָל־נְבֵלָה, *You may not eat any neveilah* — and you say that they may be eaten?! [R' Yehoshua's point was that logic does not override an explicit statement of the Torah. Logic can be used only to define the status of those items that are not discussed explicitly.]

The Boethusian conceded in the face of R' Yehoshua's argument, and replied to him: Well said!

A MUSSAR THOUGHT FOR THE DAY

Above (see *A Torah Thought for the Day*), we discussed how it was possible for the daughters of Reuel (Yisro) to think that Moshe was an Egyptian. The Midrash (1:32) offers another explanation, and illustrates it with the following parable, which gives us some insight into the outstanding character of Moshe Rabbeinu, and his exceptional *middah* of *hakaras hatov,* showing gratitude.

Once, a man bitten by a scorpion ran to the water to clean his wound. While there, he saw a child about to drown and saved his life. When the child started profusely thanking the man, he replied, "Do not thank me; rather, thank the scorpion that bit me and forced me to come here to your rescue." The same thing, explains the Midrash, occurred here, when the daughters of Yisro started thanking Moshe for saving them. He said, "Do not thank me, but thank the Egyptian man whom I killed, as this incident is what caused me to run away from Egypt, and ultimately brought me here to save you!" [Moshe's intent in telling them this was to open their eyes to the fact that any such series of events is the work of Hashem, Who is the One that must ultimately be thanked.] We find that Moshe's gratitude for his salvation from the revenge of Pharaoh was always on his mind; indeed, we find that after eighty years of being separated from his brethren and family, Moshe named his second child to commemorate the miracle of being saved from Pharaoh's sword (see *Shemos* 18:4).

Moshe's *middah* of not wishing to take credit for himself made him qualified to act as the redeemer of Klal Yisrael. The Gemara (*Megillah* 15a) states: כָּל הָאוֹמֵר דָּבָר בְּשֵׁם אוֹמְרוֹ מֵבִיא גְאוּלָּה לָעוֹלָם, *Whoever says a thing in the name of its author, brings redemption to the world. Maharal* explains: This does not mean that the act of attributing a quote to its proper source has a power to bring redemption. Rather, it means that one who is in the habit of giving credit where credit is due, rather than seeking the credit for himself, is the type of person whom Hashem will employ to bring redemption. For when redemption is brought about by someone who will not take credit for himself, this creates a greater revelation of Hashem's glory, as all will realize Who is truly responsible. This is the lesson that Moshe wished to teach the daughters of Yisro; and he succeeded, for when they came to their father, they told him: "An Egyptian man (i.e., the man who was the cause of Moshe's flight) saved us from the hands of the shepherds."

HALACHAH OF THE DAY

We have now discussed the first two steps involved in the washing of a garment, namely, soaking and scrubbing. After soaking and scrubbing a fabric, the final step in the process is wringing out the fabric. Such wringing out is considered to be an act of laundering, even when it is not accompanied by the other steps of the laundering process. Since the water that is absorbed into the fabric generally contains some dirt, when the fabric is wrung out, the cloth becomes cleaner than it had been previously.

Under Biblical law, it is forbidden only to wring out truly absorbent materials, such as wool, cotton, linen, and sponge. The Sages extended the prohibition to include any fabric that, while not truly absorbent, can trap water within its fibers, since wringing out such a fabric resembles wringing out a truly absorbent fabric. Under this Rabbinic prohibition, it is also forbidden to squeeze water out of one's hair on Shabbos. However, this applies only to hair that grows densely and traps water in it, such as hair of the head and beard, as opposed to hair that is widely spaced, such as on the arms and legs.

Materials that do not absorb or trap liquid are not subject to the prohibition of wringing. An example of this would be a nylon baby brush with widely spaced bristles, or a plastic scouring pad with widely spaced fibers, which do not trap water.

We have now completed our discussion of the first of the three categories of *laundering* that are Biblically prohibited, as we discussed earlier.

פרשת שמות
TUESDAY
PARASHAS SHEMOS

Our discussion will now turn to the second category, namely, removing dust that is absorbed in fabric.

One may not use a brush to remove dust from a garment, nor shake a garment vigorously in order to remove the absorbed dust. Some *poskim* are more stringent and prohibit shaking the garment even lightly to remove dust (or chalk) that has been absorbed into the garment. In practice, we follow the more stringent view and forbid dusting altogether, as it constitutes laundering. It is important to note, however, that the prohibition against dusting refers only to removing dust that is *absorbed into* the fabric. It does not apply to removing surface dirt which does not adhere to the fabric.

A CLOSER LOOK AT THE SIDDUR

In the third paragraph of *Krias Shema,* we recite the verse (*Numbers* 15:39):

וְהָיָה לָכֶם לְצִיצִת וּרְאִיתֶם אֹתוֹ וּזְכַרְתֶּם אֶת־כָּל־מִצְוֹת ה׳ וַעֲשִׂיתֶם אֹתָם.
And it shall constitute tzitzis for you, that you may see it and remember all the commandments of HASHEM, and perform them.

The third paragraph of *Krias Shema* is called the *parashah* of *tzitzis.* We read it twice daily because it mentions *Yetzias Mitzrayim* (the Exodus from Egypt); it is noteworthy that this mitzvah is featured so prominently in this important part of our prayers. However, we may ask: How does seeing the *tzitzis* remind us to do all of Hashem's mitzvos, and what is the reason for this mitzvah?

There is an interesting story told by Rav Luria, the *Meshivas Nefesh* (a great-uncle of the *Maharshal*), in his *sefer.* He recounts a personal encounter he had with a priest, while living in Strassburg, Germany. At that time (over 500 years ago), all Jews were commanded by the authorities to wear a yellow star. [Although this decree is mostly remembered as one of the decrees of the Nazi regime, it was actually repeated many times in history (see *Shulchan Aruch, Hilchos Shabbos* §301).]

The priest approached Rav Luria, and asked him: "Why do you wear that yellow star, and what does it symbolize?" He answered, "It is a decree from the ruler of the land that we must obey, although there is no logical reason behind it." The priest then said, "I will explain to you the reason behind it. The king is a fair and just ruler, but actually this decree is from Hashem above. It states clearly in your Torah that Hashem separated the Jews from the other nations, and He gave you mitzvos to keep. Since you are not performing mitzvos at all times, He gave some mitzvos as constant signs and reminders that you are different and are Hashem's chosen nation. *Tzitzis* is a sign on your clothing to portray that you are indeed different, and carry the responsibility to keep all of Hashem's mitzvos. But when the Jews stopped wearing *tzitzis*, Hashem sent this decree, forcing you to wear a sign of discrimination — a sign that is degrading, similar to the way people mark the mentally unstable."

We see from this story how important the mitzvah of *tzitzis* is, and how it indeed must serve to remind us that we are bound to keep all of Hashem's commandments. [*Rashi* (to *Numbers* ibid.) explains further that the numerical value of the word צִיצִית, plus the number of strings and knots on the *tzitzis,* adds up to 613, the number of mitzvos in the Torah; see also *Ramban* there.] *Tzitzis* are a badge of honor, showing ourselves and the world that we were chosen by Hashem to keep His mitzvos. This important mitzvah is thus mentioned prominently in *Krias Shema*, right after the passage exhorting us to accept all of Hashem's commandments.

QUESTION OF THE DAY:

By what name was Moshe known to the Egyptians?

For the answer, see page 54.

פרשת שמות

A TORAH THOUGHT FOR THE DAY

WEDNESDAY

PARASHAS SHEMOS

וַיֹּאמֶר אַל־תִּקְרַב הֲלֹם שַׁל־נְעָלֶיךָ מֵעַל רַגְלֶיךָ כִּי הַמָּקוֹם אֲשֶׁר אַתָּה עוֹמֵד עָלָיו אַדְמַת־קֹדֶשׁ הוּא

And [HASHEM] said, "Do not come closer to here; remove your shoes from upon your feet, for the place upon which you are standing is holy ground" (*Shemos* 3:5).

Ohr HaChaim makes the observation that the verse mentions two distinct commands that were issued to Moshe. First, he was told not to come closer; second, he was told to remove his shoes, because even the place he was already standing on was holy. He asks: Why didn't Hashem first tell Moshe to correct what he was doing wrong by taking off his shoes, and then tell him not to come closer?

Ramban's explanation provides an answer. He explains that although Moshe was far from the burning bush, the Divine Presence (*Shechinah*) was resting upon the top of the mountain, and therefore it was forbidden to tread anywhere on the mountain while wearing shoes. This, however, was a lesser prohibition than actually coming too close to the place of the *Shechinah*. Thus, Hashem warned Moshe of the greater prohibition first.

Ramban notes other places where the presence of the *Shechinah* required that one not wear shoes, such as the episode where Yehoshua was visited by the angel of Hashem (*Yehoshua* 5:15). The same was true in the *Beis HaMikdash*, where the Kohanim were required to perform the *avodah* barefoot. We may ask: What is the reason for this? Why is the wearing of shoes a problem in the presence of the *Shechinah*?

Rav Shamshon Raphael Hirsch explains that one who takes off his shoes in a holy place demonstrates that he is giving himself over fully to the holiness of that place, without maintaining any personal barriers. Similarly, no separation from the *Beis HaMikdash* is allowed for the Kohen doing the *avodah*; he must be barefooted. Indeed, the Gemara says that the floor of the *Azarah* gives holiness to the Kohen. The more a person attaches himself to a holy place, the more he will be able to feel its holiness.

Zayis Raanan (by the *Magen Avraham*) adds that after the earth was cursed (see *Bereishis* 3:17, אֲרוּרָה הָאֲדָמָה), shoes were worn to separate a man from the cursed land. But in a place of אַדְמַת קֹדֶשׁ, where the earth is blessed and no trace of the curse remains, the opposite holds true. One should strive to attach himself as much as possible to such a place.

Many other commentators are of the opinion that although the simple meaning of the commandment holds true, there is a deeper message.

Netziv, Rabbeinu Bachya, Kli Yakar and others explain that removal of one's shoes is a metaphor; in the presence of holiness, one must try to remove all of his connections to worldly pleasures. While most people cannot do this on a constant basis, there are certain times and places where this is incumbent upon everyone. For example, on Yom Kippur, when we resemble the angels, we stand in prayer throughout the day without [leather] shoes, symbolizing a full day of detachment from this world, and enjoying our closeness to Hashem. Throughout the year, whenever a person feels a yearning to visit the *Beis HaMikdash,* he must prepare himself to "take off" (i.e., rise above) his material desires.

MISHNAH OF THE DAY: SHABBOS 14:2

The following Mishnah deals with the Rabbinic prohibition of making pickling brine on the Sabbath. Since this activity resembles a part of the process of the forbidden labor of *tanning* hides, which follows the forbidden labor of *slaughtering* (above, 7:2), it is included here after the laws of *trapping* and *bruising* animals (*Tiferes Yisrael*):

אֵין עוֹשִׂין הִילְמֵי בַּשַּׁבָּת — ***We may not prepare brine on the Sabbath;***[1] אֲבָל עוֹשֶׂה הוּא אֶת מֵי הַמֶּלַח — ***but one may prepare saltwater*** וְטוֹבֵל בָּהֶן פִּתּוֹ וְנוֹתֵן לְתוֹךְ הַתַּבְשִׁיל — ***and dip his bread into it, or add*** it ***to cooked food.***[2]

A dissenting view:

אָמַר רַבִּי יוֹסֵי — ***R' Yose said*** to the Sages: וַהֲלֹא הוּא הִילְמִי בֵּין מְרוּבָּה וּבֵין מוּעָט — ***But is it not brine whether it is a large or a small***

NOTES

1. Pickling brine consists of a mixture of water, salt and oil. Salt is placed in a container to which water is then added, producing a strong solution of saltwater, to which a small quantity of oil is added for taste. The Rabbis prohibited the preparation of such brine on the Sabbath, because in doing so one appears to be preparing to pickle foods to preserve them. While there is no Biblical prohibition against pickling foods on the Sabbath, the Rabbis prohibited both pickling and the preparation of brine for pickling, because the process of pickling is similar to the process of the forbidden labor of *tanning* hides (*Rav; Meiri*).

2. The Rabbinic prohibition applies only to the preparation of the large quantities of pickling brine generally prepared when one is pickling vegetables (*Rav* from Gemara 108b). Hence, one may make small quantities of saltwater on the Sabbath (*Rav, Rambam Commentary* from Gemara ibid.). The permissible quantity is the amount he needs in order to use as a dip for his bread or to mix into a cooked dish (*Rav; Tiferes Yisrael*).

quantity?[3] וְאֵלּוּ הֵן מֵי מֶלַח הַמּוּתָּרִין — ***Rather, this is the*** type of ***saltwater that is permitted:*** נוֹתֵן שֶׁמֶן לְכַתְּחִלָּה לְתוֹךְ הַמַּיִם אוֹ לְתוֹךְ הַמֶּלַח — ***One first adds oil to the water or to the salt*** before he mixes the water and salt together.[4]

NOTES

3. R' Yose argues that to draw a distinction solely on a quantitative basis might cause people to say that only labor involving large quantities is forbidden on the Sabbath, while labor involving small quantities is permissible. Therefore, since there is no qualitative distinction between them, both large and small quantities must be prohibited because of their resemblance to the tanning process (*Rav* from Gemara ibid.).

4. R' Yose concedes that the Sages who prohibited the making of saltwater did not forbid it in all its forms. However, he maintains that the permissible form of saltwater must be qualitatively different from the prohibited kind. This is accomplished by first adding oil to the water and then adding the salt, or first adding the oil to the salt and then adding the water. In both these cases the oil hinders the proper mixing of the salt with the water, thus resulting in a weak solution unfit for tanning. He may not mix the salt and the water before adding the oil, since in the initial stages the solution would appear like that used for tanning (*Rav; Rashi*).

GEMS FROM THE GEMARA

In our commentary to the Mishnah, we cited the distinction that is made by the Gemara between pickling brine and saltwater — viz., the Rabbinic prohibition applies only to the preparation of the large quantities of pickling brine that are generally prepared for use in pickling vegetables. It is for this reason that, according to the Sages, one may make small quantities of saltwater on the Sabbath (*Rav, Rambam Commentary* from Gemara 108b).

Yerushalmi (74b), however, explains the distinction between pickling brine and saltwater in a different way. When pickling brine is prepared, it must be compounded according to a specific recipe, to insure that the various components are in proper proportion. It therefore requires a professional to prepare it; and one who puts together such a mixture appears to be preparing to cook. It is for this reason that such preparation is prohibited (and not because of its resemblance to tanning). Saltwater, on the other hand, was often used as a condiment for dipping bread while eating meals, and required no such exactitude. Therefore it may be prepared on the Sabbath, as the one who makes it does not appear to be preparing to cook (*Yerushalmi* as explained by *Pnei Moshe*; see also *Rambam, Hil. Shabbos* 22:10, who may concur with this explanation).

Another view is that pickling brine contains such a high proportion of salt that the salt does not fully dissolve. In "saltwater," however, the salt does dissolve.

[It should be noted that even the Sages, who permit the preparation of small amounts of saltwater without requiring that one change the order of combining the ingredients (as does R' Yose), agree that overly strong saltwater may not be prepared. *Yerushalmi* (14:2) writes that the permit to make saltwater applies only if the concentration of salt is weak enough that an egg that is immersed in the saltwater sinks to the bottom. If the egg floats, however, the solution is very strong, and such saltwater may not be prepared on the Sabbath. The Gemara (108b) states that this concentration is two parts of salt to one of water.]

A MUSSAR THOUGHT FOR THE DAY

The *Chofetz Chaim* finds a powerful lesson in Hashem's statement to Moshe: כִּי הַמָּקוֹם אֲשֶׁר אַתָּה עוֹמֵד עָלָיו אַדְמַת־קֹדֶשׁ הוּא, *for the place upon which you are standing is holy ground* (see *A Torah Thought for the Day*). People, he says, tend to blame their lack of spiritual growth on factors such as their surroundings, their family situation, or the like. A person thinks to himself: "If only I would be somewhere else with another group of friends, I would be able to reach a higher level than the one I am at now." The Torah tells us here, says the *Chofetz Chaim,* that this is not the case. The place that you are standing on *now* is holy! Even in your situation, it is — and can be — holy ground.

The famous dialogue between *Rav Naftali Amsterdam* and his rebbi, *Rav Yisrael Salanter,* comes to mind. "If only," Rav Naftali lamented, "I would have the brains of the *Shaagas Aryeh*, the heart of the *Yesod V'Shoresh HaAvodah*, and the rebbi's sterling character, then I would amount to something!"

"No, no, Naftali!" replied Rav Yisrael. "With *your* brains and *your* heart and *your* character you can achieve untold greatness!" Everyone has the potential to reach the highest levels of accomplishment, if he but uses the gifts Hashem has given him in the proper manner.

We can add one thought. *Ohr HaChaim* points out that the verse seems to stress that this place did not have any *previous* holiness attached to it. It was only now, through the encounter that Moshe had with Hashem in this place, that an atmosphere of holiness was created there. For the verse states, "the place . . . *is* holy ground" — not "*was* holy ground." This proves that a person can take a simple piece of land in a desert and make it a source of holiness. Through one's commitment to Torah and mitzvos, he can bring the *Shechinah* to his surroundings, wherever they may be. Unfortunately, the opposite also holds true. If God forbid one commits a sin, he can cause the *Shechinah* to withdraw, and holiness to fade.

Rav Elchanan Wasserman visited America in the 1930's to raise funds for his yeshivah in Baranovitch, which was in dire financial straits. One day he was driven to Manhattan to meet a potential donor. He sat in the back seat with his eyes closed. When the driver mistakenly drove down one of the "less spiritual" streets, Rav Elchanan cried out in pain, "Where are you taking me?" A holy man feels waves of *tumah* like a sharp sword.

On the other hand, it is told that when the Chazon Ish was taking one of his daily walks to the outskirts of Bnei Brak, he stopped in one spot and commented, "Today, two *bnei Torah* stood here and spoke in learning." When his brother-in-law, the Steipler Gaon, was questioned as to the accuracy of this incident, he replied, "Yes, it is true and easy to understand," indicating that he had no trouble understanding that a holy person would be able to detect the impact Torah has on its physical surroundings.

HALACHAH OF THE DAY

We now continue our discussion of the second category of laundering — removing dust that has been absorbed in a fabric.

There is an important difference between removing dust from a garment, and washing a garment with water. Washing with water is forbidden even if the garment is only slightly dirty. As we explained in our earlier discussion of this topic, in practice one should not even soak a clean fabric in water. When removing dust from a garment, by contrast, it is forbidden to do so only if the garment is *significantly* dirty. The factor that determines whether a garment is considered "significantly dirty" is whether the amount of dust on it would deter the owner from wearing it under normal circumstances. If there is so much dust on a garment that the person would normally choose to wear a different outfit, removing the dust is considered an act of *laundering,* and it is thus prohibited. If the amount of dust would not deter the owner from wearing the outfit, removal of the dust is not considered an act of *laundering*, and it is permitted. This determination is based on the personal attitude of each individual, and how he feels about wearing the garment in question.

If one is in doubt as to whether he would wear the garment in its dusty state, he should adhere to the following guidelines: If the fabric is of a dark color and is in relatively new condition, one can presume that the dust would deter the owner from wearing the garment. Therefore, one may not remove the dust. Otherwise, one can presume that the dust would not deter the owner from wearing the garment, and one may remove the dust.

We have now learned how to determine when a garment may be dusted. However, even in circumstances where one is permitted to remove dust from a garment, one may not use a brush, nor may one shake or rub a garment vigorously. One may only brush lightly with one's hand or a dry cloth, or shake the garment lightly.

One is permitted to ask a non-Jew to remove the dust from a garment in a situation where it is otherwise forbidden to do so (i.e., a very dusty garment that one would not wear in normal circumstances). Although we generally prohibit asking a non-Jew to do something on the Sabbath that a Jew is forbidden to do, in this case it is permitted. This is due to the fact that there are some *poskim* who maintain that removing dust from a garment is *not* considered *laundering* at all. Therefore, with regard to allowing a person to ask a non-Jew to remove dust from a garment, we rely upon the more lenient view.

A CLOSER LOOK AT THE SIDDUR

In the בִּרְכוֹת הַשַּׁחַר, the *Blessings of the Morning,* recited at the beginning of *Shacharis,* we find the blessing:

בָּרוּךְ אַתָּה ה׳ . . . שֶׁעָשָׂה לִי כָּל צָרְכִּי.

Blessed are You . . . Who has provided me with my every need.

The Gemara in *Berachos* tells us that this *berachah* should be recited when one puts on his shoes. [Most people, however, have the custom to recite all of these blessings together, in shul.] One may ask: Why is there the need to recite a separate blessing for the gift of shoes? There is already a general blessing thanking Hashem for the gift of clothing (מַלְבִּישׁ עֲרֻמִּים, *Blessed are You . . . Who clothes the naked*).

Abudraham explains that without shoes, a person would never be able to travel, and reach distant places, to carry out his ambitions. The great gift of shoes indeed allows us to achieve all our needs. Shoes are the tools that transport a person from place to place.

The *Shelah* cites the words of his teacher, the *Maharshal*: There are four levels of Creation in this world: (1) דּוֹמֵם, *lifeless objects,* such as stone; (2) צוֹמֵחַ, *growing matter,* i.e., plants; (3) חַי, *living creatures;* and (4) מְדַבֵּר, *speaking creatures* — that is, mankind, who alone possess the power of speech. Each level is nourished by those creations that are on the levels beneath it. [The earth (דּוֹמֵם) supports vegetation (צוֹמֵחַ) that provides food for animals (חַי), that are in turn consumed (or used) by Man (מְדַבֵּר).] Man was given full control over the lower levels of the world. The *pasuk* in *Tehillim* (8:7-8) states: תַּמְשִׁילֵהוּ בְּמַעֲשֵׂי יָדֶיךָ כֹּל שַׁתָּה תַחַת־רַגְלָיו צֹנֶה וַאֲלָפִים כֻּלָּם, *You give him dominion over Your handiwork; You placed everything under his feet; sheep and cattle, all of them.* So when a person takes the skin of an animal and makes shoes for walking, he is demonstrating his power to rule the whole animal kingdom as well as the levels below it. That is why we make this blessing when putting on shoes, for it shows that all of a person's needs are made available for him by Hashem.

The *Sho'el U'Meishiv* (3:124) adds that for this reason, in a holy place such as the *Beis HaMikdash*, where one must act humbly and not show off his mastery of Creation, a person must remove his shoes.

Rav Shlomo Zalman Auerbach used this idea to explain why on Yom Kippur and Tishah B'Av one is restricted only from shoes made of leather, while shoes made of other materials may be worn. The reason for not wearing leather shoes on these days is that Yom Kippur and Tishah B'Av are not times when we should be portraying our elevated status in the order of Creation; and since only shoes of leather demonstrate this ascendancy, only they are proscribed.

[It is interesting to note that the *Gra* did not make the blessing שֶׁעָשָׂה לִי כָּל צָרְכִּי on Yom Kippur and Tishah B'Av until after the fast concluded and he put on his leather shoes.]

QUESTION OF THE DAY:

Where else in Scripture do we find someone removing his shoe?

For the answer, see page 54.

A TORAH THOUGHT FOR THE DAY

וַיֹּאמֶר מֹשֶׁה אֶל־הָאֱלֹהִים הִנֵּה אָנֹכִי בָא אֶל־בְּנֵי יִשְׂרָאֵל וְאָמַרְתִּי לָהֶם אֱלֹהֵי אֲבוֹתֵיכֶם שְׁלָחַנִי אֲלֵיכֶם וְאָמְרוּ־לִי מַה־שְּׁמוֹ מָה אֹמַר אֲלֵהֶם. וַיֹּאמֶר אֱלֹהִים אֶל־מֹשֶׁה אֶהְיֶה אֲשֶׁר אֶהְיֶה וַיֹּאמֶר כֹּה תֹאמַר לִבְנֵי יִשְׂרָאֵל אֶהְיֶה שְׁלָחַנִי אֲלֵיכֶם. וַיֹּאמֶר עוֹד אֱלֹהִים אֶל־מֹשֶׁה כֹּה־תֹאמַר אֶל־בְּנֵי יִשְׂרָאֵל ה׳ אֱלֹהֵי אֲבֹתֵיכֶם אֱלֹהֵי אַבְרָהָם אֱלֹהֵי יִצְחָק וֵאלֹהֵי יַעֲקֹב שְׁלָחַנִי אֲלֵיכֶם זֶה־שְּׁמִי לְעֹלָם וְזֶה זִכְרִי לְדֹר דֹּר

Moshe said to HASHEM, "Behold, when I come to the Children of Israel and say to them, 'The God of your forefathers has sent me to you,' and they say to me, 'What is His Name?' — what shall I say to them?" HASHEM answered Moshe, "I Shall Be As I Shall Be." And He said, "So shall you say to the Children of Israel, 'I Shall Be has sent me to you.'" HASHEM said further to Moshe, "So shall you say to the Children of Israel, 'HASHEM, the God of your forefathers, the God of Avraham, the God of Yitzchak, and the God of Yaakov has dispatched me to you. This is My Name forever, and this is My remembrance from generation to generation'" (Shemos 3:13-15).

R*abbeinu Bachya* explains that on its simplest level, the verse is to be understood as follows: Hashem, in response to Moshe's request to be told His Name, told him that this Name of אֶהְיֶה, *I Shall Be*, is not only Who I am now, but it is also how I wish to be remembered throughout the generations. However, continues *Rabbeinu Bachya*, the Gemara in *Pesachim* (50a) offers a deeper look at this statement, observing that the phrase זֶה־שְּׁמִי לְעֹלָם, *this is My Name forever*, when read as it is spelled in the Torah — without the letter *vav* in the word לעלם — also may be read זֶה־שְּׁמִי לְעַלֵּם, *this is My Name, which is to be hidden*. Thus, in addition to telling Moshe that *I Shall Be* is His Name, Hashem was also telling him that this everlasting Name is generally hidden.

The *Shelah HaKadosh* (*Parashas Shemos — Torah Ohr 1*) explains this enigmatic Gemara. Ordinarily, a name — or the expression used to depict someone or something — is the "handle" used to understand the essence of that which is being referred to. In regard to Hashem, however, this is of course impossible, for a full comprehension of His true reality is beyond human capacity. Rather, when speaking of Hashem, explains the *Shelah HaKadosh*, שְׁמִי, *My Name*, refers to the full essence of how He wishes to be understood by humanity. Accordingly, since Hashem wishes that man should relate to Him on this level, Adam, the first man, was created with the lofty spiritual capacity that allowed him to understand Hashem — and become close to Him — to the fullest extent that is humanly possible. Additionally, since a person can achieve only to the extent that his environment allows him to, Adam was given a world to live in that fostered this spiritual perception.

Sadly, Adam did not withstand the temptation of the fruit of the *Eitz HaDaas,* and, following his desires instead of Hashem's commandment to refrain from doing so, sinned by eating the fruit. This action of focusing on himself instead of his relationship with Hashem did not only change Adam by resulting in his expulsion from Gan Eden and eventual death; it changed the entire world. Eating from the *Eitz HaDaas* made selfish materialism a reality as well. From now on, man would no longer live in a world where the focus of furthering a relationship with Hashem was the only goal. Because of Adam's misdeed, instead of the world naturally helping mankind become closer to Hashem, the physical world, through its tangible pleasures, beauty, and apparent lack of direction and guidance, would now serve to distract man and keep him away from achieving the spiritual greatness of reaching his intended relationship with Hashem. Instead of Hashem's Name — or Essence — being obvious to the world, לְעוֹלָם, *forever,* as was intended during Creation, this tangible reality of Hashem's existence and involvement is largely לְעַלֵּם, *to be hidden.*

The Shelah HaKadosh continues, and explains why this message — of the elevated relationship resulting from a deep connection with the Name of Hashem that was meant for mankind — was told to Moshe in answer to his question of *what is His Name*. In asking for Hashem's Name, Moshe was not only asking for a title that he could tell the Bnei Yisrael (for, as *Ramban* points out, if the Jewish people were in fact unfamiliar with Hashem and were following Moshe on blind faith alone, they could just as easily have followed Moshe without being told Hashem's Name). Rather, Moses was asking Hashem to provide him with a deeper explanation of the nature of the redemption that he had just been told to lead. He asked: What is Your Name — Essence — as it relates to Your actions during this period of history? Answering this question, Hashem told him that He was to be known as אֶהְיֶה אֲשֶׁר אֶהְיֶה, *I Shall Be As I Shall Be* — I am the Creator Whose Mastery is total, which this redemption would definitively show to the world. Moreover, continued Hashem, זֶה־שְּׁמִי לְעֹלָם וְזֶה זִכְרִי לְדֹר דֹּר, *This is My Name forever, and this is My remembrance from generation to generation*; although My essence has been לְעַלֵּם, *to be hidden,* for many generations, it is in truth לְעוֹלָם, *forever* — and the time has once again come to reveal it — making it an active *remembrance* (*Panim Yafos*). For the purpose of the Egyptian exile was to purify the Jewish people and bring them to Har Sinai to receive the Torah, which would bring humanity back to an elevated connection with Hashem — allowing them to relate to Him to the limits of human ability, a level that mankind was meant to enjoy from the outset.

MISHNAH OF THE DAY: SHABBOS 14:3

The following Mishnah deals with the taking of medications on the Sabbath. The Rabbis forbade a person who is *not* seriously ill to take medications on the Sabbath. The subject is introduced here, because, like the previous Mishnah — which dealt with saltwater — it too considers items that are ingested that are not conventional foods (*Tos. Yom Tov*):
אֵין אוֹכְלִין אֵזוֹב יָוָן בְּשַׁבָּת — ***We may not eat Greek hyssop***[1] ***on the Sabbath,*** **לְפִי שֶׁאֵינוֹ מַאֲכַל בְּרִיאִים** — ***because it is not a food of healthy people;***[2] **אֲבָל אוֹכֵל הוּא אֶת יוֹעֶזֶר וְשׁוֹתֶה אַבּוּבְרוֹאֶה** — ***but one may eat pennyroyal,***[3] ***or drink knotgrass water*** [lit., *the shepherd's staff*].[4] **כָּל הָאוֹכָלִין אוֹכֵל אָדָם לִרְפוּאָה** — ***A person may eat any foods for healing;***[5] **וְכָל הַמַּשְׁקִין שׁוֹתֶה** — ***and he may drink any beverages,***[6]

NOTES

1. A type of hyssop (Gemara 109b). It is identified by *Rambam Commentary* as lavender (see also *Aruch HaShalem*). This herb is used medicinally to kill intestinal worms (Gemara ibid.).

2. Since Greek hyssop is not eaten by healthy people, one who eats it is obviously doing so for medicinal purposes. This is prohibited by Rabbinic decree, lest one crush the herbs used in medicines. To do so would be to perform a derivative of the forbidden labor of *grinding* (*Rav; Rashi*).

3. An aromatic plant of the mint family that has clusters of small purple flowers. It yields a pungent essential oil used medicinally and as an insect repellent.

4. A low-growing weedy grass with spikelets along the leaf stems. One of its uses was as an antidote for one who drank uncovered water which may have been poisoned by a snake (*Rav* from Gemara 109b). Since healthy people also eat these foods, it is not *apparent* that one is eating them for their medicinal benefits. The Rabbis did not apply their ban on medical treatments in such cases.

5. I.e., any food eaten by healthy people may be eaten on the Sabbath — even by an ill person who intends to benefit from its medicinal properties (*Rav*; cf. *Berachos* 38a; see also *Aruch HaShulchan, Orach Chaim* 328:47).

6. The Gemara (ibid.) explains that this clause pertains to a concoction of vinegar added to water in which capers have been soaked, which is primarily used to relieve toothaches. Since healthy people only occasionally drink such a concoction, we might have thought that it falls into the category of forbidden medications. The Mishnah therefore states that *he may drink "any" beverages* on the Sabbath.

חוץ מִמֵּי דְקָלִים — ***except for the water of palm trees,*** [7] **וְכוֹס עִיקָּרִים** — ***or a potion of roots,*** [8] **מִפְּנֵי שֶׁהֵן לִירוֹקָה** — ***because they are*** used ***for*** healing ***jaundice.*** [9] **אֲבָל שׁוֹתֶה הוּא מֵי דְקָלִים לִצְמָאוֹ** — ***However, one may drink the water of palm trees to*** quench ***his thirst,*** [10] **וְסָךְ שֶׁמֶן עִיקָּרִין שֶׁלֹּא לִרְפוּאָה** — ***and he may anoint himself with root oil*** if it is ***not for healing.*** [11]

NOTES

7. The extract of palm tree roots is used medicinally. In the Land of Israel, there was a certain famous well situated between two palm trees from which such water was obtained. This water was renowned for its purgative properties (*Rav* from Gemara 110a).

8. The translation follows *Rashi* to 109b. The "cup" was a three-part mixture, consisting of a *zuz*-weight each of Alexandrian gum, liquid alum (*Rashi; Rav* has a variety of grass) and garden crocus. These were crushed and the powder was then mixed with beer and used as a remedy for jaundice. It was also used, mixed with wine rather than beer, to cure a woman experiencing an unusually long menstrual flow (*Rav*).

9. Healthy people would not normally drink these two "beverages." Rather, they were used as cures for jaundice. Hence, one who drinks these beverages is clearly doing so for medicinal purposes. They are therefore forbidden on the Sabbath (*Rashi*).

10. I.e., if he does not suffer from any ailment (*Rav; Rashi; Tiferes Yisrael*; cf. *Beur Halachah* 328:37).

11. I.e., with oil to which extracts from the roots of spices and herbs have been added (*Tos. Yom Tov*). [Anointing was a common practice, intended to keep the skin soft. Various types of oils (in liquid form) were used.]

GEMS FROM THE GEMARA

Our translation of כּוֹס עִקָּרִים as *a potion of roots* follows *Rashi* to 109b. As we explained, this potion was comprised of three ingredients: a *zuz*-weight of Alexandrian gum, a *zuz*-weight of liquid alum, and a *zuz*-weight of garden crocus.

The Gemara states that this potion was used to cure a woman with an abnormally heavy menstrual flow. However, a variation of the potion could also be used as a cure for jaundice The Gemara explains that when this potion was being taken as a cure for jaundice, it was necessary to use only [any] two of the aforementioned ingredients; they were then mixed with beer and drunk. When prepared in this manner, although effective against jaundice, the potion had an undesirable side effect — it caused sterility. This is another meaning of the name כּוֹס עִקָּרִים, as the word עִקָּרִים can also be derived from the word עָקָר, which means *a sterile person;* thus, a כּוֹס עִקָּרִים was *a cup of sterility* (*Rav* from Gemara 110a).

A woman who would drink a potion compounded of all three ingredients mixed with wine (as a cure for an unusually heavy menstrual flow), though, was *not* in danger of becoming sterile. Even in this form, however, the potion was always known as "the cup of sterility," to warn people of the undesirable side effect of the second, similar potion (*Tos. Yom Tov*).

The Gemara (110b) questions the permissibility of taking a potion that will cause sterility, apart from any Sabbath-related considerations. Surely it should be forbidden for a person to render himself incapable of fathering children! The Gemara's conclusion is that indeed, only a woman may avail herself of such a remedy, since the commandment to be *fruitful and multiply* is obligatory only upon men, not women. A man, however, may not drink this potion, since he is forbidden to cause himself to become sterile. Even an older man is forbidden to take such a potion, as even elderly men are capable of fathering children (see ibid. 111a).

A MUSSAR THOUGHT FOR THE DAY

R' *Yerucham Levovitz* (*Daas Chochmah U'Mussar* 2:79) (see also *Ohr Yechezkel — Darchei HaAvodah* p. 29) cites the *Rambam*, who, in his *Moreh Nevuchim*, notes that Hashem, after telling Moshe זֶה־שְּׁמִי לְעֹלָם, *This is My Name forever*, continues by identifying Himself further as *HASHEM the God of your forefathers, the God of Avraham, the God of Yitzchak, and the God of Yaakov.* This, explains *Rambam,* is implicitly telling us of the greatness of the *Avos;* instead of Hashem identifying Himself to Moshe simply as the Creator, the Jewish forefathers merited to become the means that Hashem uses to express Himself in this world. The way that the *Avos* achieved this lofty level, continues *Rambam*, came from their *chibur,* total attachment, to Hashem, to the exclusion of everything else, throughout every moment of their lives.

Expanding on *Rambam's* insight, R' Yerucham explains that unlike ordinary men who (as we explained in *A Torah Thought for the Day*) suffer from the consequence of Adam's sin and allow the basic physical drives of selfishness and materialism to distract them from serving Hashem and becoming closer to Him, the *Avos* were able to totally ignore these distractions and live their lives focused on the reality of Hashem and His will. One who does not focus on anything besides Hashem naturally becomes closer to Him, as did Adam before his sin.

Moreover, when there are no impediments blocking this closeness, a person becomes so refined by his connection with Hashem that a sense of perceptible Godliness can be sensed simply by looking at him. Since the *Avos* reached the epitome of closeness that was possible, they, in a very real sense, are the truest reflection of Hashem's majesty. [It was perhaps for this reason that the relationship of the *Avos* with Hashem was mentioned to Moshe. Since the *Avos* were the tangible example of the total revelation of Hashem's Name that was to be revealed through the redemption (see *A Torah Thought for the Day*), telling the Jews that the God of Avraham, Yitzchak and Yaakov would soon redeem them was the best way to describe the revelation of Godliness that would soon become manifest to the entire world at Sinai.]

This highest level of *chibur*, concludes *Rambam*, was reached only by the *Avos* and Moshe Rabbeinu. This lofty level of total connection to Hashem is far beyond what we, on our relatively low spiritual plane, are able to achieve in practice. However, looking at the *chibur* of the *Avos* allows us to begin, in a very small way, to integrate this characteristic into our own lives. *Rambam* explains that *chibur* with Hashem comes from concentrating on serving Him, without thinking of anything else. He suggests that every person can attain a measure of *chibur* — by focusing on what he is saying and being aware that he is speaking with Hashem, without any distraction or outside thoughts — when reciting the first verse of *Krias Shema* and the first blessing of the *Shemoneh Esrei.* This way, we too will spend at least a few moments a day thinking only about Hashem and His service, to the exclusion of any other drive or desire in the world.

HALACHAH OF THE DAY

We may note one additional point with regard to the prohibition against removing dust from a garment: If there is no non-Jew available to remove dust from a very dusty garment, and the owner has no other suitable garment to wear and is embarrassed to wear the dusty one, he may rub off the dust with his elbow or in some other unusual manner. Removing dust in an unusual manner is prohibited only Rabbinically, and the Rabbis granted this dispensation for the sake of human dignity [כְּבוֹד הַבְּרִיּוֹת].

We learned above that there are three categories of *laundering* that are

Biblically prohibited. We have now concluded our discussion of the first two — washing fabric with water or a cleansing agent, and removing dust that is absorbed into a fabric — and we will begin to discuss the third and final category of *laundering* that is Biblically prohibited — that of removing a stain from fabric.

It is forbidden to remove any type of stain from fabric of any color with any type of cleansing agent. It is even forbidden to use a cleanser to diminish the intensity of a stain. Moreover, as mentioned earlier, it is even forbidden to merely pour water onto the stained fabric.

This prohibition applies even if the stain is very small or very light, and would not deter the owner from wearing the garment. Furthermore, it is not necessary to remove the *entire* stain to violate the prohibition; one may not remove even part of the stain.

It is forbidden to remove a stain from fabric by rubbing or scraping it with an instrument or with one's hand or fingernail. It is permitted, however, in a case of necessity (i.e., where one has no other garment to wear) to ask a non-Jew to rub out a significant stain.

If mud or moist dirt adhered to a garment and it is still wet, one is permitted to scrape off the dirt before it dries, as long as it *does* leave a stain on the garment. Since the garment will remain soiled, removing the dirt cannot be considered an act of *laundering*. However, one may not brush or rub the garment vigorously. There are several permissible methods for removing the dirt: One may scrape it off with one's fingernail, or with the back of a spoon or knife. One may also remove the dirt by wiping it gently with a dry cloth or by rubbing the reverse side of the fabric until the dirt falls off.

A CLOSER LOOK AT THE SIDDUR

In *A Torah Thought for the Day*, we cited the Gemara in *Pesachim* (50a) that explains that Hashem's declaration of זֶה־שְּׁמִי לְעֹלָם, *This is My Name forever*, when written as it is read in the Torah — without the letter *vav* in the word לעלם — may also be understood to be stating: *This is My Name that is to be hidden*. The Gemara comments that this second reading teaches us how we, who do not live in a world where Hashem's glory is openly revealed, are to pronounce Hashem's Name. Although the Name is written י־ה־ו־ה, this is not the way it is articulated; the need to ensure that it remains *hidden* requires us to pronounce the Name differently. Thus, when praying, making *berachos*, or when reading from the Torah, Hashem's Name of י־ה־ו־ה is not pronounced in the way that it is spelled. Rather, it is pronounced as is another one of Hashem's Names — אֲדֹנָ־י, *Adono-y* (which means *my Master*).

Netziv, in his *Haamek Davar*, explains why Hashem's Name of י־ה־ו־ה is not to be used in praising Hashem, in prayer, or in *berachos* of thanks, in the present world. The Name י־ה־ו־ה alludes to Hashem's total mastery of past, present, and future (as it includes the Hebrew words for past, present and future — הָיָה הֹוֶה וְיִהְיֶה — see *Orach Chaim* 5:1). Although we unquestionably believe that Hashem is omnipresent and all-powerful, we, living in a world corrupted by Adam's sin, are unable to comprehend what this means. Thus, it is meaningless, and even insincere, for us to include these accolades in our direct praises of Him in prayer, for doing so makes our prayers appear to be nothing more than empty flattery. Instead, when it is appropriate to say Hashem's Name in prayer, the Name of Hashem used as a substitute is אֲדֹנָ־י, *Adono-y,* which, instead of focusing on Hashem's total and awe-inspiring might, speaks of His role as Master. By using this Name, we recall how He rules over every individual area of Creation, and how He sustains and guides them on a ongoing basis. This is a quality of Hashem that everyone who looks at the world is able to see.

Accordingly, rules the *Shulchan Aruch*, since the Name that we are able to relate to nowadays is אֲדֹנָ־י (*Adono-y*), the *kavannah* (focus) that a person should have in mind when reading the Name י־ה־ו־ה and pronouncing it אֲדֹנָ־י, *Adono-y,* is only that He is the Master of everything. The *Vilna Gaon* concurs with this ruling only when one is reciting Hashem's Name in most *tefillos* or blessings. However, the Gaon rules that when reciting Hashem's Name in the first verse of *Krias Shema*: שְׁמַע יִשְׂרָאֵל ה׳ אֱלֹהֵינוּ ה׳ אֶחָד, *Hear O Israel, Hashem is our God, Hashem is the One and Only,* both focuses — that Hashem is omnipresent for past, present and future, as well as His Mastery of Creation — must be kept in mind. *R' Yitzchak Hutner* (*Pachad Yitzchak — Pesach* 60:11) explains the difference between *Krias Shema* and other times that the Name is mentioned. In every other area of *tefillah* we are *praising* Hashem's greatness. In reciting the *Shema,* however, we affirm His *achdus* — total unity — by saying that *Hashem is the One and Only*. Even though we do not understand this fully now, we acknowledge that it is fact, and that it will be revealed to the world in the Messianic era. Since we are speaking of what will be revealed to us in the future, and not only of what is clear to us in the present, the restrictions that do not allow us to speak of His total dominion of Creation do not apply, and we may — and must — affirm our belief in all aspects of Hashem's Name.

A TASTE OF LOMDUS

We learned above that because Hashem's essence cannot be understood nowadays to its fullest extent, we do not pronounce the Name י־ה־ו־ה as it is written; although written י־ה־ו־ה, the Name of Hashem is pronounced אֲדֹנָ־י, *Adono-y.*

R' Akiva Eiger (*Teshuvos* 1:30) attempts to use this rule to bring an interesting proof to an apparently unrelated idea — the question of whether *kesivah k'dibur — writing is equivalent to speech.* When the Torah requires something to be "articulated," such as prayer, the recital of *Krias Shema,* or any *berachah*, may the words be written instead? Perhaps the Torah does not specifically require that the words be *verbalized*, and, in requiring that they be "said," is only instructing that they be outwardly expressed — which may be fulfilled equally by writing them down instead. In a halachic responsa dealing with this issue, R' Akiva Eiger observes that, if we are to say that the Torah is not particular that expression must involve the lips, larynx and vocal cords, and writing would in fact be an appropriate and equal substitution for speech, how would a scribe ever be able to write a *Sefer Torah* or other *kisvei kodesh*? Every time he writes Hashem's Name י־ה־ו־ה, as is appropriate, the principle of *kesivah k'dibur* states that he is "saying" it as well — transgressing the prohibition of pronouncing Hashem's ineffable Four-Letter Name! Rather, the permission to write Torah scrolls implies that *kesivah laav k'dibur — writing is not equivalent to speech*, and blessings and passages that we are commanded to "say" must in fact be articulated with the mouth.

R' Akiva Eiger himself deflects this proof, and (as is explained by *Teshuvos Avnei Nezer* to *Yoreh Deah* 306:23, and *Kehillos Yaakov, Berachos* §12), in doing so offers a clearer definition of how *kesivah k'dibur* would work. Even if it is true that *writing is the equivalent of speech,* i.e., a person is able to halachically express his ideas and inner feelings through the written word just as he can by speaking, this license does not mean that writing *always* becomes like speech, in the sense that it is *only* a means of self-expression. Unlike speech, which inherently reveals to the outside world the ideas that a person is thinking, writing may fulfill one of several purposes. A scribe writing a Torah scroll, or anybody who is copying text, is not exhibiting his inner ideas through his pen or quill in the same way that a person does when composing a letter or an author does when writing a book. The copyist is doing only a mechanical, dry act of copying. Thus, explains R' Akiva Eiger, the effectiveness of *kesivah k'dibur* is limited to when the writer intends his act of writing to be expressing the ideas that he feels inside, whether this be a *berachah*, prayer, or the like. A scribe who is writing a Torah scroll, however, has no wish that his writing Hashem's Name should be as if he is articulating it, an act which is clearly forbidden.

Interestingly, *R' Mordechai Dov Twersky,* in his *Teshuvos Eimek She'eilah* (*Yoreh Deah* §67), offers a totally different solution to R' Akiva Eiger's question of how a scribe is permitted to write Hashem's Name if it is considered as if he is "saying" it through the means of *kesivah k'dibur*. He explains that since the Gemara (*Pesachim* 50a) clearly states: אָמַר הקב״ה לֹא כְּשֶׁאֲנִי נִכְתָּב אֲנִי נִקְרָא, *Hashem says, "My Name is not said as it is written"* (teaching, as *Rashi* points out, that *two* holy Names were given — a "hidden Name" to be reserved for writing and a "revealed Name" to be used in speech), it is clear that only writing the holy Name sufficiently "hides" it. Since the prohibition to express Hashem's Name is based upon the Torah's designation of it as *hidden*, it stands to reason that if the Name is said in a way that is considered hidden, such as when writing it — as the Gemara itself says is the proper forum to use for the name of י־ה־ו־ה — no prohibition of uttering Hashem's hidden Name is being transgressed. Thus, even if *kesivah k'dibur* teaches us that the one writing the Name is also "saying" it, this form of "speech" is permitted; the fact that this expression is being done in a "hidden way" — through writing — precludes *kesivah k'dibur* "speech" from being included in the prohibition to reveal Hashem's "hidden" Name.

QUESTION OF THE DAY:

How is the Name of Hashem, I Shall Be As I Shall Be, hinted at in the Four-letter Name of Hashem (י־ה־ו־ה)?

For the answer, see page 54.

A TORAH THOUGHT FOR THE DAY

וַיֵּלֶךְ מֹשֶׁה וַיָּשָׁב אֶל־יֶתֶר חֹתְנוֹ וַיֹּאמֶר לוֹ אֵלְכָה־נָּא וְאָשׁוּבָה אֶל־אַחַי אֲשֶׁר־בְּמִצְרַיִם

So Moshe went and he returned to Yeser, his father-in-law, and said to him, "Let me go, please, and I shall return to my brethren who are in Egypt" (*Shemos* 4:18).

R*ashi* states that the reason Moshe had to obtain permission from Yeser (Yisro) to leave was that he had sworn to Yisro that he would not leave without his permission. [*Rashi* here is consistent with his comment earlier (2:21) that וַיּוֹאֶל is an expression of an oath; thus, Moshe swore not to leave without permission. See *A Mussar Thought for the Day* for more about Moshe's oath.]

It seems strange that when Moshe was commanded by Hashem to return to Egypt, he refused to go until he received permission from his father-in-law! In fact, the Midrash (4:2) points out that Moshe put his very life in great danger by delaying his fulfillment of Hashem's command. The Midrash states that from Moshe's behavior we can learn a great principle with respect to the *middah* of *hakaras hatov,* "acknowledging the good" that was done to a person: "If someone opens his door for you, you owe him your soul." Because Yisro took Moshe into his home, Moshe owed Yisro his life; this required Moshe to endanger himself rather than break their agreement.

Rav Chaim Shmulevitz adds that it must be that Moshe was convinced that Hashem wanted him to wait for Yisro's permission. However, because he did not have a specific directive from Hashem to do so, it was still a decision that put his very life in danger.

Hakaras hatov was a fundamental lesson of *Yetzias Mitzrayim. Ramban* below (20:2) notes that the first verse of the Ten Commandments states: *I am Hashem, Your God, Who took you out of Mitzrayim, from the house of slaves.* The Torah adds these words to teach us that our gratitude to Hashem for the Exodus obligates us to follow His every command. Moshe knew that it would be incorrect to start the trip that would mark the beginning of the redemption by overlooking this important *middah.* [See further in *A Closer Look at the Siddur*.]

[The Gemara in *Nedarim* (65a) learns from this verse that a *neder* (vow) or oath that was made based on someone's approval can be nullified only in front of him. According to *Rashi's* explanation of the verse, however, it is difficult to understand how this can be derived, for the verse is not speaking of nullifying the oath; Moshe was simply asking permission, in fulfillment of the terms of his oath! See *Mizrachi*, who discusses this at length.]

MISHNAH OF THE DAY: SHABBOS 14:4

The following Mishnah continues the discussion concerning the Rabbinic prohibition against medical treatments on the Sabbath:

הַחוֹשֵׁשׁ בְּשִׁינָּיו — ***One who feels pain in his teeth*** לֹא יְגַמֵּע בָּהֶן אֶת הַחוֹמֶץ — ***may not sip vinegar through them.***[1] אֲבָל מְטַבֵּל הוּא כְּדַרְכּוֹ — ***However, he may dip*** food into vinegar ***in his usual manner*** and eat it; וְאִם נִתְרַפֵּא — ***and if he is*** thereby ***cured,*** נִתְרַפֵּא — ***he is cured.***[2]

הַחוֹשֵׁשׁ בְּמָתְנָיו — ***One who feels pain in his hips*** לֹא יָסוּךְ יַיִן וְחוֹמֶץ — ***may not anoint*** them ***with wine or vinegar.***[3] אֲבָל סָךְ הוּא אֶת הַשֶּׁמֶן — ***However, he may anoint*** them ***with oil,***[4] וְלֹא שֶׁמֶן וֶורֶד — ***but not*** with ***rose oil.***[5] בְּנֵי מְלָכִים סָכִין שֶׁמֶן וֶרֶד עַל מַכּוֹתֵיהֶן — ***Princes may anoint their wounds with rose oil,*** שֶׁכֵּן דַרְכָּן לָסוּךְ בַּחוֹל — ***for such is their custom to anoint*** their bodies with rose oil even ***on weekdays.***[6]

A dissenting view:

רַבִּי שִׁמְעוֹן אוֹמֵר — ***R' Shimon says:*** כָּל יִשְׂרָאֵל בְּנֵי מְלָכִים הֵם — ***All Israel are princes***, and thus any Jew may apply rose oil to his wounds on the Sabbath.[7]

NOTES

1. Rinsing one's mouth with vinegar relieves toothaches. However, a person who does not have a toothache would not rinse his mouth with vinegar. Accordingly, one may not rinse his mouth with vinegar for a toothache [and spit the vinegar out], since it is obvious that he is doing so for medicinal purposes (*Rav*). [One may, however, sip vinegar and swallow it (*Rav* from Gemara ibid.).]

2. I.e., it is permissible to effect a cure in this manner. Eating bread or other foods dipped in vinegar was a common practice. Therefore, it is not apparent that this person is doing so for medicinal purposes (*Tos. Yom Tov*).

3. Since one anoints himself with these liquids only in order to treat his pain, his intention for medicinal purposes is obvious (*Rav; Rashi*).

4. Since healthy people also anoint themselves with oil, he may anoint the painful area with it as well (*Tiferes Yisrael*).

5. Since rose oil is expensive, healthy people anoint themselves with it only for medicinal purposes. Since its purpose is obvious, its application falls under the prohibition on medical treatments (*Rav*; *Rashi*).

6. Since, owing to their wealth, princes use rose oil to anoint themselves even on weekdays, it is not automatically apparent that its application to a painful area on the Sabbath is for medicinal purposes (*Rav; Rashi; Tiferes Yisrael*).

7. R' Shimon's position is that the halachah does not discriminate between different groups. Whatever is permitted for one group should be permitted for another (*Rashi* to 111b; cf. *Tosafos*).

GEMS FROM THE GEMARA

The Gemara (111b) states in the names of Rava and R' Chiya bar Avin that Rav held that the law follows R' Shimon, but not for his reason; i.e., one is permitted to anoint himself with rose oil on the Sabbath, but not because of the reason stated by R' Shimon. Thus, Rav does not actually follow R' Shimon's opinion on this matter.

The Gemara then clarifies this statement: It does *not* mean that Rav, who permits the use of rose oil, does so only because it is his opinion that the use of rose oil has no therapeutic effect (and there is therefore no reason for it not to be used). That cannot be correct, for since the Mishnah teaches that princes may smear rose oil on their wounds, it is evident that rose oil does heal. [If rose oil does not heal, it would not have been necessary for the Tanna Kamma to state that it may be used (by princes) on the Sabbath. Thus, we see that even the Tanna Kamma, who argues with R' Shimon, maintains that rose oil does heal (*Rashi*). It does not seem likely that Rav would disagree with both R' Shimon and the Tanna Kamma (*Sfas Emes*).]

Rather, when the Gemara states that according to Rav, the law follows R' Shimon, who permits the use of rose oil, but not for his reason, it means that the permit of Rav is not as inclusive as that of R' Shimon. R' Shimon holds that rose oil is permitted even in places where it is expensive, and thus not commonly used. His reason, as explained in the Mishnah, is that the halachah does not distinguish in such matters between different groups of people, and whatever is permitted for princes must therefore be permitted for anyone. Rav, on the other hand, holds that only if it is common it may be used, but not if it is not common. For this reason, Rav permitted the use of rose oil only in locales where rose oil was common. [Even the Tanna Kamma agrees that in a locale where commoners use rose oil for non-healing purposes, they may anoint their wounds with it, since its general use is not evidently medicinal. Rav permitted the use of rose oil only in such locales, and thus is consistent with the Tanna Kamma's view (*Rashi*).]

QUESTION OF THE DAY:

What were the seven names of Yisro?

For the answer, see page 54.

A MUSSAR THOUGHT FOR THE DAY

The *Yalkut* (*Shemos* §169) states that when Moshe was interested in marrying Tzipporah, the daughter of Yisro, Yisro had a peculiar request: "I will give you my daughter if you agree to give up your firstborn to *avodah zarah;* you are free to bring up any subsequent children as Jews." Moshe agreed, and he even accepted this bargain upon himself with an oath.

To understand these words literally is very difficult. How could Moshe even consider agreeing to such terms, much less make an oath to adhere to them?! *Radvaz* (6:2168) asks this question, and says that Moshe did not really accept these terms. Rather, he allowed Yisro to be fooled into thinking that he had. [Since Yisro deceived himself, and was not directly misled by Moshe, this was permitted.]

Rav Dessler, in *Michtav MeiEliyahu* (1:153), explains that this Midrash is not be taken literally at all. He cites an important principle in the name of *Maharal*: Many times, when *Chazal* tell us that a person said a particular thing, it does not always mean that those actual words were uttered. Rather, *Chazal* are revealing to us the hidden feelings that person has regarding a particular subject. When a person is determined to do something, he is automatically pulled in that direction, with an even greater force than if he had made an oath to do so. *Chazal* sometimes do this to magnify the danger (or the goodness) of a particular matter. [Thus, by exposing his children to the ways of Yisro, Moshe created a situation where it was possible that his son could stray to *avodah zarah.*]

Baal HaTurim (2:16) explains Moshe's rationale: Moshe knew quite well that he could easily convince his father-in-law of the true path in life and bring him closer to Hashem, as he ultimately did. Thus, he felt safe in allowing Yisro to think that he had agreed to such an oath. He nevertheless was punished, as his grandson Yonasan son of Gershom did ultimately serve as a priest to *avodah zarah* (see *Bava Basra* 109b-110a for further details). Moshe had no intention of complying with the oath, but because he allowed himself to even speak of such an idea, the Torah sees this as an indication — albeit very minute — that he would agree to attach himself to one who served *avodah zarah*. [According to *Targum Yonasan* (4:24), Yisro held Moshe back from performing the *milah* upon his eldest son because of the oath that Moshe had made, a delay that indeed almost caused Moshe's death (see there).]

From this we can see how careful we must be not to allow ourselves to befriend or join groups that are removed from Torah values, even if we think that we are strong in our beliefs and no one can change us. The Torah shows us that even our great teacher Moshe was adversely affected by such a connection.

HALACHAH OF THE DAY

Yesterday, we discussed some of the details of the prohibition against removing a stain from fabric, the third of the methods Biblically prohibited under the category of *laundering.* We will now continue discussing other aspects of this prohibition.

We discussed the scenario of wet mud that adhered to a fabric, and said that as long as it leaves a stain, there are permissible methods of removing the dirt. However, if the mud has dried onto the fabric, the above mentioned methods may not always work. This is not due to the prohibition of *laundering*, since the dirt will leave a stain behind. Rather, it is due to another factor. When one removes dried dirt from a garment, the dirt will crumble, thereby causing one to transgress the prohibition of טוֹחֵן, *grinding*. Although one is not interested in grinding the dirt, this is nonetheless prohibited Rabbinically. Thus, if the dirt consists of something that has never been previously ground up (e.g., mud), one is forbidden to remove it. If it consists of an item that was previously ground up (e.g., mashed potato), one is permitted to remove it by one of the aforementioned methods, since there is no prohibition against grinding something that was previously ground [אֵין טוֹחֵן אַחַר טוֹחֵן]. Likewise, if the dirt consists of a food item that does not grow from the ground (e.g., eggs), one is permitted to remove it by one of the previously mentioned methods, since the prohibition of *grinding* does not pertain to such items.

In a case of necessity, one is permitted to ask a non-Jew to remove any type of dirt, as long as it leaves a stain on the fabric.

It is important to note, with respect to the entire preceding discussion, that the permissible methods of removing wet mud or the like from fabric apply only when a stain will be left on the cloth after the dirt is removed. If no stain will remain, one may not scrape off the dirt, since this is considered *laundering*.

Earlier, in our discussion regarding washing clothing with water, we mentioned that soaking fabric in clean water is forbidden according to many *poskim* as an act of *laundering*. There are circumstances where our Sages prohibited even soaking fabric in dirty water. The concern of the Rabbis was that a person might wring out the liquid, which would constitute a forbidden act. This Rabbinical prohibition applies only when the fabric is sufficiently wet that if one touches the fabric with his hand, the hand will become wet enough to transfer moisture to another item it subsequently touches. Also, a significant part of the fabric must be saturated, enough that a person would want to wring it out. The liquid that the fabric is soaking in must also be a clear one (including a light-colored liquid such as lemonade or white wine), so that the fabric will be *relatively* clean when it is wrung out; and it must be a liquid that will not leave behind a strong odor (for otherwise there is no point in wringing it out). The fabric must be an item that one cares to wring out, such as clothing, and not an item that a person will simply leave saturated with liquid. When all of these conditions are present, it is Rabbinically forbidden to soak the fabric even in dirty water.

A CLOSER LOOK AT THE SIDDUR

When we daven *Shemoneh Esrei* during the *Shacharis* prayer, we are required to be סוֹמֵךְ גְּאוּלָּה לִתְפִלָּה, *connect redemption to Prayer* (i.e., *Shemoneh Esrei*). This means that as soon as we complete reciting the blessing speaking of redemption that immediately precedes the *Shemoneh Esrei* (the *berachah* of *Gaal Yisrael*), we must begin the *Shemoneh Esrei* without delay. This requirement applies to the *Maariv* prayer as well. [Although in the case of *Maariv* there are prayers that interpose between *Gaal Yisrael* and *Shemoneh Esrei,* the Gemara tells us that those prayers also deal with redemption, and do not constitute an interruption between *geulah* and *tefillah.*]

The Gemara in *Berachos* praises one who adheres to this, and calls him a "*ben Olam Haba.*" This would seem to be a large measure of reward for what appears to be a very simple practice. *Rabbeinu Yonah* in *Berachos* gives two explanations for the sizable reward:

(1) When we speak of redemption in our *tefillah,* we are remembering that Hashem took us out of Egypt to make us His servants. At that point, we ceased to be slaves of Pharaoh, and we became slaves of Hashem, bidden to serve only Him. When we pray the *Shemoneh Esrei,* we are performing the service of Hashem (as we have noted in

earlier studies, prayer is עֲבוֹדָה שֶׁבְּלֵב, *service of the heart*). Thus, one who connects redemption with *tefillah* shows his *hakaras hatov* to Hashem by fulfilling the purpose of his redemption.

(2) Mentioning the miracles of *Yetzias Mitzrayim* and the *Yam Suf* (Sea of Reeds) serves to strengthen a person's *bitachon*, trust in Hashem. The Bnei Yisrael at the *Yam Suf* had no choice but to place their trust in Hashem, and through their *bitachon* they were saved. By reiterating this in our prayers, and understanding and believing that this is the only way anyone can be saved from any harm, we reach the proper level of readiness to begin our *Shemoneh Esrei,* in which we ask Hashem for our needs. One who connects *geulah* and *tefillah* — that is, he reaches a high level of *bitachon* upon contemplating the redemption, and transfers that to his Prayer — is truly deserving of being called a *ben Olam Haba.*

פרשת שמות

SHABBOS

PARASHAS SHEMOS

A TORAH THOUGHT FOR THE DAY

וַיָּשָׁב מֹשֶׁה אֶל־ה׳ וַיֹּאמַר אֲדֹנָי לָמָה הֲרֵעֹתָה לָעָם הַזֶּה לָמָּה זֶּה שְׁלַחְתָּנִי. וּמֵאָז בָּאתִי אֶל־פַּרְעֹה לְדַבֵּר בִּשְׁמֶךָ הֵרַע לָעָם הַזֶּה וְהַצֵּל לֹא־הִצַּלְתָּ אֶת־עַמֶּךָ. וַיֹּאמֶר ה׳ אֶל־מֹשֶׁה עַתָּה תִרְאֶה אֲשֶׁר אֶעֱשֶׂה לְפַרְעֹה כִּי בְיָד חֲזָקָה יְשַׁלְּחֵם וּבְיָד חֲזָקָה יְגָרְשֵׁם מֵאַרְצוֹ

And Moshe returned to HASHEM *and he said, "My master! Why have You done evil to this people — why have You sent me? From the time I came to Pharaoh to speak in Your Name, he has acted with evil to this people; but You did not save your people!" And* HASHEM *said to Moshe, "Now you will see what I shall do to Pharaoh, for through a strong hand he will send them out, and with a strong hand he will drive them from his land"* (*Shemos* 5:22-6:1).

In this passage, we find Moshe, anguished by the fact that his mission of mercy to redeem the Jews from bondage has resulted in even harsher burdens for them, approaching Hashem with the question: "Why?" As *Rashi* explains: If it was not Your will to free them at this point in time, why did You send me now? If I am to be their redeemer, why was it necessary for me to begin as an accomplice in their oppression?

It is difficult to find a direct answer to Moshe's question within Hashem's reply. Indeed, *Rashi* understands Hashem's rejoinder as reproof to Moshe (which continues into the next *parashah*). Hashem told Moshe: "You have questions about My actions? When I promised Avraham that he would see offspring from Yitzchak, and then I commanded him to bring him upon the Altar, he had no questions; he instantly obeyed. But you are questioning me!" For this, Moshe was punished. Hashem said: "*Now* you will see . . ." *Rashi* explains: You will see what happens *now,* to Pharaoh, but you will not live to see the miracles that occur when the seven Canaanite nations are conquered as the Jews enter Eretz Yisrael (see also *Sanhedrin* 111a).

Rabbeinu Bachya, however, does see an answer to Moshe in Hashem's reply. It is the way of man to assume that the righteous should never suffer, and the wicked should never prosper; but that is not the way of Hashem. Sometimes the righteous must suffer, to pave the way for greater reward in the future; and sometimes the wicked must be rewarded for good deeds that they performed. As we learned earlier (see *A Torah Thought for the Day*, Monday), the suffering of the Jews in Egypt allowed them to leave after only 210 years in Egypt, instead of 400 years. Thus, Hashem told Moshe, "Do not be impatient. *Now* you will see; in the end, Pharaoh and the Egyptians will receive their just deserts, while the Jews will leave triumphantly, as a free nation."

For another understanding of Hashem's reply, see *A Mussar Thought for the Day*.

MISHNAH OF THE DAY: SHABBOS 15:1

Tying and *untying* knots are two of the labors that are Biblically forbidden. The following Mishnah discusses the status of various knots: וְאֵלּוּ קְשָׁרִים שֶׁחַיָּיבִין עֲלֵיהֶן — ***And these are knots for which we are liable*** to a *chatas*:[1] קֶשֶׁר הַגַּמָּלִין — ***the camel driver's knot,***[2] וְקֶשֶׁר הַסַּפָּנִין — ***and the sailor's knot.***[3] וּכְשֵׁם שֶׁהוּא חַיָּיב עַל קִישּׁוּרָן — ***And just as one is liable for tying them,*** כָּךְ הוּא חַיָּיב עַל הֶיתֵּרָן — ***so is one liable for untying them.***[4]

רַבִּי מֵאִיר אוֹמֵר — ***R' Meir says:*** כָּל קֶשֶׁר שֶׁהוּא יָכוֹל לְהַתִּירוֹ בְּאַחַת מִיָּדָיו — ***Any knot that one can untie with one of his hands,*** אֵין חַיָּיבִין עָלָיו — ***we are not liable for*** tying ***it.***[5]

NOTES

1. I.e., these are the knots referred to above (7:2), where tying a knot and untying a knot are enumerated as two of the primary categories of forbidden labor.

Only knots bearing similarity to those used for tying together torn threads in the curtains of the Mishkan, or the nets of those who fished for the *chilazon* [the aquatic creature from which the *techeiles* dye was manufactured] entail Biblical liability (*Rav, Rashi* from Gemara 74b). Moreover, one is liable only for tying professional knots that are intended to remain permanently (*Rav; Rambam, Commentary* and *Hil. Shabbos* 10:1; cf. *Rashi; Rosh*).

2. The septum of a camel's nose was punctured, and a leather thong was inserted through the hole. The ends of the thong were then knotted permanently, to form a ring to which ropes or reins could be attached (*Rav*).

3. The prow of the ship was punctured, so that a rope could be inserted and knotted to form a ring. The long ropes used to tie a ship in place while in dock were fastened to this ring (*Rashi*). The ends of the rope that made up this ring were tied by the sailors with a permanent knot (*Rav*).

4. I.e., the same knots for which one is liable for tying, he is also liable for untying.

The forbidden labor of *untying* took place in the Mishkan, when those who trapped the *chilazon* would untie the knots in their nets to readjust them (*Rav* from Gemara 74b; *Rashi*). However, as is the case with all forbidden labors, one is liable only for untying a knot if he does so for a constructive purpose. If he does so destructively, he is exempt (*Rambam, Hil. Shabbos* 10:7; see above, 13:3).

5. I.e., even if one tied a knot with the intent that it remain permanently in place, if he tied it loosely enough that he can untie it with one hand, he is not liable to a *chatas* (*Rav; Rashi*; see the end of the next Mishnah).

GEMS FROM THE GEMARA

The Mishnah stated: *R' Meir says: Any knot that one can untie with one of his hands, we are not liable for it.*

The Gemara (111b) in the name of Rav Achadvoi the brother of Mar Acha inquires: What is the status of a bow according to R' Meir? The Gemara explains that the question of whether one would be liable for tying a bow is dependent on the reason that R' Meir exempts a person who ties a knot that can be untied with one hand. Do we say that R' Meir exempts a person who ties such a knot because any such knot is not deemed to be significant, since it is so easily untied? If this is the case, then when one ties a bow as well, since it can be untied with one hand, he should also not incur liability. Or perhaps the reason of R' Meir is because a knot that can be untied with one hand is [obviously] not tight, and one is not liable for tying if he ties such a loose knot. If this is the case, one who ties a bow would be liable, even though it can be untied with one hand. The Gemara leaves the question unresolved.

The halachah does not accord with R' Meir. Thus, one is liable for tying a permanent knot even if it can be untied with one hand.

[*Rambam* and *Rif* rule that one is liable for violating the *melachah* of *tying* only for tying a professional knot. Now, *Taz* states that a *professional* knot implies a *strong* knot. One might ask: Surely, a knot that can be untied with a single hand is not a very strong knot. How, then, can it be that one would be liable for tying such a knot?

We may answer that although it would seem that a knot that can be untied with a single hand would not qualify as a strong knot, this is not necessarily the case. The commentators define a strong knot either as a knot that will not come apart on its own (*Beur Halachah* to 317:1), or a knot that cannot be pulled open [without being untied (*Mirkeves HaMishneh*)]. Even a knot that can be untied with a single hand can meet one or both of these criteria. Thus, it is possible for a knot that can be untied with one hand to still qualify as a strong knot.]

QUESTION OF THE DAY:

Why did Moshe question the fact that Pharaoh had not heeded his request to free the Jews, when Hashem had already told him (see above, 4:21) that Pharaoh would not listen?

For the answer, see page 54.

A MUSSAR THOUGHT FOR THE DAY

Above, in *A Torah Thought for the Day,* we noted that when Moshe asked Hashem why He had caused the plight of the Jews to worsen when Moshe came upon the scene, Hashem did not answer him directly, but merely told him that he would now see the redemption that would soon follow. Another understanding of the verse is offered by *R' Reuven Feinstein,* according to which Hashem *did* explain to Moshe why He had caused him to fail in his initial attempt.

R' Reuven explains that the key to understanding Hashem's reply lies in its opening words: "Now you shall see what *I* will do to Pharaoh." The Exodus from Egypt was more than a miraculous event and the fulfillment of Hashem's promise to Avraham; it was a clear proof to the Jews, to Egypt, and to the entire world that Hashem was the Master, in total control of the world, and that He had chosen the Bnei Yisrael as His special nation. [Indeed, the opening words of the Ten Commandments read: *I am HASHEM, Your God, Who took you out of Egypt.*] It was for this reason that Hashem performed such spectacular miracles during the Exodus, including the Ten Plagues and the miracles at the *Yam Suf.* It was an absolutely essential component of the Exodus that the Jews, along with the rest of the world, be shown the true might and glory of Hashem.

But there was a difficulty. The messenger chosen to lead the Jews forth from Egypt was the righteous Moshe, the man whose level of prophecy would be unique, who served as the faithful shepherd of the nation at a level never again seen. It would be all too easy for the downtrodden Jews to seize upon Moshe as their savior, and give no thought at all to the One who sent Moshe. If this were to happen, the Exodus would simply serve to catapult Moshe's status to near-Divine proportions, while doing nothing to strengthen the belief in Hashem that would be central to the acceptance of the Torah and the formation of the Jewish nation.

For this reason, says R' Reuven, it was necessary to prove to the Jews from the outset that Moshe was a messenger, and no more. He came to Pharaoh, made his request — and failed badly. Thus, it was made clear to all the Jews that his subsequent successes were not a result of his personal greatness, but a reflection of Hashem's Will.

This is what Hashem told Moshe: Had you been blessed with immediate and total success, everyone would attribute it to you, and not to Me. But "*now*" that all have seen that you are but a fallible man, you shall see what *I will do* to Pharaoh. It will be clear to all that the redemption that is to come is *My* doing, and My doing alone. That is the reason your initial efforts ended in failure.

HALACHAH OF THE DAY

Yesterday, we began discussing the topic of soaking fabric in dirty liquid, and discussed the circumstances when it would be Rabbinically prohibited: The fabric must be sufficiently wet, the liquid it is soaking in must be clear and relatively odorless, and the fabric must be of a type that one would care to wring out.

For these reasons, the prohibition against saturating a fabric does not apply to towels and rags, which people generally do not mind leaving saturated. It also does not apply to saturating fabric with a liquid so filthy that it will badly soil the fabric and require washing afterward. And it also does not apply to merely moistening a clean fabric, or saturating an insignificant portion of the fabric.

The most common application of saturating fabric is when cleaning up a spilled liquid. We will now discuss some rules that apply, based on the guidelines mentioned above.

If a small amount of liquid spilled, one is permitted to wipe it up even with a garment (e.g., an apron), provided that the garment will not become thoroughly saturated.

If a large amount of a clear liquid spilled, one may not blot it with a garment, but may use a towel, rag or paper towel to clean it up.

If a large amount of a colored liquid or a liquid with a strong odor spilled, one is permitted to wipe it up with a garment or towel. However, when wiping up after a colored liquid has spilled, one should preferably use a rag or paper towel to avoid transgressing the *melachah* of צוֹבֵעַ, *dyeing.*

In order to ensure that people would not come to wring out wet garments on Shabbos, our Sages decreed that wet, saturated fabric not be used or moved at all on Shabbos, much like *muktzeh*. This applies only to fabric that one would be inclined to wring out. Thus, saturated fabric may not be moved only when the conditions outlined above are present: The fabric must be sufficiently wet so that one's hand, when touching the fabric, becomes wet enough to transfer the moisture to another item it subsequently touches; a significant part of the fabric must be saturated; the liquid that the fabric is soaking in must be a clear one that does not have a strong odor; and the fabric must be of a type that one cares to wring out, rather than leave it saturated, such as clothing.

If all these conditions are not present, the fabric is not *muktzeh,* and may be moved. Even when it is forbidden to move the fabric, two people may move it together, since they will remind each other not to wring it out. Also, once the fabric dries, even one person may move it.

A CLOSER LOOK AT THE SIDDUR

As we discussed last week, the *Shemoneh Esrei* prayers of the Sabbath do not contain the lengthy catalog of personal requests that make up the central portion of the weekday *Shemoneh Esrei*. Nevertheless, the central blessing of the Sabbath *Shemoneh Esrei* does contain a short section of requests, which are of a more general (and also somewhat more spiritual) nature than the weekday requests.

We begin with the request, קַדְּשֵׁנוּ בְּמִצְוֹתֶיךָ, *sanctify us with Your mitzvos. Eitz Yosef* explains that the performance of mitzvos sanctifies a person's *neshamah* (soul) and endows it with radiance. Thus, on the spiritual day of the Sabbath it is appropriate to ask Hashem for assistance in attaining greater spiritual heights. Also included in this request is a plea that the *Beis HaMikdash* be rebuilt, so that we may perform the mitzvos of the sacrificial service.

The next request is וְתֵן חֶלְקֵנוּ בְּתוֹרָתֶךָ, *and grant us our share in Your Torah.* The Sabbath, when one is freed from the pressures of the workweek, is an ideal time to delve into the study of the Torah. We ask Hashem to grant us the *siyata d'Shmaya,* Heavenly assistance, that we require to excel in our Torah learning. We speak of "our share" of Torah because every Jew is given the capability to take the Torah he learns and make it uniquely his (see *Kiddushin* 32b); this is accomplished through concentrated study and the learning of Torah for its own sake (*lishmah*). We pray that we be able to reach this level of commitment to our studies.

The third request is שַׂבְּעֵנוּ מִטּוּבֶךָ, *satiate us with Your goodness.* This wording is especially appropriate on the Sabbath, when we are all guests at Hashem's table; as the Gemara in *Beitzah* (16a) tells us, funds spent to honor the Sabbath are reimbursed by Hashem. Here, we ask Hashem to provide us not only with the minimum that we need, but to provide enough that we will be satiated, and able to thank Him for His beneficence with full hearts.

We will continue our discussion of these requests next week.

ANSWERS TO QUESTIONS OF THE DAY

Sunday:

This expression alludes to the fact that the family of Yaakov descended to Egypt only to sojourn there (see *Bereishis* 47:4), and never considered themselves as having truly arrived to stay (*R' Yehoshua of Belz*).

Monday:

It is the ritual of כַּרְפַּס, in which we dip a vegetable into saltwater. The saltwater symbolizes the tears of the oppressed Jews, while the word כַּרְפַּס contains the letters ס׳ פָּרֶךְ — *sixty [myriads of Jews were forced to endure] harsh labor.*

Tuesday:

Ibn Ezra states that the name given to Moshe by the Egyptians was Munyus (מוניוס).

Wednesday:

In *Megillas Rus,* we find that Boaz, the redeemer of Naomi's fields, removed his shoe (*Rus* 4:8; see *Rashi* there). [Interestingly, according to *Daas Zekeinim* here, Boaz gave the redeemer his *glove,* not his shoe.]

Thursday:

The Four-letter Name of Hashem contains the letters of the words היה, הוה and יהיה, which mean *He was, He is,* and *He will be* (see *A Closer Look at the Siddur*). Thus, it points to Hashem's eternal nature.

Friday:

Re'uel, Yesser, Yisro, Chovav, Chever, Keini, and Putiel (see *Rashi* to *Shemos* 18:1).

Shabbos:

Ramban explains that Moshe knew that Pharaoh would not listen to him and *release* the Jews, but he had thought that their bondage would at least be relaxed somewhat. Instead, it was intensified.

פרשת וארא

Parashas Va'eira

פרשת וארא

SUNDAY

PARASHAS VA'EIRA

A TORAH THOUGHT FOR THE DAY

וַיְדַבֵּר אֱלֹהִים אֶל־מֹשֶׁה וַיֹּאמֶר אֵלָיו אֲנִי ה׳

God (Elohim) *spoke to Moshe and said to him, "I am HASHEM"* (*Shemos* 6:2).

There are two obvious questions pertaining to the language of this verse. First, why does it use two verbs to refer to Hashem's speaking (first וַיְדַבֵּר and then וַיֹּאמֶר), since there appears to be only one statement? Second, what is the difference in connotation between the two verbs used?

Rashi explains that וַיְדַבֵּר אֱלֹהִים implies a harsh form of speech (indicated either by the verb form דבר itself, or by its juxtaposition to the Name Elokim, which is the Name associated with Hashem's Attribute of Strict Justice [*Middas HaDin*]). These words are meant to convey a rebuke to Moshe for having complained (see above, 5:22): לָמָה הֲרֵעֹתָה לָעָם הַזֶּה, *Why have You done evil to this people?,* thereby casting aspersion on Hashem's behavior toward Bnei Yisrael. Following this rebuke, the verse begins its narrative by stating וַיֹּאמֶר אֵלָיו, *and He said to him.* Hashem then relates to Moshe the reasons for sending him to redeem the Jews; the first reason being simply — אֲנִי ה׳, *I am HASHEM.* The Name Hashem symbolizes God's trait of trustworthiness — the promise that He will abide by His principle of rewarding those who are obedient and faithful to Him, and punishing those who are not. As used in this verse, it signifies Hashem's affirmation to keep His as yet unfulfilled promise to the *Avos,* to give Eretz Yisrael to their children.

Ramban, however, states that the phrase וַיֹּאמֶר אֵלָיו is to be understood as a continuation of the reprimand, pointing out to Moshe that his doubts and reluctance to undertake the assigned mission forced God to reveal to Moshe His Name "Hashem," whereas the Name אֵל שַׁדַּי (which signifies a lesser medium of prophecy) was a sufficient revelation to establish the unswerving faith and allegiance of the *Avos. Ramban* notes that this interpretation is borne out by the Midrash, which states: "Many times I revealed Myself to Avraham, Yitzchak and Yaakov without telling them that My Name is Hashem, as I told you, and yet they did not question My behavior. Nor did they ask Me for My Name as you did."

These two interpretations also differ in how they will understand Hashem's statement in verse 3: וּשְׁמִי ה׳ לֹא נוֹדַעְתִּי לָהֶם, *and My Name HASHEM I have not made known to them.* According to *Rashi,* it means: I have not yet revealed My Name Hashem to them by fulfilling My promise. According to *Ramban,* it means: It was not necessary for Me to inform them that My Name is Hashem.

Ramban does not clarify why the verse begins with the Name Elokim and ends with the Name Hashem. *Reb Berel Soloveitchik,* following the general theme of the *Ramban,* answers this question while elaborating on the nature of the rebuke. He cites Midrashim that state that when Moshe asked Hashem why He had mistreated His nation, Hashem's Attribute of Strict Justice (*Middas HaDin*) wanted to kill Moshe for these words. However, when Hashem saw that his intentions were for the benefit of and in sympathy with Bnei Yisrael, he restrained the *Middas HaDin,* and allowed His Attribute of Mercy (*Middas HaRachamim*) to save Moshe. Hashem reprimanded Moshe by highlighting to him that, unlike the *Avos,* he could not survive the judgment of *Middas HaDin* (indicated by the Name Elokim) without the intervention of *Middas HaRachamim* (referred to as Hashem).

MISHNAH OF THE DAY: SHABBOS 15:2

The following Mishnah considers the status of impermanently tied knots:

יֵשׁ לְךָ קְשָׁרִין שֶׁאֵין חַיָּיבִין עֲלֵיהֶן כְּקֶשֶׁר הַגַּמָּלִין וּכְקֶשֶׁר הַסַּפָּנִין — ***There are knots for which we are not liable*** to a *chatas,* ***as*** opposed to ***the camel driver's knot and the sailor's knot,*** for which we are liable.[1]

The following knots may be tied deliberately on the Sabbath:

קוֹשֶׁרֶת אִשָּׁה מִפְתַּח חֲלוּקָהּ — ***A woman may tie the opening of her robe,***[2]

NOTES

1. After making this general statement, the Mishnah does not go on to describe these knots. The Gemara explains them to be: (a) the knot by which the reins are tied to the nose ring of the camel, and (b) the knot by which the ropes are tied to the ship's ring. These are sometimes left tied for a week or two at a time, and are then untied. Similarly, any knot made to remain tied for a specific, limited period of time does not entail liability (*Rav; Rashi* to Gemara 112a). [Although the tying of these knots entails no Biblical liability, it is, nevertheless, Rabbinically prohibited to tie them.]

2. This robe opens in the front and has two straps, one extending from the top of each corner. The right strap was tied over the left shoulder, and the left strap over the right shoulder, thereby closing the garment. Since this knot is made to be tied and untied the very same day, it bears no resemblance to the Biblically prohibited permanent knot, and it is permissible to deliberately tie it on the Sabbath (*Rav; Rashi*).

וְחוּטֵי סְבָכָה — or the *strings of a cap,*[3] וְשֶׁל פְּסִקְיָא — *or of a girdle,*[4] וּרְצוּעוֹת מִנְעָל וְסַנְדָּל — *or straps of a shoe or sandal,*[5] וְנוֹדוֹת יַיִן וָשֶׁמֶן — or leather *canteens of wine or oil,*[6] וּקְדֵירָה שֶׁל בָּשָׂר — *or* the cover of *a pot of meat.*[7]

רַבִּי אֱלִיעֶזֶר בֶּן יַעֲקֹב אוֹמֵר — *R' Eliezer ben Yaakov says:* קוֹשְׁרִין לִפְנֵי הַבְּהֵמָה בִּשְׁבִיל שֶׁלֹּא תֵצֵא — *One may tie* a rope *in front of* the stall of *an animal so that it* will *not go out.*[8]

The Mishnah returns to a position taken by the Sages: קוֹשְׁרִין דְּלִי בִּפְסִקְיָא — *One may tie a pail with a girdle,* אֲבָל לֹא בְּחֶבֶל — *but not with a rope.*[9] רַבִּי יְהוּדָה מַתִּיר — But *R' Yehudah*

NOTES

3. A netlike hat worn on the head (*Rav*). Since a woman is particular about her hair, she will not slip the net off without first untying the strings holding the net to her hair, for fear of pulling out some of her hair. It is therefore a knot which is undone every day (*Tos. Yom Tov* from Gemara 112a).

4. This was a wide belt with laces tied at its ends (*Rav; Rashi*). Although it is possible to remove this girdle by slipping it down over the feet and allowing the laces to remain tied permanently, it is not customary for a woman to do so because it is a breach of modesty. Hence, it was tied and untied every day (*Tos. Yom Tov* from *Rashi* 112a).

5. [A *shoe* is made of soft leather while a *sandal* is made of hard leather (see *Yevamos* 12:1).] The Gemara differentiates between various knots on a shoe or sandal — e.g., the permitted knot that one fastens each day when putting on the shoe and unfastens when removing it — which is permitted by our Mishnah — and the permanent knot that fastens the bottom of the strap to the shoe or sandal, which one is forbidden to tie or untie on the Sabbath.

6. The openings of these canteens were flaps which were tied together, and which were untied in order to fill or drink from the canteen. Moreover, even the knots of a canteen with two openings may be tied and untied. Although it is possible to pour the wine or oil through one opening, thus leaving the second one permanently closed, this was not customarily done, since it would then be difficult to pour out a large amount at once. Consequently, we do not consider these knots permanent, and they may be tied and untied on the Sabbath (*Rav; Tos. Yom Tov* from Gemara 112b).

7. Occasionally, a piece of cloth was tied over the top of a pot, and removed when the pot was emptied. Since the knot fastening the cloth to the top of the pot is a temporary one, it may be tied on the Sabbath. Even if a pot had spigots through which its contents can be removed without untying the cloth, nevertheless, the cloth may be tied and untied; since it was not customary for the pot to be emptied through the spigots, the knots in the cloth are regarded as temporary (*Rav* from Gemara 112b).

8. I.e., we may tie a rope across the opening of a cattle stall in order to prevent the animal from leaving the stall (*Rav; Rashi*).

9. I.e., one may suspend a pail from the top of a well by tying a girdle to the pail and to the top of the well.

Since one needs the girdle, he will surely not leave it tied permanently to the pail. Consequently, there is no danger of the knot becoming permanent. One who ties a

permits it.[10]

The Mishnah concludes:

כְּלָל אָמַר רַבִּי יְהוּדָה — ***R' Yehudah stated a general rule:*** **כָּל קֶשֶׁר שֶׁאֵינוֹ שֶׁל קַיָּימָא אֵין חַיָּיבִין עָלָיו** — ***Any knot that is not permanent, one is not liable for it.***[11]

NOTES

rope to a pail, however, will probably leave it there permanently. It is therefore prohibited (*Rav*).

10. The Gemara explains that even R' Yehudah does not permit tying an ordinary rope to a pail, since this will certainly become a permanent knot. He permits only tying a weaver's rope to the pail, since the weaver, who needs the rope for his work, will not leave it tied permanently to the pail. The Sages, on the other hand, prohibit its use, since one might use an ordinary rope for this purpose, not realizing that there is a difference between a weaver's rope and an ordinary rope. A girdle, however, cannot be confused with a rope (*Rav; Tiferes Yisrael* from Gemara 113a).

11. This statement does not pertain to R' Yehudah's previous ruling. Rather, R' Yehudah here disputes the statement of R' Meir recorded in the previous Mishnah. There, R' Meir declared that any knot capable of being untied with one hand does not incur liability. R' Yehudah counters that this rule is incorrect. Rather, liability depends solely on whether the knot is permanent or not (*Ran; Tos. Yom Tov;* cf. *Tosafos; Shenos Eliyahu*).

GEMS FROM THE GEMARA

The Gemara (112b) cites a Mishnah in Tractate *Keilim* (17:1): The measure by which all wooden utensils of homeowners lose their *tumah* is a hole the size of pomegranates; i.e., if the utensil has a hole of this size, it loses its *tumah*.

[To explain: Utensils that have become *tamei* lose their *tumah* by being reduced to a state in which they are no longer usable. The size of a hole that renders a utensil unusable depends on the utensil's regular function and customary use. Whatever the necessary size is, once the *tumah* has departed, it does not return if the utensil is repaired. Now, a homeowner does not discard a utensil if it has a hole smaller than the size of a pomegranate, but instead keeps it to contain larger items. However, when it has a hole the size of a pomegranate, he discards it as totally useless. Hence, it does not retain its *tumah* (*Rashi*).]

Chizkiyah inquired regarding this Mishnah: If the utensil developed a puncture the size of an olive and he sealed it, and it developed another olive-size puncture next to the plug and he sealed it, and he continued in this manner until he completed a plug the size of a pomegranate, what is the law? Does its *tumah* depart in this fashion, or not?

פרשת וארא

SUNDAY

PARASHAS VA'EIRA

R' Yochanan resolved the inquiry from a Mishnah (*Keilim* 26:4) that states that a sandal from which one ear (i.e., one side of the connection between the sandal's top and its sole) broke off, and it was repaired, retains its *tumah* of *midras* [a category that includes any item that was leaned on, sat upon, or stepped on by certain people who are *tamei*]. However, if the second ear then broke off, even if it was repaired, it becomes *tahor* from the *midras tumah,* but it remains *tamei* at a lesser level, as having touched a *midras* (see *Rashi* there for an explanation of this point).

R' Yochanan related that he and his fellow students once asked Chizkiyah: Why, when the second ear of the sandal breaks, does the sandal not retain *tamei midras,* as the first ear is already repaired, and the sandal is still usable? Chizkiyah responded that the new ears are not considered part of the original sandal. Therefore, once both ears have broken off, what remains of the *original* sandal has been rendered useless. Thus, its *tumah* has departed. The usable, repaired sandal is a new creation (a פָּנִים חֲדָשׁוֹת — literally, a *new face*), and it has never become *tamei* as a *midras.*

Here too, extrapolates R' Yochanan, in the case of the utensil which had been repeatedly punctured and repaired until its repaired area reached the size of a pomegranate, a new face has come into being here, and this "new" utensil never became *tamei.*

Chizkiyah was so impressed with the comparison that he exclaimed about R' Yochanan: "This is no mere mortal!" Others said that Chizkiyah exclaimed: "One such as this is a great person!"

A MUSSAR THOUGHT FOR THE DAY

One might conclude that when the trait of mercy prevails and exacting justice is not administered, justice has been compromised and, indeed, failed. *Mesillas Yesharim* (Chapter 4) however, states that this is incorrect, for just as Hashem does not forget any good deed, He does not dismiss any bad deed entirely (see *Bava Kamma* 50a).

Thus, the trait of justice cannot be eliminated even by Hashem's mercy. What then is the role of *Middas HaRachamim* (the Attribute of Mercy)? *Mesillas Yesharim* answers that Hashem's mercy tempers the Attribute of Strict Justice in three ways. Whereas the *Middas HaDin* would require an immediate, severe, and unalterable retribution, the *Middas HaRachamim* acts to defer the punishment, lessens its severity, and offers complete exoneration if the person undertakes true repentance, including remorse

פרשת וארא

SUNDAY

PARASHAS VA'EIRA

and anguish over his deeds. With these easings of the *Middas HaDin* in place, it is possible for the world to endure, as every sinner will not be immediately destroyed. But the *Middas HaDin* will also be satisfied, either at a later date if the person does not repent, or through the pain and sorrow that repentance elicits, if he does.

In commenting upon this *Mesillas Yesharim, Rav Yerucham Levovitz* (in *Daas Chochmah U'Mussar* 1:369) posits that we have difficulty in understanding the notion of Hashem as being One Who "loves justice" (as we say daily in *Shemoneh Esrei*), because we view justice as punishment and vengeance, rather than as a trait of Hashem, fundamental to the order of the world. Thus, the prophet Michah says (6:8): הִגִּיד לְךָ אָדָם מַה־טּוֹב וּמָה־ה׳ דּוֹרֵשׁ מִמְּךָ כִּי אִם־עֲשׂוֹת מִשְׁפָּט וְאַהֲבַת חֶסֶד וְהַצְנֵעַ לֶכֶת עִם־אֱלֹהֶיךָ, *He has told you, O man, what is good and what HASHEM seeks from you — only the performance of justice, the love of kindness, and walking humbly with your God.*

Love of kindness and proper execution of justice are demanded by Hashem, are characterized as good, and must be harmonious. In explaining that the *Middas HaDin* cannot be dismissed, Rav Yerucham cites the Gemara in *Yoma* (22b) that discusses why Shaul HaMelech was led into a situation (the war against Amalek) that culminated in his mistakenly sparing the life of Agag, and losing his kingdom as a result. The Gemara concludes that Shaul had sinned by renouncing his honor, when he did not respond to insults hurled at him by those who opposed his appointment as king. Moreover, he repeated this offense by not allowing the people to kill those scoffers after his victory over Ammon. The Gemara wonders why this behavior was not considered commendable, in light of Rava's dictum: Anyone who lets his right to respond to an insult pass (and instead ignores the matter entirely), Heaven will let all of his sins pass as well! The Gemara answers that the scoffers in this case did not even ask for forgiveness. Rav Yerucham explains: Although one might think that such a high level of magnanimity is even more admirable, it is not, for such behavior is tantamount to a total dismissal and rejection of the concept of justice.

QUESTION OF THE DAY:

Where else in the Torah do we find that Hashem said to someone, "I am HASHEM"?

For the answer, see page 111.

HALACHAH OF THE DAY

We mentioned yesterday that the Sages decreed wet clothing to be *muktzeh,* so that one would not come to wring the clothing out on Shabbos. This prohibition applies only to clothing that one is not wearing. If, however, the clothing a person is wearing becomes saturated (i.e., he is caught in a storm), they do not become *muktzeh.* It is, however, still forbidden for one to wring out the clothing. Furthermore, one may not even shake or brush the water off his clothes. If one's socks become saturated, he may continue walking even though through his walking water will be squeezed out of the wet socks. Since he has no intention of squeezing out the water, and the act is being done in an unusual manner, it is permitted. Additionally, even if one was not wearing an article of clothing when it became saturated, but he intended to wear it and has no suitable replacement, it is not considered *muktzeh,* and he may wear it on Shabbos.

There is a general rule of *muktzeh* stating that if an item is unfit for use during the twilight period at the onset of Shabbos, it is deemed *muktzeh* and may not be used or moved the entire Shabbos. In accordance with this rule, laundry that is wet at the onset of Shabbos would normally be considered *muktzeh.* There is, however, an exception to this rule. If one is *certain* that the wet clothing will dry and become fit for wearing at some point during Shabbos, the clothing does not become *muktzeh,* and may be worn when it dries.

There are times when one performs a permissible act, but because of circumstances he gives the impression that he is engaged in forbidden activity. This misconception may often result in one or both of the following two problems: people may think or speak ill of the one doing the suspect action, or people may mistakenly learn from these misunderstood actions that things that are in reality forbidden are actually permissible. For these reasons, in many situations the Sages forbade otherwise permissible activities, in order to avoid these pitfalls. This concept is called *mar'is ayin,* literally translated as: *the way the eye sees.*

Due to the prohibition of *mar'is ayin,* our Sages prohibited the hanging of wet clothing to dry on Shabbos. While the hanging of the clothing is in itself permissible (in a case where the clothing is not considered *muktzeh*), the Sages prohibited it, since one who sees someone hanging clothing to dry may mistakenly assume that the clothing was also washed on Shabbos. Thus, even if clothing becomes wet inadvertently, such as when one is caught in a rainstorm, it is forbidden to hang one's clothing up in the manner one would hang freshly laundered clothing to dry.

A CLOSER LOOK AT THE SIDDUR

The very first prayer of the day is *Modeh Ani*, which is recited immediately upon awakening. The prayer ends with the words, רַבָּה אֱמוּנָתֶךָ, *great is Your faithfulness.* This praise underscores the fundamental importance of our trust in Hashem's faithfulness in watching over us. *Iyun Tefillah* relates this phrase to the verse in *Eichah* (3:23): חֲדָשִׁים לַבְּקָרִים רַבָּה אֱמוּנָתֶךָ, *They are new every morning; great is Your faithfulness,* and cites the following Midrash (*Tehillim* §25): "It is customary in the world that people give items to someone for safekeeping. The watchman may exchange or mix up the different items, not recognizing their differences or their owners. But this never happens to the Holy One, Blessed is He, Who is the Lord of Truth. Does one wake up in the morning seeking his soul and not finding it, or finding it in another's body and a foreign one in his own?" The Midrash then cites Rav Aleksandri, who illustrates an additional element of praise to Hashem, using a similar metaphor. "A person may give a new article to someone for safekeeping, and after some time it is returned to him worn and used. The Holy One, Blessed is He, however, is given a tired, worn-out soul and in the morning returns it rested and rejuvenated."

Chasam Sofer, commenting on this phrase, translates it to mean, "great is Your faith *in us.*" Imagine, says the Chasam Sofer, if a person would lend a valuable object to someone, or give it to him to watch, and later observe him mishandling or jeopardizing it. If he were able to repossess the object, would he risk giving it back to that person a second or even a third time? Of course not! But Hashem has boundless faith in us. Though we are careless and abusive in the treatment of our souls, which Hashem has entrusted to us, He returns them to us again and again, confident that we will use them properly in His service.

No less inspirational is the end of the Midrash, which understands רַבָּה אֱמוּנָתֶךָ in the sense that Hashem is trustworthy in fulfilling His promises. Rav Simon says, "From the fact that You renew us each day, we believe and acknowledge that You will also return our souls to us at the time of תְּחִיַּת הַמֵּתִים, The Ressurection of the Dead" (since sleep is somewhat analogous to death — see *Bava Basra* 10a). Rav Aleksandri adds: "From the fact that You renew us each day even while we are in exile, we know that You will one day redeem us."

A TORAH THOUGHT FOR THE DAY

וַיְדַבֵּר ה׳ אֶל־מֹשֶׁה וְאֶל־אַהֲרֹן וַיְצַוֵּם אֶל־בְּנֵי יִשְׂרָאֵל וְאֶל־פַּרְעֹה מֶלֶךְ מִצְרָיִם לְהוֹצִיא אֶת־בְּנֵי־יִשְׂרָאֵל מֵאֶרֶץ מִצְרָיִם

And HASHEM spoke to Moshe and to Aharon and He commanded them regarding the Children of Israel and regarding Pharaoh, king of Egypt — to take the Children of Israel out of the Land of Egypt (*Shemos* 6:13).

The commentaries are bothered by the fact that this verse, literally translated, would seem to say that Moshe and Aharon were to tell *both* Pharaoh and the Jews to take the Children of Israel out of Egypt! While it is understandable that Moshe and Aharon were to deliver a message to Pharaoh instructing him to permit the Jews to leave Egypt, what was the message that they were to tell the Jews?

Answering this question, *Rashi* explains that this verse, understood in the context of the preceding one (v. 12): הֵן בְּנֵי־יִשְׂרָאֵל לֹא־שָׁמְעוּ אֵלַי, *Behold, the Children of Israel have not listened to me,* was a response to Moshe's complaints to Hashem. It was Moshe, not the Jews, who was the recipient of a directive from Hashem concerning the Children of Israel. Hashem reminded Moshe that even though the Jews *did not heed Moshe because of shortness of breath and hard work* (as stated in verse 9), he was nonetheless required to endure their complaining and always lead them slowly with compassion. Moreover, adds *Ibn Ezra,* Hashem told Moshe that he must never become angry with the Jews if they do not obey him.

Rabbeinu Bachya, in one approach, explains Hashem's message to Moshe similarly, but he offers a different explanation as well. According to his second approach, Hashem was in fact commanding Moshe to deliver a message to the Bnei Yisrael; namely, that the Jews were to rid themselves of the idols they had become accustomed to serving while in Egypt.

The *Satmar Rebbe,* in his *Divrei Yoel,* offers a deeper look at these two interpretations. He explains that when Moshe complained to Hashem that the Jews refused to listen to him *because of shortness of breath and hard work,* the Midrash (*Shemos Rabbah* 6:5, and *Eitz Yosef*), wonders why hard work would make the Jews ignore a prophecy that would save them from this excruciating labor, when the exact opposite should have been the case. The Satmar Rebbe explains that *hard work* refers to the difficult effort required to give up idols. The Jewish people, when faced with the need to decide between idolatry and redemption, simply were not interested in leaving Egypt. When Moshe protested to Hashem that he could not redeem a people who were so connected to their idols that they were not interested in leaving, Hashem's response was twofold;

while Moshe was correct, and was therefore bidden to teach the Jews about the folly of idolatry, he was told to deliver this message without anger or frustration, but with compassion, one small step at a time, until finally, the Jews would be ready for redemption. [According to this, the two approaches of *Rabbeinu Bachya* actually complement one another; the Jews were to be commanded to give up their idolatry, and Moshe was enjoined to treat them with greater compassion.]

The *Yerushalmi* (*Rosh Hashanah* 3:5) understands the verse more literally, and indeed explains that a message was to be given to the Jews concerning their freedom. The message was: After they would be freed from Egypt, enter the Land of Israel and set up a society, they were to be careful regarding the laws of freeing their own Jewish slaves or bondsmen. Although this mitzvah would not go into effect for many years, a precondition of freedom is agreeing not to mistreat others; this merit of not unduly subjugating a fellow Jew, even one who sold himself as an indentured servant, explains *Korban HaEidah,* would make the Jewish people worthy of being redeemed from their own slavery (see *Korban HaEidah* there). [Sadly, the Jewish people did not fulfill this mitzvah properly, and the *Yerushalmi,* continuing, states that the first exile came about because they neglected to properly free their slaves at the *Yovel* year. Thus, the failure to maintain the precondition of redemption resulted in exile. See *Yirmiyahu* 34:12-14.]

This merit was even more necessary, points out *R' Dovid Kviat* in his *Succas Dovid,* when we consider that the Jews did not really deserve to leave Egypt. As we explained above, they were idol worshipers and, on the surface, not interested in listening to Moshe. Thus, the redemption could not come solely on the basis of the merits of the Jewish people; rather, it came about because Hashem, in His great *chesed,* heard their groans and cries, and was fulfilling the treaty that He had made with Avraham. Accordingly, the Bnei Yisrael had to do something on their own to make themselves worthy of redemption. This commitment not to mistreat their own slaves in the future was a merit that would allow them to become free men.

QUESTION OF THE DAY:

Why was the command in our verse directed explicitly to both Moshe and Aharon?

For the answer, see page 111.

MISHNAH OF THE DAY: SHABBOS 15:3

Since the previous Mishnah dealt with tying knots in clothing, such as tying the opening of a robe or the strings of a girdle, the following Mishnah discusses other rules regarding the adjustment of clothing on the Sabbath, albeit ones that are not specifically relevant to the forbidden labor of *tying* a knot (*Tos. Yom Tov*):

מְקַפְּלִין אֶת הַכֵּלִים — ***One may fold garments,*** [1] **אֲפִילוּ אַרְבָּעָה וַחֲמִשָּׁה פְּעָמִים** — ***even four or five times,*** [2] **וּמַצִּיעִין אֶת הַמִּטּוֹת מִלֵּילֵי שַׁבָּת לְשַׁבָּת** — ***and one may make the beds on the night of the Sabbath for the Sabbath*** daytime,[3] **אֲבָל לֹא מִשַּׁבָּת לְמוֹצָאֵי שַׁבָּת** — ***but not on the Sabbath for the night after the Sabbath.*** [4]

Prior to the adoption of the present, fixed calendar, it was possible for Yom Kippur to occur immediately preceding or following the Sabbath — i.e., on a Friday or a Sunday. The Mishnah considers what activities may be performed on one of these holy days for the sake of the other:

NOTES

1. One who takes off his clothes on the Sabbath may fold them to wear them later on the same day. However, such folding may nevertheless be prohibited if it appears to be intended to press out any wrinkles which may have formed. The Rabbis therefore prohibited many instances of folding. They are as follows: (a) Two people may not fold a garment together, since they stretch the garment between them, thus flattening the wrinkles completely, they *appear* to be making major adjustments in the garment. (b) Even one person may fold only new garments — which are stiff and not easily wrinkled — as the folding of such clothing is of only minor benefit. Old clothes, however, may not be folded, since folding substantially improves their appearance. (c) New garments may not be folded unless they are white; if they are colored, they may not be folded, since folding substantially improves their appearance (*Rashi; Rav;* cf. *Rambam, Hil. Shabbos* 22:22). (d) Even if all the above conditions are met, nevertheless, the Rabbis permitted one to fold his garment only if he has nothing else to wear on the Sabbath; if he has other garments, he may not fold this one (*Rav* from Gemara 113a; *Rashi*).

2. I.e., one may make whatever number of folds is necessary (*Meiri; Tiferes Yisrael*). [*Rashi* apparently explains this to mean that he may fold and refold the garment as many times during the day as necessary, as long as he still needs it for use on the Sabbath.]

3. I.e., we may prepare the beds on the night of the Sabbath for sleeping on them anytime during the Sabbath (*Rambam Commentary; Tos. Yom Tov*).

4. Since this, too, is a form — albeit a minor one — of adjusting an article (e.g., the bed) for use, it is permitted only when necessary for use on the Sabbath (*Rambam, Hil. Shabbos* 13:7; cf. *Raavad* ad loc.).

רַבִּי יִשְׁמָעֵאל אוֹמֵר — *R' Yishmael says:* מְקַפְּלִין אֶת הַכֵּלִים וּמַצִּיעִין אֶת הַמִּטּוֹת מִיּוֹם הַכִּיפּוּרִים לְשַׁבָּת — *One may fold garments and make the beds on Yom Kippur for the Sabbath;*[5] וְחֶלְבֵי שַׁבָּת קְרֵיבִין בְּיוֹם הַכִּיפּוּרִים — *and fats of the Sabbath* sacrificial offerings *may be offered on Yom Kippur,*[6] אֲבָל לֹא שֶׁל יוֹם הַכִּיפּוּרִים בְּשַׁבָּת — *but* those *of Yom Kippur* may *not* be offered *on the Sabbath.*[7] רַבִּי עֲקִיבָא אוֹמֵר לֹא שֶׁל שַׁבָּת קְרֵיבִין בְּיוֹם הַכִּיפּוּרִים — *R' Akiva says: Neither may those of the Sabbath be offered on Yom Kippur,* וְלֹא שֶׁל יוֹם הַכִּיפּוּרִים קְרֵיבִין בְּשַׁבָּת — *nor may those of Yom Kippur be offered on the Sabbath.*[8]

NOTES

5. I.e., if Yom Kippur falls on a Friday, he may make these preparations on Yom Kippur for the sake of the Sabbath.

Since the sanctity of the Sabbath is greater than the sanctity of Yom Kippur [as manifest in the difference in punishments: desecration of the Sabbath carries the more stringent punishment of court-imposed execution for willful transgression, whereas desecration of Yom Kippur bears the lesser punishment of excision (*kares*)], preparations may be made on Yom Kippur for the Sabbath (*Rav*).

6. I.e., if Yom Kippur falls on Sunday, the fats of any Sabbath day sacrificial offerings not yet consumed by the conclusion of the Sabbath may be offered that night, even though it is Yom Kippur. Here too, since the sanctity of the Sabbath is greater than that of Yom Kippur, its needs may be fulfilled on Yom Kippur.

7. However, since the sanctity of the Sabbath is greater than that of Yom Kippur, if Yom Kippur falls on Friday, the fats of Yom Kippur's sacrificial offerings may not be offered on the Sabbath (*Rav*).

8. R' Akiva regards the sanctities of both days as equal for these purposes, and therefore we may not take care of the needs of the one day on the other day (*Rav*).

[R' Akiva agrees that the sanctity of the Sabbath is greater than that of Yom Kippur. However, he demonstrates from certain Biblical verses that with respect to burning the sacrifices of one day on the other they are regarded as equal (*Tos. Yom Tov*).]

GEMS FROM THE GEMARA

Our Mishnah discusses laws that apply to the care of garments on the Sabbath. The Gemara (113a) digresses to discuss the general subject of changing one's clothes in honor of the Sabbath.

Rav Huna said: If one has clothing other than his weekday ones into which to change for the Sabbath, he should change into them; and if he does not have other clothing into which to change, at the very least he should let down the hems of his weekday clothing.

[It was the custom of poor people, who performed manual labor to

earn a livelihood, to hitch the hems of their clothing up (by tucking some fabric under their belts — see *Ran*) in order that the hems would be lifted high off the ground and not interfere with their work. Wealthy people, however, who stayed at home, did not have such a concern, and wore their hems long, reaching to the ground. Rav Huna states that even one who does not have a separate change of clothing should let down his hems on the Sabbath, in the manner of wealthy people, so as to make the clothing appear finer in honor of the Sabbath (*Rashi*).]

Rav Safra challenged this ruling: "But surely this appears like haughtiness!?"

The Gemara answers: Since he does not do this every day, and only today he does so, it does not appear like haughtiness; i.e., it is clear that he is doing so solely to honor the Sabbath.

The Gemara then expounds a verse in *Isaiah* (58:13) on the subject of Sabbath clothing: The verse states: וְכִבַּדְתּוֹ מֵעֲשׂוֹת דְּרָכֶיךָ, *and you honor it by not doing your ways.* The Gemara explains: *And you honor it* teaches that your Sabbath garments should not be like your weekday garments. The Gemara then comments that this understanding of the verse (which relates *honor* to *garments*) is in consonance with the practice of R' Yochanan, who used to refer to his clothes as "those [things] that honor me." [Clothes bring honor to their wearer (*Rashi*). Similarly, by changing into special garments, one honors the Sabbath.]

A MUSSAR THOUGHT FOR THE DAY

As we explained in *A Torah Thought for the Day,* the *Yerushalmi* (*Rosh Hashanah* 3:5) states that before Hashem freed the Jewish people from Egyptian slavery, He charged them with the future mitzvah of freeing a Jewish bondsman at the onset of the *Yovel* year; this, explain *Korban HaEidah* and *Succas Dovid,* would serve as a merit to allow the Bnei Yisrael freedom. *R' Chaim Shmulevitz* (*Sichos Mussar* §31) comments that besides the great merit that was created for the Bnei Yisrael by their accepting to free their future servants, the Torah is teaching us another message by relating that Hashem chose to instruct them specifically in this mitzvah while they were still in Mitzrayim. When a person is challenged to perform an otherwise difficult mitzvah, he must seize the opportunity to commit to carrying it out while it is easiest for him to do so. He can then carry this momentum throughout his life, to anchor

himself during the more difficult times to come.

To allow us to better understand the hardship involved in freeing a servant, let us try to picture how a master who has a servant working for him feels as the *Yovel* year approaches. Many years earlier, this person contracted a Jewish indentured servant. After the initial period of six years of servitude elapsed, the servant decided to remain with his master, and to serve him until the *Yovel* year (see *Shemos* 21:5-6). Thus, such a servant has been trained for many years, and the master has used him for many jobs over the years, profiting greatly from his work. Additionally, after the six-year term elapsed, the master did not have to pay for the additional work. If he frees this servant, he will lose this windfall, and be left with nobody to carry out these duties, leading to great expense. With all of this in mind, it is very understandable why a master would have a very difficult time freeing his servants at *Yovel.*

What is the answer to this? What is the only way that a master can overcome his desires and fulfill the Torah's commandment of freeing his Jewish bondsman? *R' Chaim Shmulevitz* explains that the only way a person will free his servant is if he understands this servant's deep longing for freedom. This is only possible when he, the master, is also a slave yearning for freedom. Of course, this is not usually the case. It was for this reason that Hashem charged the Jewish people with this mitzvah while they were still in Egypt, where it was natural for the Jewish people to understand and accept it; only a people who literally still tasted the bitterness of slavery could fully commit to overcome their selfishness and free their own slaves many years in the future. Once the painful initial commitment was undertaken by using the inspiration of the moment, concludes R' Chaim, it was much easier to maintain this standard in the future, even when these feelings were no longer present.

R' Chaim points out that everybody, at one time or another, has feelings of *his'orerus,* inspiration to better serve Hashem. What a person must do during these times is to seize the inspiration of the moment and use these feelings to make meaningful changes in his life; by doing so, he will be carried through future, more difficult times as well.

HALACHAH OF THE DAY

We learned yesterday that one may not hang wet clothing to dry on Shabbos in the manner that freshly washed laundry is hung, so that an onlooker should not mistakenly think that the clothing was washed on Shabbos. We will now further elaborate on this halachah.

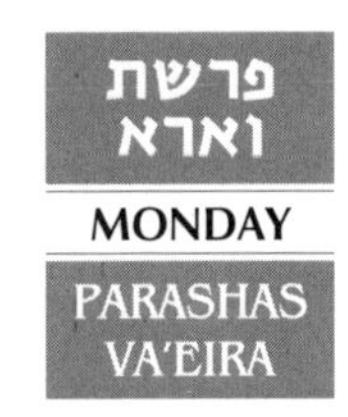

The prohibition against hanging wet clothing to dry on Shabbos applies only to clothing that is saturated to the point where a person touching the wet garment and then touching another garment will transfer moisture from the first garment to the second one.

We learned that the wet clothing cannot be hung in the *same manner* as one would generally hang his freshly laundered clothing. This includes hanging clothing in the same area where freshly laundered clothing is normally hung, such as on a clothesline, or in the laundry room or bathroom. It is, however, permissible for one to hang clothing in an area where one does not normally hang laundry, such as in a clothing closet where dry clothing is hung, or over the back of a chair. Furthermore, one is permitted to hang wet clothing in an area that is normally used for drying laundry, if it is hung in a manner that is unusual for fresh laundry. Thus, if the garment is hung in crumpled shape or is visibly dirty, it will be apparent that it is not freshly laundered.

Some *poskim* rule that this prohibition, which is based on the above explained rule of *mar'is ayin,* does not apply to garments that are normally dry-cleaned, such as suits and coats. Since these garments are not laundered in the usual fashion, nobody observing them hanging will suspect that they were washed on Shabbos.

It is forbidden to place a wet garment or towel near any source of heat where it can be heated to the temperature of *yad soledes bo* (as we discussed above in our studies of the *melachah* of *cooking,* this temperature can be as low as 110 degrees Fahrenheit). If the moisture in the garment is heated to that extent, one violates the *melachah* of *cooking* as well as the *melachah* of *bleaching,* since the hot water purges the fabric of dirt. The Sages therefore prohibited one from placing a damp item near a source of heat even temporarily, if placing it there for any length of time would allow it to reach *yad soledes bo.* Examples of actions forbidden because of this include draping a wet garment or towel near an oven or fire, over a radiator, or even over a hot pot that was removed from the fire (*a kli rishon*).

A CLOSER LOOK AT THE SIDDUR

Above, we discussed the mitzvah of freeing Jewish slaves upon the arrival of the *Yovel* year. The Gemara in *Rosh Hashanah* (8b) states that during the ten days between Rosh Hashanah and Yom Kippur, newly freed Jewish bondsmen did not return home, although they were no longer required to work. Rather, they would remain in the homes of their masters, *eating and drinking and rejoicing with their crowns on their heads,* and would return home after Yom Kippur. The commentaries offer several explanations of what the Gemara means when it states that the bondsmen sat *with their crowns on their heads. Rashi* comments that since they were now, for all practical purposes, free men, they were permitted to do as they pleased, which included, should they wish to do so, wearing a crown, the ultimate symbol of royalty and freedom.

Meiri explains differently. According to his view, the bondsmen would actually wrap turbans around their heads to demonstrate that they were now free people. Moreover, upon doing so, they would recite the *berachah* of עוֹטֵר יִשְׂרָאֵל בְּתִפְאָרָה, *Blessed are You . . . Who crowns Yisrael with splendor,* that is recited among the morning *berachos.* For, as the *Yerushalmi* teaches, an indentured servant under the command of a master may not wear a head covering, for it bespeaks dignity and freedom.

Mishnah Berurah (46:9) observes that unlike many of the morning *berachos,* such as פּוֹקֵחַ עִוְרִים, *Blessed are You . . . Who opens the eyes of the blind,* and מַלְבִּישׁ עֲרֻמִּים, *Blessed are You . . . Who clothes the naked,* the blessing of *Who crowns Yisrael with splendor* is one of the two blessings (along with אוֹזֵר יִשְׂרָאֵל בִּגְבוּרָה, *Blessed are You . . . Who girds Yisrael with might*) that specifically mentions the Jewish people. The reason for this distinction is that unlike sight and clothing — which all people need and Hashem privileges everyone to enjoy — a head covering is not a basic necessity. Rather, it is unique to a Jew's mission in life, of living in constant awareness of Hashem above. The Gemara in *Shabbos* (156b) teaches us: *Cover your head from awe of your master.* Thus, this *berachah* thanks Hashem for entrusting the Bnei Yisrael with this mission, for it is through this constant subordination to Hashem that we may rise to our own perfection as well (*Rav Hirsch*).

A servant, however, is unable to have total awe of Hashem and concentrate only upon the awe of Heaven, for he must fulfill his obligations to another, lesser, master as well; only a free person can enjoy the privilege and responsibility of single-minded service of Hashem. Accordingly, explains *Meiri,* a slave or servant does not make the daily blessing of *Blessed are You . . . Who crowns Yisrael with splendor.* Only now, upon being released from the obligation to their masters and once again enjoying the right to do as they pleased, would the former servants exhibit their new status by donning a head covering and publicly making this *berachah.*

The commentaries explain that there is actually another, connected focus behind the *berachah* of עוֹטֵר יִשְׂרָאֵל בְּתִפְאָרָה, *Blessed are You . . .*

Who crowns Yisrael with splendor. Besides thanking Hashem for a head covering and the intrinsic honor and splendor that we gain by maintaining this awareness of our constant relationship to Him, we are praising Him for giving us the mitzvah of *tefillin shel rosh* (the phylacteries worn upon the head), which is called a פְּאֵר, *crown of glory. Tefillin* brings glory to the wearer, explains *Tur* (*Orach Chaim* §25), because (in addition to fulfilling a mitzvah in the Torah) wearing *tefillin shel rosh* causes that: וְרָאוּ כָּל־עַמֵּי הָאָרֶץ כִּי שֵׁם ה׳ נִקְרָא עָלֶיךָ וְיָרְאוּ מִמֶּךָּ, *All the other peoples of the earth will see that the Name of HASHEM is proclaimed upon you, and they will revere you* (*Devarim* 28:10). The "Name of Hashem" that the people will see, explains the Gemara, refers to the *tefillin shel rosh,* whose outer case displays two of the letters of Hashem's Name, indicating the unique Divine presence that rests on the Jewish people. It is in thanks to Hashem for this great gift of *tefillin shel rosh* which, properly fulfilled, gives us great honor in the eyes of all of mankind, that we praise Him as the One *Who crowns Yisrael with splendor.*

A TASTE OF LOMDUS

We explained in *A Torah Thought for the Day* that the Jews were charged with the mitzvah of freeing a Jewish slave at the onset of the *Yovel* year even before they left Egypt. It is noteworthy that the process by which a slave must be freed takes place not all at once, but in several stages. As we mentioned above (see *A Closer Look at the Siddur*), the Gemara in *Rosh Hashanah* (8b) explains that at the beginning of *Yovel* — Rosh Hashanah — Jewish bondsmen ceased working for their masters. However, they did not return home until after Yom Kippur, when, as the Torah commands in *Parashas Behar* (*Vayikra* 25:9-10), the *shofar* was blown, proclaiming their newfound freedom. During the ten-day period between Rosh Hashanah and Yom Kippur, bondsmen did not continue to work — for the *Yovel* year had already begun — nor were they permitted to leave the homes of their masters. Rather, states the Gemara, during this time, the newly freed bondsmen stayed in the homes of their former masters, and were free to eat, drink and enjoy themselves, all at the master's expense.

Turei Even is puzzled by the need for this extended procedure; why was the process of freeing a bondsman stretched out over this time? If Rosh Hashanah was the beginning of *Yovel,* the bondsmen should have been free to leave immediately, and if their freedom depended on blowing the *shofar,* why weren't they required to work until Yom Kippur?

Answering his own question, *Turei Even* explains that a closer look at the laws of *Yovel* explains why this status of intermediate freedom was needed. The Gemara states that although every fiftieth year was potentially designated as *Yovel,* its status was not automatic. Rather, *Yovel's* uniqueness — both its sanctity and its laws — depended on a number of criteria that had to be met; namely, blowing the *shofar* after Yom Kippur, and the willingness of masters to free their Jewish bondsmen and return eligible ancestral holdings to their original owners (see *Rambam, Hilchos Shemittah V'Yovel* 10:13). Accordingly, at a time when there was no property to be returned, or no bondsmen waiting to be freed, or the *shofar* was not blown, *Yovel* and its special laws, such as the need to refrain from working the land and the emancipation of slaves, would not commence. While the possibility of two of these criteria — the availability of property restoration and freedom — were ascertainable before the onset of *Yovel* (for it would be apparent whether or not there were fields and bondsmen to be returned and freed), the *shofar,* however, was blown ten days after *Yovel* had started. This meant that although the time for *Yovel* had already begun, it was unclear, depending on whether or not the *shofar* would be blown, if this year would in fact become sanctified, allowing all of *Yovel's* laws to take effect.

It was for this reason that the bondsmen did not continue working after Rosh Hashanah. Since the *shofar* would possibly, and most probably, be blown in a few days time, this year would be *Yovel,* granting them freedom and exempting them from further service to this master. However, the possibility that the *shofar* would *not* be blown precluded these people from returning home as truly free men. Thus, on the one hand, the slaves remained in their masters' houses, living at the masters' expense as they had done throughout their servitude; but, because in a few days time they would probably be retroactively freed when the blowing of the *shofar* sanctified the year as *Yovel* from its onset, they were totally absolved from any work-related responsibilities. Only after the *shofar* was actually blown after Yom Kippur were these men able to return home, for *Yovel* — and their freedom — had definitely begun.

Turei Even observes that the concept of the master being unable to compel the slave to work once the *potential* date of *Yovel* has arrived, because it might later be retroactively declared as *Yovel,* has a parallel in another halachic context — the status of the thirtieth day after Rosh Chodesh Elul during the times of the *Beis HaMikdash.* Unlike nowadays, when the Jewish months are either twenty-nine or thirty days in length,

based on a set calendar, the date on which Rosh Chodesh of each month would occur during the Temple era was not fixed, and was based on the testimony of witnesses in *beis din.* If acceptable witnesses came on the thirtieth day of the month and testified that they had seen the new moon the previous night, it was determined that today was in truth not the last day of the old month; rather, it was Rosh Chodesh, the first day of the new one. If, however, no witnesses would arrive during the course of the day, the old month would finish "full," with thirty days, and Rosh Chodesh would be on the thirty-first day. Thus, on the evening and morning of the thirtieth day, it was always unknown whether witnesses would come during the course of the day, and establish it as Rosh Chodesh.

While this uncertainty did not make a difference during most of the year, on Rosh Hashanah (since, as it is on every holiday, work is forbidden from the previous night), a problem arose; even though witnesses had not yet come and testified, the possibility of witnesses establishing today as Rosh Chodesh — and Rosh Hashanah — meant that work would be retroactively forbidden from the festival's onset. Accordingly, even though the new month had not yet been declared, the chance that witnesses would come later on in the day and sanctify the entire day retroactively precluded work from ever being done, beginning with the previous night. However, just as a bondsman's status during the ten days between Rosh Hashanah and Yom Kippur (although he was permitted to act like a free man — see *A Closer Look at the Siddur*) was not absolute, and he was not allowed to return home until it was definitely *Yovel,* the Rosh Hashanah *mussaf* sacrifices were *not* offered out of doubt. Even though work was prohibited on the chance that the day was holy, sacrifices were not offered until witnesses came and definitely established the day as Rosh Hashanah.

A TORAH THOUGHT FOR THE DAY

הוּא אַהֲרֹן וּמֹשֶׁה אֲשֶׁר אָמַר ה׳ לָהֶם הוֹצִיאוּ אֶת־בְּנֵי יִשְׂרָאֵל מֵאֶרֶץ מִצְרַיִם עַל־צִבְאֹתָם. הֵם הַמְדַבְּרִים אֶל־פַּרְעֹה מֶלֶךְ־מִצְרַיִם לְהוֹצִיא אֶת־בְּנֵי־יִשְׂרָאֵל מִמִּצְרָיִם הוּא מֹשֶׁה וְאַהֲרֹן

This is Aharon and Moshe to whom HASHEM *said, "Take the Children of Israel out of Egypt according to their legions." They are the ones who spoke to Pharaoh, king of Egypt, to take the Children of Israel out of the land of Egypt; this is Moshe and Aharon* (*Shemos* 6:26-27).

In verse 26, Aharon is mentioned before Moshe, while in the next verse, Moshe is mentioned first. *Rashi* explains that the Torah sometimes mentions one first and sometimes the other first to teach us that the two of them are שְׁקוּלִין, *equal.*

One may ask: How can we explain that Aharon and Moshe were equal? Granted, Aharon was a great *tzaddik.* But can he be considered the equal of Moshe Rabbeinu, the master of all the *nevi'im,* who spoke to Hashem face to face, and ascended to Heaven to receive the Torah? Surely Moshe was on a level unto himself!

R' Moshe Feinstein (in his *Darash Moshe*) explains that greatness is not defined by a person's accomplishments, but rather by the person's success in fulfilling the tasks for which Hashem equipped him and sent him to this world. Every person enters the world with unique abilities and a specific set of tasks to accomplish. Some are given tremendous ability, and expected to achieve a great deal, while others are endowed with lesser abilities, and correspondingly, smaller tasks. But every person's job is identical — use the skills you have been given to the utmost, to accomplish as much as you can.

It is true, says R' Moshe, that Aharon was not a Moshe. But he was not supposed to be, as he was not given the gifts of a Moshe. He did, however, succeed in utilizing all of his God-given abilities to accomplish the tasks set for him in this world, just as Moshe did. For this reason, he was indeed equal to Moshe — for both of them fulfilled their tasks to the fullest. And any person who fully utilizes all of his abilities is as great as Moshe and Aharon.

With this idea, R' Moshe explains an incident recorded in the Gemara (*Bava Basra* 10b). The Gemara relates that Yosef the son of R' Yehoshua was very ill, and his soul left his body, and then returned (in what we would refer to today as an "out-of-body experience"). His father asked him, What did you see (when your soul glimpsed the next world)? He replied, עוֹלָם הָפוּךְ רָאִיתִי, *I saw an upside-down world,* where עֶלְיוֹנִים לְמַטָּה וְתַחְתּוֹנִים לְמַעְלָה, *great ones were below, and lowly ones were above!* His father responded, עוֹלָם בָּרוּר רָאִיתָ, *You glimpsed a world of clarity,* for this is the truth. The simple way to understand the Gemara is that Yosef glimpsed kings and powerful men on a low level, and was surprised by their lack of status in the next world; his father then told him that these matters have no value in the next world. But R' Moshe is unsatisfied with this interpretation. Surely, he asks, Yosef knew that power on this earth is meaningless in the next world! Why would he characterize such a sight as "upside-down"?

R' Moshe therefore explains that Yosef indeed saw great, learned sages in positions of lesser prominence than more simple folk, and it was this that he could not understand. His father therefore explained to him that the simple folk who were being honored were deserving of such reward because they had used their God-given abilities to achieve a large proportion of the tasks that Hashem had set for them. The learned Sages who were below them, continued R' Yehoshua, although they had accomplished a great deal, could have accomplished even more; they left a greater percentage of their potential unrealized, and therefore were relegated to a lesser status in the next world. This, explained R' Yehoshua, is the way of Hashem's judgment.

MISHNAH OF THE DAY: SHABBOS 16:1

The Mishnah begins a discussion of which items may be saved from a fire on the Sabbath:

כָּל כִּתְבֵי הַקֹּדֶשׁ — ***All Holy Scriptures*** (i.e., Torah scrolls or scrolls of the other books of the Bible), מַצִּילִין אוֹתָן מִפְּנֵי הַדְּלֵיקָה — ***may be saved from a fire*** on the Sabbath,[1] בֵּין שֶׁקּוֹרִין בָּהֶן — ***whether we read from them*** publicly in the synagogue on the Sabbath (such as scrolls of *Nevi'im,* from which the *haftarah* is read), וּבֵין שֶׁאֵין קוֹרִין בָּהֶן — ***or whether we do not read from them*** (such as scrolls of *Kesuvim* [Hagiographa]),[2] אַף עַל פִּי שֶׁכְּתוּבִים בְּכָל לָשׁוֹן — and ***even if they are***

NOTES

1. I.e., they may be removed from a house or courtyard where a fire has broken out, as long as they themselves have not caught fire (*Meiri*).

2. The weekly *haftarah* selection is never read from *Kesuvim.* Furthermore, and as the Mishnah will go on to explain, the Rabbis forbade even private individuals to read *Kesuvim* on the Sabbath. Nevertheless, even *Kesuvim* scrolls may be rescued from a fire (*Rav; Rashi*).

written in any language besides Hebrew, טְעוּנִים גְּנִיזָה — *they* (i.e., the translated Scriptures) *warrant being hidden away* (i.e., they may not be discarded in an unprotected area where they may come to disgrace).[3]

The Mishnah now explains its statement that *Kesuvim* are not read on the Sabbath:

וּמִפְּנֵי מַה אֵין קוֹרִין בָּהֶם — *And why do we not read from them* on the Sabbath? מִפְּנֵי בִיטּוּל בֵּית הַמִּדְרָשׁ — *On account of neglect of the study hall.*[4]

The Mishnah continues discussing the permit to save sacred writings from the fire:

מַצִּילִין תִּיק הַסֵּפֶר עִם הַסֵּפֶר — *We may save the container of a scroll together with the scroll,* וְתִיק הַתְּפִילִין עִם הַתְּפִילִין — *and the container of tefillin together with the tefillin* (i.e., when saving a scroll of the Scriptures or a pair of *tefillin* from a fire on the Sabbath, their containers may be saved along with them), וְאַף עַל פִּי שֶׁיֵּשׁ בְּתוֹכָן מָעוֹת — *and even though there is money in them* (i.e., even though in addition to the scroll of the Scripture or *tefillin* these containers also contain money, which is *muktzeh,* they may still be rescued). וּלְהֵיכָן מַצִּילִין אוֹתָן — *And to where may we* take them to *save them?* לְמָבוֹי שֶׁאֵינוֹ מְפוּלָּשׁ — *To an alley that is not open.*[5] בֶּן בְּתֵירָא אוֹמֵר — *Ben*

NOTES

3. Thus, the Mishnah means to say the following: All books of the Scriptures, whether of the sort that are read on the Sabbath or not, are to be saved from a fire on the Sabbath, *if they are written in Hebrew.* If they are written in a foreign language, *although they may not be saved from a fire on the Sabbath,* they must, at other times, be put away in a repository for holy objects when they become worn out (*Rav, Rashi* from Gemara 115a; see, however, *Gems from the Gemara*).

4. In Talmudic times, it was customary for the Sages to deliver lectures on the Sabbath to the general population regarding various halachos. This could not be done during the week, when most people were occupied with earning a livelihood. In order to insure attendance, the Rabbis prohibited the reading of *Kesuvim* on the Sabbath during the lecture hours (i.e., before the noonday meal), since people would become engrossed in them and fail to attend the lectures. Since the lectures pertained to daily observances, it was more beneficial for the public to attend the lectures than to study *Kesuvim.* After the noonday meal, it was permissible to read from the *Kesuvim* (*Rashi; Rav* from Gemara 116b; see *Tiferes Yisrael* for why this decree is no longer operative).

[*Kesuvim* was regarded as the most interesting part of Scriptures, as evidenced by the fact that its books were read to the Kohen Gadol on the night of Yom Kippur to keep him awake. See *Yoma* 7:1.]

5. In this context, an *alley that is not open* refers to an alley enclosed on three sides, with a post at the open end. On the other hand, the *alley that is open* to which Ben Beseira refers below is one enclosed on three sides, without a post at the open end (*Rav* from Gemara 117b). [This is in contradistinction to the prevalent meaning of מָבוֹי שֶׁאֵינוֹ מְפוּלָּשׁ — viz., any alley that is enclosed on three sides — and מָבוֹי מְפוּלָּשׁ — viz.,

Beseira says: **אַף לַמְּפוּלָּשׁ — *Even to [an alley] that is open.*** [6]

NOTES

an alley that is open at both ends.]

The Mishnah here follows the opinion of R' Eliezer, that an alley with three walls requires two side-posts on the fourth side if it is to satisfy the Rabbinic requirements for permitting carrying in it or into it from a private domain. This requirement, however, is only for usual, optional carrying. For the purpose of saving Scripture or *tefillin,* R' Eliezer permits carrying even into an alley with only one post at its mouth (*Rav* from Gemara ibid.).

6. I.e., R' Eliezer permits removal of a Torah scroll to an alley without any post at all affixed to its open end (*Rav* from Gemara ibid.).

GEMS FROM THE GEMARA

The Gemara (115a) explains that our Mishnah follows the view of Rabban Gamliel, who maintains that books of the Scriptures may not be written in any language other than Hebrew — or, in the case of the Pentateuch, Greek (*Megillah* 1:8). Accordingly, it would be forbidden to read foreign-language translations of the Scriptures on *any* day of the week — not just on the Sabbath. Consequently, one would be forbidden to save these translations from a fire. [This is in contrast to the books of *Kesuvim* which may be read on part of the Sabbath, as well as during the week, and therefore may be saved from a fire on the Sabbath.] Nevertheless, while on the one hand they may not be saved from a fire on the Sabbath, on the other hand it is forbidden to simply discard them. Rather, they must be put away in a repository for holy objects (*genizah*). [This was a room or vault where holy objects no longer fit for use were placed. Eventually, when the place became filled it would be sealed.]

Rashi cites the opinion of his teachers, who state that Rabban Gamliel's prohibition against translating Scriptures applies only to *Kesuvim.* On the other hand, since *Nevi'im* had already been translated by Yonasan ben Uziel (a pupil of the Tanna Hillel) into Aramaic, it was permissible to translate them into other languages too. *Rashi* himself, however, maintains that although Yonasan ben Uziel translated *Nevi'im,* he did not commit his translation to writing, but only recited it orally. There was therefore no precedent to translate *Nevi'im* in writing.

Later during the Tannaic and Amoraic periods, the Sages realized that the Torah was becoming forgotten by the people. They therefore permitted the Oral Law to be committed to writing. This originally included books of Mishnah only. Subsequently, Aggadah, *Siddur,*

Gemara, and other holy books were written down as well. The Sages also permitted the translation of Scriptures. Additionally, they permitted the Scriptures to be written in any script, with any type of ink. Since today all these books may be written, in our day and age they too are to be rescued from a fire on the Sabbath (*Tos.* from *Gittin* 60a; *Shulchan Aruch* 334:12). Moreover, in this context, printed books are treated the same as handwritten ones (*Magen Avraham* 334:17, 284; *Turei Zahav* 284:2).

A MUSSAR THOUGHT FOR THE DAY

We explained in *A Torah Thought for the Day* that Hashem judges people not simply for the number of their accomplishments, but by the percentage of their potential that they succeeded in realizing. Thus, every person must measure himself not against others, but against what *he* is able to accomplish.

This mind-set can help us to understand what seems to be a paradox — the fact that Moshe, the greatest *navi* and perhaps the most exalted person who ever lived, is described by the Torah as *exceedingly humble, more than any man on the face of the earth* (*Bamidbar* 12:3). How was it possible for Moshe — who performed the mighty plagues that brought Pharaoh and the Egyptians to their knees, and who ascended to the heavens to debate with the angels and receive the Torah — to envision himself as a humble person?

According to what we have learned, however, the difficulty can be resolved. The fact that a person accomplishes great things in his life is no reason for him to become arrogant, as he still may be far from completing the goals that Hashem has set for him. Indeed, he cannot even feel superior to any other individual, for even if his accomplishments far outweigh those of another, that other person may have completed a higher percentage of his allotted tasks; and a person is certainly not entitled to be arrogant because of gifts that Hashem has given to him and not to others!

Rav Yosef Leib Bloch points out that one can also attain humility by measuring himself against the infinite and eternal Creator. Obviously, all mortal accomplishments pale in relation to the glory of Hashem. Thus, the more that a person can perceive Hashem's greatness, the easier it will be for him to appreciate how minute his own accomplishments are on a cosmic scale, and to realize that they are no reason for

arrogance. It was precisely because Moshe achieved a closeness to Hashem beyond that of any other mortal, that he was able to comprehend his insignificance to such a great extent. This enabled him to become the most humble of men despite his exalted status and his vast accomplishments.

HALACHAH OF THE DAY

Another Rabbinic prohibition related to laundering is the prohibition of wiping mud on a clean towel. Since a muddy towel is unfit for further use, and mud can easily be rinsed off, the Sages were concerned lest one forget and rinse off the muddy towel, in violation of the prohibition against laundering. Thus, if one's shoes become muddy, he should not wipe them on a clean towel.

It is permitted, however, to wipe one's wet, muddy shoes on a doormat, rag or paper towel, since no one will be disturbed if these items become soiled; therefore we are not concerned that one will mistakenly come to rinse the mud off them. [It should be noted that rubbing off *dry* mud is forbidden, due to the prohibition of *grinding*.]

It is forbidden to cover a bucket of water with a cloth, lest the cloth fall into the bucket and the person come to wring it out on Shabbos. However, if the cloth is designated as a cover for the bucket, it may be used for that purpose, since it is assumed that even if it falls in, one will not bother to wring it out.

It is forbidden to walk near a body of water where there is a danger of falling in, since one's clothes would then become soaked and he might wring them out. For example, one should not walk on the ledge of a swimming pool. Similarly, one may not walk on a frozen body of water unless he is certain that the ice is thick enough to support his weight.

Now that we have delineated the rules that govern the *melachah* of laundering, let us see how they may be applied to some common situations that may occur on Shabbos.

Carpet is subject to the restrictions against laundering, since it is made from fabric. May one clean carpeted floors on Shabbos?

Applying the rules set forth above, we may arrive at the following conclusions:

As we have seen previously, the removal of dust or particles of dirt is forbidden only when the dirt has become absorbed or otherwise trapped between the fibers of the fabric. The simple removal of surface dirt is permissible. For this reason, the halachah is that if crumbs or other food particles fall on a carpet and come to rest on top of it, but do not become embedded between the carpet's fibers, they may be removed on Shabbos.

A CLOSER LOOK AT THE SIDDUR

This week, we will continue our discussion of the tenth of the Thirteen Fundamental Principles (י״ג עיקרים) enumerated by *Rambam,* which states:

> אֲנִי מַאֲמִין בֶּאֱמוּנָה שְׁלֵמָה שֶׁהַבּוֹרֵא יִתְבָּרַךְ שְׁמוֹ יוֹדֵעַ כָּל מַעֲשֵׂה בְנֵי אָדָם וְכָל מַחְשְׁבוֹתָם שֶׁנֶּאֱמַר ״הַיֹּצֵר יַחַד לִבָּם הַמֵּבִין אֶל־כָּל־מַעֲשֵׂיהֶם״.
>
> *I believe with complete faith that the Creator, Blessed be His Name, knows all the deeds of human beings, and all of their thoughts, as it is stated: "He Who fashions all their hearts together, Who comprehends all of their deeds."*

Discussion of this principle would be incomplete without addressing a major theological question that it engenders: If Hashem "knows" all that men will do, how is it possible to say that man has *bechirah,* free choice? If it is known to Hashem that a person will do good, then it would seem that the person has no choice but to be good. But the fact that man is not constrained to be good or evil, but rather is free to choose the path he wishes, is axiomatic to our faith. How are these two principles to be reconciled?

Rambam addresses this question in his *Hilchos Teshuvah,* and comments that the answer is "broader than the land and wider than the sea." He then cautions that true understanding of the matter requires careful thought and consideration. After these prefaces, he cites his own words in *Hilchos Yesodei HaTorah* (Chapter 2), where he explains the fundamental difference between "knowledge" of man as opposed to "knowledge" of Hashem. The essence of *Rambam's* answer is that since the very nature of Hashem's knowledge is beyond our comprehension, we need only know that it does not contradict our free will, although it is difficult for us to understand why.

Raavad is dissatisfied with *Rambam's* approach, and remarks that it is unwise to bring up a question of such magnitude and then leave the answer as based upon one's faith. It would have been better, says *Raavad,* to leave the question unasked. However, after making this observation,

Raavad offers his own, more easily understood, approach. He explains that the knowledge possessed by Hashem is not a decree, which compels a person to act in a certain way. Rather, it is born of the fact that Hashem is above the constraints of time; to Him, past, present and future are one and the same. Thus, Hashem knows what a man will do because He knows the choices that will be made, not because man has no choice. [A modern analogy might be made to a film recording. One who watches the film knows what all the characters therein have done; but that does not mean that the people in the film had no free will! Hashem has the power to access the "film" of all that was and all that will be, and therefore the acts and thoughts of men are clearly revealed to him.]

[*Raavad* notes that there is no one definitive, final answer to this question, and he offers his approach as only one solution. Many other commentators have spoken of this, and a thorough analysis is beyond the scope of our work. For further discussion, see *Kuzari* 5:19-20.]

QUESTION OF THE DAY:

Why does the Torah choose to mention Aharon first in the first verse, and Moshe first in the second verse, instead of vice versa?

For the answer, see page 111.

A TORAH THOUGHT FOR THE DAY

וַאֲנִי אַקְשֶׁה אֶת־לֵב פַּרְעֹה
And I will harden Pharaoh's heart (*Shemos* 7:3).

Many commentators raise the following theological question: If Hashem was the cause of Pharaoh's intransigence, why was he punished? The fundamental basis of reward and punishment is dependent on free will, which was apparently taken from Pharaoh in this instance.

There are many approaches suggested to answer this question. *Rambam* says (*Shemoneh Perakim* §8) that there are instances when wickedness is so severe and entrenched that Hashem insists on exacting full punishment from the wicked person. To ensure this, Hashem removes that person's ability to do *teshuvah,* which He ordinarily provides to all people in His great mercy. Thus, Pharaoh, who of his own free will had imposed horrible bondage and terrible decrees upon the Jews, would definitely be punished, as Hashem eliminated his ability to do *teshuvah. Ramban* seems to concur with this position, citing a Midrash that states that when Hashem warns someone repeatedly to repent and he does not do so, he will "lock him out of the door of repentance, to punish him for his sins." *Sforno* maintains that if there were any possibility that Pharaoh would fully repent and be truly remorseful, acknowledging his sinfulness and subjugating himself to Hashem's will, his repentance would have been accepted. But mere acquiescence to let the Jews leave based on fear of loss of his kingdom would not suffice. Therefore Hashem removed his ability to accede to Moshe's demand.

Abarbanel, after a lengthy repudiation of *Rambam's* position, suggests two other solutions: (1) While it is true that no wickedness is too great to preclude repentance, this rule is limited to those deeds between man and Hashem. However, for iniquities and injustices directed at man there can be instances where no repentance is sufficient. Just as a tribunal is mandated to mete out punishment to a murderer or thief regardless of his contrition, so too Hashem metes out punishment for sins against the Jewish people. Pharaoh, who robbed, enslaved and "embittered the lives" of Jews to a far greater extent than authorized by Hashem, had to be punished, and no amount of remorse or prayer would be accepted. (2) The repeated refusal of Pharaoh to heed Moshe's request was entirely of his own free volition, but **resulted** from the methodology of the plagues. Had Hashem simply struck Egypt with a plague that would remain in force until Pharaoh relented, that acquiescence would not be a result of choice; rather it would be based on a clear realization that his adversary, Hashem, was stronger. However, since the plagues lasted for a short time and then disappeared, Pharaoh was able to convince himself that they were not the work of Hashem, but rather the result of some celestial activity or other abberant natural occurrence. With each plague, Pharaoh was faced with a choice of believing whether it was Hashem's work or not. Though each plague increased in severity or in its miraculous nature, Hashem hardened Pharaoh's heart just enough so that he would be able to make a choice between good and evil. Each time, Pharaoh chose not to send out the Jews — and for this, he was punished.

MISHNAH OF THE DAY: SHABBOS 16:2

The following Mishnah continues to consider the Rabbinic laws concerning the rescue of items from a fire on the Sabbath:

מַצִּילִין מְזוֹן שָׁלֹשׁ סְעוּדוֹת — ***One may save*** enough ***food for*** the ***three meals*** that one is obligated to eat on the Sabbath. **הָרָאוּי לְאָדָם לְאָדָם** — ***What is fit for people*** may be saved ***for people,*** **הָרָאוּי לִבְהֵמָה לִבְהֵמָה** — and ***what is fit for animals*** may be saved ***for animals.***[1]

The Mishnah elaborates on the three-meal rule:

כֵּיצַד — ***How so*** (i.e., under what circumstances may one save enough food for three meals)? **נָפְלָה דְלֵיקָה בְּלֵילֵי שַׁבָּת** — If ***fire broke out on the Sabbath*** [i.e., Friday] ***night*** before the person ate, since all three meals

NOTES

1. I.e., three meals' worth of food fit for human consumption may be saved for every person who requires it, and a supply of animal food may be saved for one's cattle.

Since a person is required to feed his animals before he himself sits down to eat (*Berachos* 40a), in order to partake of the three Sabbath meals he must have sufficient fodder for three feedings of his livestock (*Tiferes Yisrael*).

In contrast to the Scriptures and *tefillin* of the previous Mishnah, the foodstuffs in our Mishnah may be removed only to an area into which one is otherwise permitted to carry — i.e., a yard properly enclosed on its fourth side, and incorporated by an *eruvei chatzeiros,* if necessary (*Rav;* see the end of Mishnah 3). Although the owner is transferring the foodstuffs to a yard into which he is otherwise permitted to carry, the Rabbis nevertheless restricted removing any more than these minimum food requirements. They did so for fear that in his haste to save his property he might extinguish the fire (*Rav* from Gemara 117b). By limiting the amount of food he can save to what is needed for the Sabbath, they removed the element of haste from his salvage efforts, thereby making it unlikely that he will forget the prohibition against extinguishing the fire (*Tos. Yom Tov*).

remain to be eaten that Sabbath, מַצִּילִין מְזוֹן שָׁלֹשׁ סְעוּדוֹת — *he may save* enough *food for three meals;* בְּשַׁחֲרִית — if it broke out *in the morning* before the meal, since he has eaten one of the three Sabbath meals, מַצִּילִין מְזוֹן שְׁתֵּי סְעוּדוֹת — *he may save* only enough *food for two meals;* בְּמִנְחָה מְזוֹן סְעוּדָה אַחַת — if it broke out *in the afternoon* after the first meal of the day was eaten, he may save only enough *food for one meal.*

A dissenting view:

רַבִּי יוֹסֵי אוֹמֵר — *R' Yose says:* לְעוֹלָם מַצִּילִין מְזוֹן שָׁלֹשׁ סְעוּדוֹת — *One may always save* enough *food for three meals.*[2]

NOTES

2. R' Yose maintains that since the Sabbath mandates three meals, the Rabbis did not differentiate between the various times of the day. Rather, they made a general rule permitting the removal of enough food for three meals (*Rav; Rashi; Tiferes Yisrael*).

GEMS FROM THE GEMARA

In its elaboration of the three-meal rule, our Mishnah ruled that if fire broke out on Friday night before the person ate, since he still must eat all of the three Sabbath meals, he may save enough food for three meals; if the fire broke out in the morning before the meal, since he has only two remaining Sabbath meals to eat, he may save only enough food for two meals; if it broke out in the afternoon before the final meal, since there is only one Sabbath meal left to eat, he may save only enough food for one meal.

Intriguingly, in the case of the fire breaking out at night, *Rav* and *Rashi* state, "before he ate," while concerning the fire breaking out in the morning, they state, "before the meal." One reason given for this change in phraseology is as follows: Since the Sabbath evening meal may be eaten anytime during Friday night, even though the usual suppertime has passed, one may save food for three meals, as long as he has not yet eaten. In the daytime, however, if one has not eaten until the afternoon, he can no longer fulfill his obligation to eat the morning meal. *Rav* and *Rashi* therefore state regarding the daytime Sabbath meal that the fire broke out "before the meal," so as to indicate that he may save food for two meals only if the usual mealtime has not yet passed. If it has passed, even though he himself has not yet eaten, he may save only enough food for one meal (*Bach* to *Orach Chaim* §334).

Others explain the change in phrasing differently. In view of the Baraisa quoted in the Gemara (118a), stating that one may wash the dishes after the morning meal of the Sabbath for the noon meal, and after the noon meal for the late afternoon meal, it appears that it was customary for them to eat a light breakfast [a repast similar to what is known today as a *Kiddush*] in the morning, and then to eat the regular Sabbath meal at noon, followed by another meal (the *seudah shelishis*) in the late afternoon. Therefore, *Rav* and *Rashi* state that the fire broke out "before the meal," to indicate that even if one has eaten breakfast, as long as he has not yet eaten the regular Sabbath meal, he may still save food for the two meals that customarily followed this breakfast (*Pri Megadim, Orach Chaim, Mishbetzos Zahav* 334:1).

A MUSSAR THOUGHT FOR THE DAY

The Gemara in *Niddah* (70b) poses the following contradiction between two verses. One verse (*Yechezkel* 18:32) states: כִּי לֹא אֶחְפֹּץ בְּמוֹת הַמֵּת, *For I do not desire the death of the one who should die,* while a second verse (*Shmuel I* 2:25) states: כִּי־חָפֵץ ה׳ לַהֲמִיתָם, *For HASHEM desires to kill them!* The Gemara explains that the first verse refers to those who are doing *teshuvah,* whereas the other refers to those who are not doing *teshuvah.*

Rav Yisrael Salanter (*Ohr Yisrael* §30) explains this Gemara in light of his general thesis that every person has the ability and obligation to alter and rectify his deficient or sinful character traits, and outlines three distinct levels which one must climb to attain spiritual perfection and complete *teshuvah:* (1) awareness of one's shortcomings; (2) conquest of these shortcomings in a behavioral way, though one is still emotionally and intellectually bound to them; (3) complete intellectual renunciation of these weaknesses, and transformation of them into positive qualities. Rav Yisrael maintains that awareness comes as a result of הִתְפָּעֲלוּת, an emotional arousal by an individual which will lead to the realization that he is spiritually lacking, and is on a ruinous path because of this corrupt trait. Someone who is stirred, either through *mussar* or *tochachah* (rebuke), becomes a candidate for complete *teshuvah,* and will be afforded the time and tools to reach this goal, by the mercy of Hashem. This person is called "one who is doing *teshuvah.*" Someone, however, who remains unmindful, unmoved, and indifferent to his objectionable ways is considered "one who is not doing *teshuvah*" and he will be stripped of Hashem's special kindness.

Rav Yisrael stresses that the identification of a person as "one who will not do *teshuvah*" is not based on Hashem's knowledge of the future, but on His impeccable assessment of one's intellectual and emotional capacity for *teshuvah* at the time of judgment. *Rav Aharon Kotler* (in his *Mishnas Rav Aharon*) finds a parallel to this concept in the case of a *ben soreir u'moreh,* a rebellious son who is punished by death because his wanton behavior will surely lead to a bad end, though his current sins are not punishable by death. Rav Aharon explains that his punishment is not for the sins that he will commit, but for the sin of possessing an incorrigible nature that will dominate and dictate continued destructive behavior, despite parental pleadings and judicial penalties. The absence of hope that he will mend his ways mandates that he be put to death. Commenting further on Rav Yisrael's interpretation of the Gemara, Rav Aharon maintains that even one serious flaw that is completely ignored by a person may relegate him to the status of "one who is not doing *teshuvah,*" particularly if it is one which influences others, for he then may be viewed as one who desecrates Hashem's Name. Cognizant of the fact that one may be a slave of habit and unwilling to completely abandon a particular *middah* or action, Rav Aharon urges that a person who possesses an undesirable trait should at least attempt to limit it in some way or refrain from indulging it at some particular time. By so doing, he will instill in himself a modest sense of wrongdoing, and will avoid the disaster of being called "one who does not do *teshuvah.*"

HALACHAH OF THE DAY

Yesterday, we began discussing the cleaning of carpeted floors on Shabbos.

As we have learned, the removal of dust or dirt that has become trapped between the fibers of a fabric is prohibited only when the fabric is considered to be significantly dirty. Accordingly, if a small amount of dust or dirt became embedded between the carpet's fibers, but it is not enough to significantly impact the appearance of the carpet, one may sweep out the dirt. However, if the carpet has become significantly dirty, with many crumbs or particles of dirt trapped between the fibers, one may not sweep out the dirt. One may lift off only the crumbs that are sitting on the surface of the carpet. If a non-Jew is available, one may ask the non-Jew to sweep up all of the dirt.

Many *poskim* prohibit the use of non-powered carpet sweepers on Shabbos for varying reasons. Some say that since these sweepers are highly effective, their use must be considered a form of laundering. Others maintain that these sweepers have a tendency to pull fibers out of the carpet, a [Rabbinic] violation of the *melachah* of קוֹרֵעַ, *tearing.* Still others maintain that the use of such a tool is prohibited under the rule of עוּבְדָא דְחוֹל, *weekday activity,* activities prohibited because they are not within the spirit of the day of Shabbos. Practically speaking, one should not use a carpet sweeper on Shabbos even in the cases where it is permissible to clean the dirt from the carpet. Rather, one should use a broom in keeping with the guidelines set forth above. One may, however, instruct a non-Jew to use a carpet sweeper on Shabbos.

It is forbidden under all circumstances to pour water on a carpet, either to remove a stain or to prevent a stain from setting. Furthermore, one may not ask a non-Jew to pour water on a carpet.

If a moist food item, such as a clump of mashed potatoes, fell onto a carpet, the following rules would apply:

If the dirt is noticeable to the extent that it spoils the appearance of the carpet enough to be embarrassing, and the removal of the dirt will not leave behind a stain, then it is forbidden for one to peel or scratch off the dirt. He may, however, ask a non-Jew to remove it. If the dirt will leave behind a stain after being removed, one may remove the dirt himself, since this cannot be considered laundering.

If the dirt is not very noticeable, one may peel or scratch it off even if the removal of the dirt will not leave behind a stain.

A CLOSER LOOK AT THE SIDDUR

Near the conclusion of the *Ne'ilah* service (which is recited at the close of Yom Kippur), after the final *Vidui* (confession of sins), we find a prayer called אַתָּה הִבְדַּלְתָּ אֱנוֹשׁ מֵרֹאשׁ, *You have separated man from the beginning . . .* The main theme of this prayer is reassurance to the congregation that Hashem in His mercy affords us the opportunity to repent, and in fact, desires our repentance, so that we may live. In the prayer, we find two verses cited from *Yechezkel.* One (18:23) reads: הֶחָפֹץ אֶחְפֹּץ מוֹת רָשָׁע . . . הֲלוֹא בְּשׁוּבוֹ מִדְּרָכָיו וְחָיָה, *Do I desire at all the death of the wicked . . . is it not so that if he returns from his [evil] ways, he will live?* And the second (ibid. v. 32) reads: כִּי לֹא אֶחְפֹּץ בְּמוֹת הַמֵּת . . . וְהָשִׁיבוּ וִחְיוּ,

For I do not desire the death of the one who dies . . . Repent and live! These two verses appear to be carrying the same message. *Malbim,* however, interprets them as follows. The first verse is speaking of one whose repentance is total, and rooted in the love of Hashem. This type of repentance is characterized by genuine remorse and grief over one's past misdeeds. The second verse, however, refers to one who fears Divine retribution and wishes to change his ways, but has not reached the level where he can feel truly remorseful about his past. Nevertheless, the verse assures us that this level of repentance will also be accepted. *Malbim* explains that this is true for two reasons: (1) Hashem does not wish death upon anyone who has shown even some sorrow and willingness to better himself; (2) through his improved behavior, the penitent will eventually come to repent fully, and elevate his state of righteousness.

The Gemara tells us that there is a difference between these two types of *teshuvah.* If one reaches the level of repenting out of the love of Hashem (תְּשׁוּבָה מֵאַהֲבָה), then his past sins become transformed to merits, in recognition of the great moral and emotional upheaval that the penitent underwent to overcome and reject his previous behavior. One who repents out of fear of retribution, however, does not merit this reward. Although such a person has shown a willingness to use his free will differently, he has not fully cast away his sins. His past misdeeds are therefore not fully erased, but are re-categorized as inadvertent ones, the result of some negligence or weakness. Using this idea, we can perhaps explain why the first verse refers to the penitent merely as a wicked man, while the second refers to him as "the one who dies." For the second verse speaks of someone who has not cast away his prior sins; truly, but for Hashem's mercy, he still deserves to die. The first verse, however, speaks of one who has "returned from his [evil] ways," completely regretting and renouncing his prior misdeeds. Thus, while he is described as a former sinner, he is not characterized as "one who dies."

QUESTION OF THE DAY:

When did Hashem harden Pharaoh's heart?

For the answer, see page 111.

פרשת וארא

THURSDAY

PARASHAS VA'EIRA

A TORAH THOUGHT FOR THE DAY

וְשָׁרַץ הַיְאֹר צְפַרְדְּעִים וְעָלוּ וּבָאוּ בְּבֵיתֶךָ . . .
וּבְתַנּוּרֶיךָ וּבְמִשְׁאֲרוֹתֶיךָ

And the river shall swarm with frogs, and they shall ascend and come into your palace . . . and into your ovens and into your kneading bowls (*Shemos* 7:28).

The Gemara in *Pesachim* (53b) derives an important halachic principle from this verse. Todos of Rome asked: From where did Chananya, Mishael, and Azaryah learn that they should give up their lives to the fiery furnace? They learned this from the frogs in Egypt. They said: If the frogs, that are not commanded to sanctify Hashem's Name, did so [by entering the ovens], we, who are so commanded, must surely do so!

Tosafos ask: Why did they need the lesson from the frogs? Nevuchadnezzar was attempting to have them bow to an *avodah zarah* (idol), and the prohibition against *avodah zarah* is one of the three cardinal sins for which one is required to give up his life rather than transgress! *Tosafos* offer two answers: (1) *Rabbeinu Tam* says that the statue to which Nevuchadnezzar ordered them to bow was not a true *avodah zarah,* as it was not representative of a deity. Rather, it was an *andarta,* a sculpture of Nevuchadnezzar himself, which was made for his own honor and to which he expected his subjects to bow down as a sign of respect rather than worship. Although one is not permitted to bow to such a statue in any event, it is not necessary to give up one's life to avoid doing so. Nevertheless, Chananya, Mishael and Azaryah chose to refuse, to sanctify Hashem's Name. (2) *Ri* explains that the statue was indeed a true *avodah zarah.* Chananya, Mishael and Azaryah, however, had the option to flee, as Daniel had done, rather than defy Nevuchadnezzar. They learned from the frogs that they were permitted to remain and take advantage of the opportunity to perform the mitzvah of sanctifying Hashem's Name.

Meiri, in his initial interpretation, solves the problem by asserting that one is permitted to transgress the prohibition against *avodah zarah* rather than be killed as long as the perpetrator is forcing him to do so for his own benefit, and not for the sake of forcing a Jew to sin. Since Nevuchadnezzar's motive was to instill fear and respect for himself, it would have been permitted for them to bow to the statue. *Meiri* later recants this position, and explains in accord with *Rabbeinu Tam.*

Tos. Rid presents a completely different approach. He explains that the statue was indeed an *avodah zarah,* and Chananya, Mishael and

Azaryah were indeed obligated to sacrifice their lives rather than bow to it. The Gemara means to ask only how they knew that they could say to Nevuchadnezzar: "Behold, our God Whom we worship is able to save us. He will rescue us from the fiery burning furnace and from your hand." How were they so confident that they would miraculously survive? [Although they entertained the possibility that they would not survive, as indicated in the latter half of the *pasuk*, it is clear that they assumed they would.] This confidence was learned from the behavoir of the frogs, who entered the hot ovens of the Egyptians but were not harmed. [The Midrash says that after the plague, all the frogs died except those that had gone into the ovens.]

MISHNAH OF THE DAY: SHABBOS 16:3

The following Mishnah continues to list the items that can be saved from a fire on the Sabbath:

מַצִּילִין סַל מָלֵא כִּכָּרוֹת — ***One may save*** from his burning house ***a basket full of loaves,*** אַף עַל פִּי שֶׁיֵּשׁ בּוֹ מֵאָה סְעוּדוֹת — ***even though it has*** enough loaves ***in it*** *for* ***a hundred meals,***[1] וְעִיגּוּל שֶׁל דְּבֵילָה — ***and a round cake of pressed figs,***[2] וְחָבִית שֶׁל יַיִן — ***and a barrel of wine.*** וְאוֹמֵר לַאֲחֵרִים — ***And he may tell others:*** בּוֹאוּ וְהַצִּילוּ לָכֶם — ***"Come and save*** food or drink ***for yourselves";***[3] וְאִם הָיוּ פִּיקְחִין — ***but if they were wise,*** עוֹשִׂין עִמּוֹ חֶשְׁבּוֹן אַחַר הַשַּׁבָּת — ***they make a reckoning with him after the Sabbath*** for their wages as laborers.[4]

NOTES

1. Since he is removing a single basket from the house, which he must in any case be permitted to remove since it contains the loaves necessary for his three meals, the Rabbis did not require him to remove any additional loaves from the basket (*Rav*).

2. Dried figs were customarily pressed into large round cakes. This cake [as well as the barrel of wine mentioned next] contains much more than was needed for three meals (*Rav*).

3. By announcing that they may save for themselves, he relinquishes his title to the property, and it becomes הֶפְקֵר, *ownerless.* Accordingly, others may retrieve it for themselves (*Rashi* from Gemara 120a).

4. I.e., they may accept wages for effecting the rescue. Generally, wages may neither be paid nor accepted for work done on the Sabbath, even if that work is permissible. For example, one may not pay someone for watching his field or his child on the Sabbath, though such work in no way violates the Sabbath laws (*Bava Metzia* 58a; *Shulchan Aruch* 306:4,5). Only if one is being paid a weekly, monthly, or yearly rate, may the Sabbath work be included (ibid.).

In the case of this Mishnah, however, their efforts to save the food were not made

The Mishnah cites a dispute concerning the location to which the items may be taken:

לְהֵיכָן מַצִּילִין אוֹתָן — ***To where may they*** remove these items to ***save them?*** לְחָצֵר הַמְעוֹרֶבֶת — ***To a courtyard*** whose houses are ***unified*** by means of an *eruv.*[5] בֶּן בְּתֵירָא אוֹמֵר — ***Ben Beseira says:*** אַף לְשֶׁאֵינָהּ מְעוֹרֶבֶת — ***Even to*** a courtyard whose houses are ***not unified*** by an *eruv.*[6]

NOTES

for the purpose of earning wages on the Sabbath, because the food rescued was actually ownerless and therefore rightfully the property of the rescuers. It is therefore their prerogative to "sell" the food back to its owner for compensation of their exertions (*Rav; Rashi*).

The Mishnah deals here with God-fearing people, who, knowing that the householder relinquished title to the food under duress, refuse to take advantage of the situation, though they are legally entitled to do so. On the other hand, they are not that pious that they would rescue the food completely gratis. They may, therefore, make a reckoning after the Sabbath (*Rav*). Truly pious people, however, would not accept any money, so as not to benefit financially from toil on the Sabbath (*Rav, Rashi* from Gemara 120a).

5. I.e., one may carry the food out only to a place into which carrying is permitted even according to Rabbinic law. Hence, since the Rabbis prohibited carrying from a privately owned house into a communally owned courtyard unless all the houses sharing the yard have been unified by an *eruv,* the food may be carried out only in such a yard. Similarly, one may take out food from one courtyard to another only if the two courtyards have been unified by an *eruv* (see *Rambam, Hil. Shabbos* 23:20).

Even so, the Rabbis limited the amount one may save because they were afraid that if one were permitted to try and save all his property, he might, in his haste to save it, forget that it is the Sabbath and extinguish the fire (*Rashi* from Gemara 117b).

6. Ben Beseira maintains that foodstuffs may be removed to a courtyard lacking an *eruv chatzeiros.* In contrast, however, to his ruling above in Mishnah 1 — permitting the removal of scrolls of Scripture or *tefillin* even to a courtyard without any enclosure whatever on its fourth side — here he agrees that foodstuffs may be removed only to a courtyard properly enclosed on its fourth side.

GEMS FROM THE GEMARA

The Gemara (120a) notes a contradiction between our Mishnah and the previous Mishnah: The previous Mishnah taught that one is permitted to save a maximum of only three meals' worth of food from a burning house, and not more. Why, then, does our Mishnah rule that one may save a basket even if it contains enough bread for a hundred meals?

The Gemara, in the name of Rav Huna, answers that in our Mishnah we are discussing a case where one comes simply to save (i.e., remove) from a burning house a basket of food as it is; whereas in the previous Mishnah, we were discussing a case where one wishes to bundle items together (i.e., he wishes to gather together several baskets of food, and place them inside a single container for removal). Thus, in the case of our Mishnah, where he comes simply to save a basket of food, he may save it regardless of how many loaves of bread are in it. [Since he is performing only a single act (removing a basket of bread from the burning house), it makes no difference how much he saves in removing that basket (*Rashi*).] But if one comes to bundle together baskets of food and remove them, he may bundle and remove only enough food for three meals. [Since collecting each basket requires a separate effort, the Rabbis did not permit one to remove more than three meals' worth of food, even if in the end he will place all of the baskets in a single large container and remove them together (*Rashi*).]

The Gemara presents another resolution in the name of Rav Abba bar Zavda in the name of Rav: Both our Mishnah and the previous Mishnah are discussing a case where one comes to bundle together containers before removing them. However, in our Mishnah we are discussing a case where the items are being removed to *that* courtyard, whereas in the previous Mishnah, we were discussing a case where the items are being removed to a more distant courtyard. [According to this approach, the distinction is explained as follows: Removing items to a farther courtyard involves more effort. The Rabbis did not permit making this more extensive effort for more than three meals' worth of food.]

A MUSSAR THOUGHT FOR THE DAY

One of the most basic character traits that a person is expected to possess is *derech eretz,* proper respect. Perhaps the most famous statement concerning the principle of *derech eretz* is found in *Pirkei Avos* (3:21). R' Elazar Ben Azaryah says: אִם אֵין תּוֹרָה אֵין דֶּרֶךְ אֶרֶץ; אִם אֵין דֶּרֶךְ אֶרֶץ אֵין תּוֹרָה, *If there is no Torah, there is no derech eretz; if there is no derech eretz, there is no Torah. Rabbeinu Yonah* explains that without knowledge of Torah, one will not understand his obligations to his fellow man (such as honesty in business). But one must first try to perfect his

personal qualities, such as proper *derech eretz,* thus enabling the Torah to reside within him. For Torah cannot reside in the body of one who is devoid of good character traits.

Tos. Yom Tov explains that Torah and *derech eretz* are not prerequisites for each other; rather, they complement each other. There are numerous references in Midrashim, *meforshim,* and works of *mussar* that illustrate the concept of *derech eretz.* Among them is *Rashi's* explanation of Hashem's statement (*Bereishis* 1:26): *Let* **us** *create man. Rashi* explains that although the angels of the Heavenly court certainly did not assist Hashem in the creation of man, Hashem wished to teach the quality of humility, using language which seemingly sought their counsel and approval for this important project. This lesson even took precedence over the dangerous opening that it gave heretics to "prove" that there are multiple creators.

In this vein, *R' Chaim Shmulevitz* (5732:18) cites a *Midrash Tanchuma* that states that Chananya, Mishael, and Azaryah, having survived the heat and flames of the furnace, remained there until ordered out by Nevuchadnezzar. They declared, "We will not go out without the permission of the king, and will abide by his word. Through his command we were thrown in, and by his command we will go out." The Midrash then continues, stating that Noach, too, remained in the Ark until ordered to leave by Hashem, using a similar refrain. "Just as I did not enter the Ark without Hashem's permission, so I will not leave without His permission." R' Chaim understands this Midrash to be teaching the importance of *derech eretz,* a central governing principle for proper personal and interpersonal conduct. Though Noach was virtually a slave to the welfare of the animals, suffering indignity, sleeplessness, and even injury, he still had the capacity to wait patiently in the Ark until he was instructed to leave. Even more amazing is the case of Chananya, Mishael, and Azaryah, who were apparently thrown to their deaths, and yet chose to treat the king with respect.

QUESTION OF THE DAY:

Why did all the frogs die after the plague of frogs ended (except for the ones that had entered the ovens)?

For the answer, see page 111.

HALACHAH OF THE DAY

We will now continue our discussion of cleaning carpets on Shabbos:

Even in situations where it is permissible for one to remove dirt from the carpet on Shabbos, one may not rub the carpet vigorously or use a brush in order to remove the dirt. One may brush the dirt off only lightly, using his hand or a cloth. If necessary, one may instruct a non-Jew to rub or brush out the dirt.

The preceding guidelines pertain only to food items, such as mashed potatoes that were previously ground up. Substances that were never ground up that have become caked on a carpet may not be scraped off due to the violation of the *melachah* of טוֹחֵן, *grinding*. Once again, however, one may ask a non-Jew to scrape the dirt off.

Another practical question: May one make a wet compress using a washcloth on Shabbos?

It is preferable not to make a wet compress on Shabbos by saturating a cloth with water. If possible, the compress should be prepared prior to the onset of Shabbos, so as to avoid any possibility of doing *melachah* on Shabbos.

If a compress must be made on Shabbos, one of the following procedures should be used:

One may soak the cloth in a colored liquid such as apple juice. Since the cloth will take the color of the liquid, this cannot be seen as an act of laundering. Alternately, one may spill water on the floor, thereby making the water somewhat unclean, and then saturate the cloth with this water. Once again, since the water being used to saturate the cloth is not clean, this is not viewed as laundering.

If none of these options is practicable, one may take a clean cloth and saturate it with clear water for the sake of an ill person. It is important to note that while using the compress, one must take care not to squeeze the liquid from the cloth.

Yet another question: May one clean his shoes on Shabbos?

It is permitted to dust off leather shoes with a rag or towel. One may also pour water onto leather shoes if he can avoid wetting the cloth stitching. It is forbidden, however, to pour water on shoes constructed from absorbent fabric, such as canvas sneakers. With respect to removing dust and dirt from such shoes, all of the guidelines enumerated above with regard to absorbent fabrics pertain to shoes as well.

If shoes become muddy on Shabbos, one may remove the mud, while it is moist, with a rag or paper towel, but not with an ordinary towel.

When using a rag, one is permitted to rub only gently, not vigorously. If the mud has dried, one may not scrape it off, as this would be a violation of the *melachah* of *grinding*.

It is forbidden to polish shoes with any type of polish on Shabbos. Furthermore, it is forbidden to re-brush shoes that had been polished prior to Shabbos.

This concludes our discussion of the *melachah* of *laundering*.

A CLOSER LOOK AT THE SIDDUR

In the prayer of *Krias Shema*, which we recite twice daily, the second verse states: וְאָהַבְתָּ אֵת ה׳ אֱלֹהֶיךָ, *You shall love HASHEM, your God.* There are many interpretations of this seminal verse, dealing with the laws of this mitzvah, its nuances, and methods of its implementation. Among these is a Baraisa in *Yoma* (86a) which beautifully sets forth the connection that must exist between one's relationship with Hashem and how one must behave with respect to his fellow man. The Baraisa states: *You shall love HASHEM, your God* — this teaches that the Name of Heaven shall *become beloved* through you. A person should study Scripture, learn Mishnah, and serve Torah scholars, and his dealing with people should be conducted in a pleasant manner. What do people say about this person? "Fortunate is his father who taught him Torah. Fortunate is his teacher who taught him Torah. Woe unto people who do not learn Torah . . . See how pleasant are his ways, how refined are his deeds!" Regarding such a person, Scripture says (*Yeshayah* 49:3): וַיֹּאמֶר לִי עַבְדִּי־אָתָּה יִשְׂרָאֵל אֲשֶׁר־בְּךָ אֶתְפָּאָר, *You are My servant Israel through whom I am glorified.* The Baraisa continues, describing an individual who learns Torah but whose deeds are unpleasant. People say of him: "Woe unto his father who taught him Torah. Woe unto his teacher who taught him Torah. See how perverse are his deeds and how ugly are his ways!" Regarding him Scripture says (*Yechezkel* 36:20): עַם־ה׳ אֵלֶּה וּמֵאַרְצוֹ יָצָאוּ, *these are the people of Hashem, but they departed His land.*

This Baraisa sums up the importance of *derech eretz,* not merely for its intrinsic qualities of integrity and decency, but as an instrument of bringing glory to Hashem's Name (see *Rambam, Hil. Yesodei HaTorah* 5:11 and *Hil. Dei'os* 5:13). *R' Meir Simchah of Dvinsk* (the *Meshech Chochmah*) highlights this idea in his explanation of the three phrases in the verse: וְאָהַבְתָּ אֵת ה׳ אֱלֹהֶיךָ בְּכָל־לְבָבְךָ וּבְכָל־נַפְשְׁךָ וּבְכָל־מְאֹדֶךָ, *You shall love HASHEM with all your heart, and with all your soul, and with all your*

פרשת וארא

THURSDAY

PARASHAS VA'EIRA

resources. It is understandable, he says, that when faced with a dire situation requiring martyrdom, a person can successfully meet the challenge, for his very identity as a Jew is being put to the test. This enables him to call forth all of his spiritual reserves. That is the lesson of *with all your heart and with all your soul.* But in his daily affairs, religious or mundane, one tends to be less vigilant and concerned with their proper performance. In order to stress that one has the same obligation of making Hashem's Name beloved in these spheres, the Torah added the phrase *with all your resources,* which encompasses all circumstances and all matters.

פרשת וארא

FRIDAY

PARASHAS VA'EIRA

A TORAH THOUGHT FOR THE DAY

וְשַׂמְתִּי פְדֻת בֵּין עַמִּי וּבֵין עַמֶּךָ

I shall make a distinction between My people and your people (*Shemos* 8:19).

R*ashi* explains that in this verse Hashem promised to make a separation between His people and Pharaoh's people, but does not clarify in what way this promise differs from the promise of וְהִפְלֵיתִי, *I will separate* (v. 18), which foretold that Goshen, the province of the Jews, would be spared from the plague of wild animals. *Sforno* and *Ramban* explain that this verse is adding another dimension to the miraculous differentiation between Goshen and Egypt; namely, even if Jews were to find themselves in Egypt proper, where Egyptians were being attacked, the Jews would be safe and protected. In this sense, says *Ramban,* the word פְּדֻת connotes *salvation*. [Indeed, both *Targum Yonasan* and *Onkeles* translate פְּדֻת here as פֻּרְקָן, *salvation.*]

Rashbam makes the point that the concept of *separation* and the concept of *salvation* and *redemption* are closely related, for the latter protect or remove one from the power and influence to which he should have been or, in fact, had been subjected. Thus, any Jews in Egypt proper, which had been attacked by the swarms of wild animals, should have been in the same danger as the Egyptians, and only Hashem's ability to orchestrate this "differentiation" saved them (see *R' Shamshon Raphael Hirsch)*.

Abarbanel explains that, although *Ramban's* portrayal of the expanded miracle is correct, this is not the meaning of the word פְּדֻת in the verse. He translates פְּדֻת as *redemption*, and explains that Hashem is saying that as a **result** of the plague of wild animals, Pharaoh would be awed by the animals' ability to distinguish between Egypt and Goshen. This would cause Pharaoh to recognize the power of Hashem and emancipate the Jews. Thus, וְשַׂמְתִּי פְדֻת means, *I will establish a redemption*, for after this plague, the Jews would no longer be viewed as slaves, but as the redeemed nation of Hashem. [This in fact came to pass, as seen by Pharaoh's capitulation: *Go, bring offerings to your God, in the land* (v. 21).]

Netziv (*Haamek Davar*) argues that the concept of פִּדְיוֹן, *redemption*, requires substituting something of value for the redeemed item. He therefore proposes a novel approach to explain this verse. He suggests that there were Jews who did not wish to leave Egypt, and who deserved to die. However, Hashem protected them, to ensure that no one would discredit Him by drawing attention to the Jews who died.

On the other hand, if there were foreign non-Egyptians who found themselves in Egypt during the plague, they suffered along with the Egyptians, though innocent of any particular sin. These non-Egyptians served as the "redemption" for the Jews who deserved punishment. This is what the verse means when it says that Hashem would *redeem* the Jews — he would substitute the non-Egyptians in their stead.

MISHNAH OF THE DAY: SHABBOS 16:4

The following Mishnah continues to list the items that may be saved from a fire on the Sabbath:

וּלְשָׁם — ***And to there,***[1] מוֹצִיא כָּל כְּלֵי תַשְׁמִישׁוֹ — ***he may take out all the utensils that he*** needs to ***use*** for his meals.[2] וְלוֹבֵשׁ כָּל מַה שֶּׁיָּכוֹל לִלְבּוֹשׁ — ***And he may put on all*** the clothing ***that he can wear,*** וְעוֹטֵף כָּל מַה שֶּׁיָּכוֹל לַעֲטוֹף — ***and wrap*** himself in ***all*** the clothing in ***which he can wrap*** himself,[3] and walk out of the house with them on.[4] רַבִּי יוֹסֵי אוֹמֵר — ***R' Yose says:*** שְׁמוֹנָה עָשָׂר כֵּלִים — He is permitted to put on and remove from the house only ***eighteen garments.***[5] וְחוֹזֵר וְלוֹבֵשׁ

NOTES

1. I.e., to whatever area foodstuffs may be removed (as explained in the previous Mishnah), these items may also be removed. As we saw in the previous Mishnah, the removal of items to a courtyard lacking an *eruv chatzeiros* is the subject of a dispute between the Tanna Kamma and Ben Beseira (*Rav*).

2. I.e., he may carry out all utensils required for the meals of that Sabbath (*Rav; Rashi*). For example, cups and jars (*Rashi*), and other table utensils (*Magen Avraham* 334:9).

3. Certain garments, such as turbans and shawls, were not made to be "put on," but were merely wrapped around the body.

4. I.e., he may put on even more articles than one would normally wear (see *Ran*).

5. The Gemara identifies these eighteen garments as: (1) a cloak, (2) a quilted coat, (3) a wide belt worn over the garments, (4) a vest, (5) an undershirt, (6) a belt worn on the undershirt, (7) a hat, (8) an inner cap, (9,10) a pair of shoes, (11,12) a pair of leggings, (13,14) a pair of gloves that covers the arms as far as the elbows, (15,16) two kerchiefs (worn but used to dry oneself), (17) a small shawl that covers the head and shoulders, (18) a scarf (*Rav*). R' Yose rules that only these eighteen garments [which were commonly worn in Talmudic times] may be worn for the purpose of removing them from a burning house. Any other garments worn in addition to these are superfluous, and hence would constitute a burden that one would be forbidden to wear in a public domain. Therefore, one may not wear them to remove them from the scene of the fire — even if his intention is to wear them out to a courtyard in which he may normally carry — for fear that in his state of turmoil he will forget and continue wearing them out into a public domain (*Tos. Yom Tov* from *Ran*).

ומוציא — ***And*** after he has finished removing the first set of clothing to safety, ***he may return*** to the house ***and put on*** more ***clothing and take*** them ***out*** of the house as well. וְאוֹמֵר לַאֲחֵרִים בּוֹאוּ וְהַצִּילוּ עִמִּי — ***And he may say to others, "Come and save with me."***[6]

NOTES

6. The phrasing here differs from the phrasing of the previous Mishnah. Whereas there, in regard to saving food, the Mishnah states that he says to others, "Come and save *for yourselves,*" here, in regard to saving clothing, the Mishnah states that he says, "Come and save *with me.*" Why the difference? Since the amount of food one may save is contingent upon the number of meals that individual has already eaten (as explained in Mishnah 3), and since at the outbreak of the fire it is possible that either the owner or the bystander has already eaten a meal while the other has not, the amounts that each may remove are not necessarily equal. Therefore, it would be imprecise for the Mishnah to phrase the owner's appeal as, "Come and save *with me,*" implying that both can save the same amount. Rather, it is more correct to phrase that appeal as, "Come and save *for yourselves*" — i.e., each according to what he is permitted to save. Since with regard to clothing, however, there are no limitations, the Mishnah phrases the appeal as "Come and save *with me,*" i.e., as much as I do (*Rav*).

GEMS FROM THE GEMARA

We explained in the previous Mishnah (see note 3 there) that in saying to others, "Come and save for yourselves," one relinquishes his title to the objects that he is bidding the others to save, and they become ownerless. Accordingly, others may retrieve them for themselves (*Rashi* from Gemara 120a).

Ran posits that a formal renunciation of title is unnecessary. He contends that since the property is irretrievably lost to its owner in any case (because the halachah forbids him to save it), it is *automatically* regarded as ownerless. *Ran* cites as proof of this principle the rule that an object swept out to sea, once it is irretrievably lost to its owner, may be salvaged and kept by anyone (*Bava Metzia* 24a-b). According to *Ran,* the point of the Mishnah is the opposite of the point according to *Rashi,* for *Ran* holds that the Mishnah is teaching that even though he is telling them to salvage what they can in the hope that they will return the items to him, they are still permitted to save the items even if they *do* return them to him, since legally the items are ownerless and they are not *bound* to return them.

R' Yitzchak Abohab, siding with *Rashi,* draws a distinction between something *physically* irretrievable — which is automatically deemed ownerless — and something that is physically retrievable, but which the halachah prevents one from retrieving — which is not regarded as ownerless until the owner declares it to be ownerless (cf. *Beis Yosef, Orach Chaim* §334).

Other authorities assert that because the owner has the option of announcing before non-Jews, "Anyone who extinguishes the fire will not lose" (Gemara 121a) — thus hinting to the non-Jewish populace that they will be rewarded for their services in extinguishing the fire — the items are regarded as retrievable. Accordingly, they are not automatically ownerless, unless the owner formally renounces his ownership of them (*Bach* §334).

Magen Avraham (334:11) goes further, adding that since it is possible for the owner to find Jews who are well-disposed toward him and who would rescue the threatened items and return them to him, they do not automatically become ownerless unless he formally renounces his ownership.

A MUSSAR THOUGHT FOR THE DAY

R' *Shamshon Raphael Hirsch* suggests that the phrase "between My people and your people" is a reference to the differing perspectives possessed by the people of the two nations. He states: "The fact that the Jews — who, unarmed and unable to defend themselves, should have been the first victims — were untouched by the universal calamity will be the mark of differentiation between My people and your people; between those who place their dependence only on human powers, and those who give themselves over entirely to Hashem and His commands."

This concept of dependence and reliance on Hashem, which we know as בִּטָּחוֹן, *trust*, is at the very core of our belief system, and we have addressed it before in our studies. It is basic to our belief, and has application to virtually every aspect of life.

Today, we will focus on one aspect, namely, the consequences of achieving a level of *bitachon*. One might think that surrendering oneself completely to trust in Hashem is detrimental, because it highlights one's vulnerability and utter helplessness without His help, leading to fear and depression. The masters of *mussar*, however, teach us that the truth is quite the opposite.

Chovos HaLevavos (in his *Shaar HaBitachon*) says: "He who trusts in

God is firmly assured that God will provide his sustenance . . . at all times and all places, just as He provides for the unborn child, and for the chick in the egg . . ." Furthermore, he says, "among the secular advantages of his trust in God are a heart at rest, without worldly cares; a tranquil spirit, liberated from mental disturbance." In a similar vein, *R' Yosef Yoizel Horowitz* (*Madreigas HaAdam* — Ways of Trust §1) declares: "The essence of trust in Hashem is the tranquility it affords and the relief from pressures of the world; one who trusts in Hashem is saved from squandering his soul and living like a wanderer; he need not chase after people to flatter them . . . His entire behavior is serene, in the absolute knowledge that nothing can add or detract from what his Creator decreed for him, even by a hairbreadth."

The clear inference of these passages is that the recognition of Hashem's mastery over all areas of life is a liberating force, rather than a debilitating one. This concept is illustrated in the simple, yet extraordinarily profound saying of Ben Zoma in *Pirkei Avos* (4:1), which asks, אֵיזֶהוּ עָשִׁיר? הַשָּׂמֵחַ בְּחֶלְקוֹ, "Who is rich? He who is happy with his lot." *Rashi* concludes that even the wealthiest person who is discontented with his lot will be in a constant state of fear and despondency, and is considered a pauper.

Because our world *appears* to operate naturally, and be subject to a good measure of human control, this fundamental principle is easily forgotten and difficult to internalize. It is therefore necessary to continually remind ourselves of its truth and its lessons, and to rejoice in the freedom that it can bring.

HALACHAH OF THE DAY

The *melachah* of מְנַפֵּץ, *combing*, follows *laundering,* and is the third of the thirteen labors necessary for the processing of wool. Wool, in its natural raw state, is comprised of tightly tangled clumps of fibers that cannot be spun into thread while in this entangled state. Therefore, after the fibers have been cleaned, it is necessary to comb them out, so that the separate fibers can then be spun and formed into a usable product (thread). It is also necessary to comb out the wool fibers before dyeing them, for if the wool is dyed while it is tangled together, the dye will not reach each part of every fiber, and the resulting color will not be uniform. *Combing* was performed during the construction of the Mishkan

as a necessary step in the production of the tapestries and other fabrics used in the Mishkan.

Since, as we have explained, the purpose of this *melachah* is to render the wool fibers suitable for further processing into finished fabric, it follows that the *melachah* would apply to any material from which one may produce a usable fabric. For this reason, the *melachah* is not restricted only to fibers of the sort that are commonly used in the production of clothing, such as wool or cotton. Rather, it applies equally to the fibers of synthetic materials such as polyester, as well as to fibers of straw, strands of rubber, or any other material that may be processed and ultimately woven into a fabric-like material.

Since live hair is completely unsuitable for being spun into thread, the *melachah* of *combing* does not apply to the combing of live hair. However, as we have discussed earlier, it is forbidden under certain circumstances for one to comb his hair on Shabbos, due to the possibility that this will violate the *melachah* of *shearing* (see *Halachah of the Day, Parashas Vayechi,* Friday, for the parameters of this prohibition).

For the same reason, one who combs a wig, whether it is made of human hair or synthetic fibers, will not violate the *melachah* of *combing.* [Again, see above as to when there is an issue of *shearing* in these cases.]

Because this *melachah* applies to the preparation of raw materials for spinning into thread, there are few examples of common applications of this *melachah.*

A CLOSER LOOK AT THE SIDDUR

Our total dependence on Hashem for our welfare, sustenance, and salvation is beautifully and succinctly depicted in the prayer: בְּרִיךְ שְׁמֵהּ דְּמָרֵא עָלְמָא, *Blessed is the Name of the Master of the universe,* which we recite whenever we take the Torah Scroll from the ark to read from it. Written in Aramaic, it is based on the *Zohar* that asserts that the Heavenly gates of mercy are opened when the congregation readies itself to read the Torah. After extolling the greatness of Hashem and beseeching Him for His mercy and munificence, the prayer continues, "It is You Who nourishes all and sustains all; You control everything. It is You Who controls kings, and kingship is Yours . . . Not in any man do I put my trust, nor on any angel do I rely — only on the God of Heaven, Who is the God of truth, Whose Torah is truth . . . In Him do I trust, and to His glorious and holy Name do I declare praises . . ."

The close relationship between recognizing our dependence on Hashem and redemption may be seen in the composition of Psalm 130, which begins with the phrase: מִמַּעֲמַקִּים קְרָאתִיךָ ה׳, *From the* **depths** *I called You, HASHEM,* a reference to supplication under the most trying circumstances of exile, poverty and lowliness (*Ibn Ezra*). Following one's admission of guilt for sinning and his begging for forgiveness, the supplicant says, יַחֵל יִשְׂרָאֵל אֶל ה׳ כִּי עִם ה׳ הַחֶסֶד, *Let Israel hope to HASHEM, for with HASHEM is kindness,* וְהַרְבֵּה עִמּוֹ פְדוּת, *and with Him is abundant redemption.* Because it weaves together the themes of repentance, forgiveness, reliance on Hashem and redemption, this Psalm is recited by many congregations as a preamble to the section of *Krias Shema* and its blessings during the Morning service on the High Holy Days, whose main function is to elicit acceptance of Hashem's kingship. For the same reason, it is widely recited during times of community distress.

The phrase "**abundant** redemption" in the verse cited above has several connotations. *Metzudas David* explains that the sense of the verse is that there is ample reason for hope, for just as He has redeemed us **many** times in the past, He will redeem us again; His power of redemption remains undiminished.

Baal HaTurim points out that the word פְּדֻת, *redemption,* as it appears in *Parashas Va'eira* (*Shemos* 8:19) is spelled deficiently, without a *vav,* whereas פְּדוּת in Psalm 130 is spelled מָלֵא — with a *vav*. This indicates to us that whereas the salvation discussed in *Va'eira* was limited, as it involved only protecting the Jews from the plague, the future salvation and redemption will be complete and all-encompassing.

QUESTION OF THE DAY:

Why was the plague of wild animals the first one in which Hashem stated that a distinction would be drawn between Goshen and the rest of Egypt?

For the answer, see page 111.

A TORAH THOUGHT FOR THE DAY

כִּי בַּפַּעַם הַזֹּאת אֲנִי שֹׁלֵחַ אֶת־כָּל־מַגֵּפֹתַי אֶל־לִבְּךָ
For this time I shall send all My plagues to your heart (*Shemos* 9:14).

A simple reading of *Rashi* seems to indicate that the words *all My plagues* teach us that מַכַּת בְּכוֹרוֹת, *the plague of the firstborn,* is equal in severity to all the other plagues. Many commentators are mystified by this *Rashi,* since the subject of this verse is a warning about בָּרָד, *hail*, not the plague of the firstborn! *Mizrachi* suggests that *Rashi* is not referring to the plague of the firstborn, which would be vowelized as מַכַּת בְּכוֹרוֹת, but to a plague on the ripened harvest, which is vowelized מַכַּת בַּכּוּרוֹת. Thus, *Rashi* refers to the harvest that was destroyed by the hail. In this sense, the severity of the plague is rooted in its decimation of the ready food supply. [Similarly, some emend the word בְּכוֹרוֹת to בַּצוֹרֶת, *famine.*]

However, there are two difficulties with this interpretation. First, if hunger and famine are considered the worst of afflictions, then the plague of locust should have been considered worse than the hail, since it destroyed all the produce remaining after the hail, causing even more acute starvation. Furthermore, *Rashi* (*Shemos* 4:23) stated earlier that the plague of the firstborn was indeed the harshest plague!

Kli Yakar notes two other difficulties with the verse. First, why does the verse state that this plague was to be sent to Pharaoh's *heart,* a description not found in connection with any other plague? Furthermore, why indeed did the plague of hail affect only the ripened produce (as the Torah later states in v. 32)? *Kli Yakar* explains that Hashem was giving the following statement to Pharaoh: "I will send you one plague which, if you are wise, will induce you to take to heart my warning regarding the plague of the firstborn." Although Moshe warned Pharaoh of this impending calamity at the very outset of their dialogue (see *Rashi* to *Shemos* 4:23), Pharaoh failed to grasp or feel the enormity of its horror, and he dismissed it as an idle threat. Hashem, therefore, launched the plague of hail in a way that paralleled the coming plague of the firstborn, in that it specifically struck the *firstborn crop,* which is exceptionally treasured by mankind. The fact that this plague caused Pharaoh to admit, "I have sinned," for the very first time, confirms that the loss of his "firstborn" crop caused him more pain and grief than any previous plague.

Thus, the warning to Pharaoh should be understood as follows. "I am

sending a message to your heart regarding the *plague of the firstborn,* which will be the most catastrophic plague. If you are so anguished and distraught by the loss of your first and most cherished fruit, how much more intense and magnified will be the loss of your human firstborn!" *Kli Yakar* concludes that this is indeed a very precious interpretation.

MISHNAH OF THE DAY: SHABBOS 16:5

The previous Mishnahs have discussed what items may be rescued from a fire on the Sabbath. The following Mishnah discusses what may be done to *contain* a fire:

רַבִּי שִׁמְעוֹן בֶּן נַנָּס אוֹמֵר — ***R' Shimon ben Nannas says:*** **פּוֹרְסִין עוֹר שֶׁל גְּדִי** — ***We may spread a young goat's hide***[1] **עַל גַּבֵּי שִׁידָּה תֵּיבָה וּמִגְדָּל שֶׁאָחַז בָּהֶן אֶת הָאוּר** — ***over a carriage, trunk or closet on which a fire has taken hold,***[2] **מִפְּנֵי שֶׁהוּא מְחָרֵךְ** — ***because*** the hide ***singes*** but does not burn.[3] **וְעוֹשִׂין מְחִיצָּה בְּכָל הַכֵּלִים בֵּין מְלֵאִין בֵּין רֵיקָנִים** — ***And we may make a partition*** in the path of a fire ***with all*** kinds of ***vessels, whether full or empty,***[4] **בִּשְׁבִיל שֶׁלֹּא תַּעֲבוֹר הַדְּלֵיקָה** — ***so that the fire should not*** be able to ***spread*** beyond them.[5] **רַבִּי יוֹסֵי אוֹסֵר בִּכְלֵי חֶרֶס חֲדָשִׁים מְלֵאִין מַיִם** — ***R' Yose prohibits*** doing so with ***new earthenware vessels filled with water,***[6] **לְפִי שֶׁאֵין יְכוֹלִין לְקַבֵּל אֶת הָאוּר** — ***because***

NOTES

1. I.e., a raw hide which is still moist, and therefore is more fire-resistant (*Rashi*).

2. I.e., he may spread it over the part of the object that has not yet caught fire, to prevent the fire from spreading there (*Rambam, Hil. Shabbos* 12:5). This is permitted because one is not extinguishing the fire, but merely preventing the fire from spreading to the area covered by the hide.

3. Thus, it protects these wooden boxes from burning (*Rav; Rashi*). [The Mishnah is not giving *the reason* that one is permitted to spread a kid's hide over burning boxes, but rather is stating the *purpose* for doing so (*Rambam Commentary*).]

4. I.e., whether they contain water or are empty (*Rav; Rashi*).

5. It is permissible to place the vessels in the path of the fire even if the heat will burst the vessels, thereby releasing the water and quenching the fire. This fits into the category of גְּרַם כִּבּוּי, *indirectly causing a fire to be extinguished,* rather than extinguishing it by direct effort.

The causation (rather than direct performance) of a forbidden labor is usually Rabbinically prohibited. However, in this case of financial loss, the Rabbis did not prohibit it (*Shulchan Aruch* and *Rama* 334:22).

6. This refers to new earthenware vessels that have not hardened sufficiently to be able to endure the heat of a fire (*Rav; Rashi*).

they cannot withstand the fire, וְהֵן מִתְבַּקְעִין וּמְכַבִּין אֶת הַדְּלֵיקָה — ***and*** therefore ***they*** will ***burst and extinguish the fire.***[7]

NOTES

7. R' Yose maintains that causing a fire to be extinguished is Rabbinically prohibited even in this case that involves financial loss (*Rav; Rambam Commentary*). [Nevertheless, R' Yose forbids making the partition only with vessels that will *definitely* burst.]

GEMS FROM THE GEMARA

In the course of its analysis of our Mishnah, the Gemara (120b) cites a Baraisa, in which the Rabbis taught that if a lit lamp is on top of a board, and one wishes to move the board, it is permitted to shake the board and let the lamp fall down; and if the lamp is thereby extinguished, it is extinguished (and this is not forbidden because of the possibility that the lamp might be extinguished).

[Since the lamp is *muktzeh* and may not be carried, someone who wishes to carry the board must first endeavor to remove the lamp from it. He cannot simply remove it by hand, since it is *muktzeh.* Therefore, he must remove it indirectly, by shaking the board and allowing it to fall off. (Indirect movement of *muktzeh* is permitted in such a case; see Mishnah below, 21:2.) Although this may result in extinguishing the fire of the lamp, since it is not his intention to extinguish it, nor is it inevitable that he will do so, it is permitted.

Tosafos, however, find this ruling difficult. Why, they ask, is one allowed to shake the lamp off the board, when some of its oil is sure to be spilled as a result — and removing oil from a burning lamp is in itself a violation of the forbidden labor of extinguishing! (see *Beitzah* 22a). *Tosafos* therefore explain that the Baraisa is speaking of a lamp that has no more oil in it. Alternatively, the Baraisa does not speak of an oil lamp, but rather of a wax candle (*Rashba;* see also *Meiri*).]

The Gemara then cites the Tannaim of the academy of R' Yannai, who clarified that the Rabbis allowed one to shake off the lamp and carry the board only in a case where one had forgotten and unintentionally left the lamp on the board before the Sabbath. However, if one *intentionally* leaves a lamp on top of a board with the intent that the lamp remain atop the board for the Sabbath, the board becomes a *bassis l'davar ha'assur,* a base to a forbidden object (i.e., to an object that is *muktzeh*), and the board itself is treated as *muktzeh*. Consequently, one would *not* be allowed to move or shake the board.

פרשת וארא

SHABBOS

PARASHAS VA'EIRA

A MUSSAR THOUGHT FOR THE DAY

Although it is obvious that the study of *mussar* enables the student to acquire knowledge and understanding of what is proper behavior and what is not, the main function of this study is to enable the person to be convinced of its truth, internalize it as part of his character, and act upon it accordingly. This is generally known as שִׂימָה בְּלֵב, *placing it in the heart*.

The verse in *Mishlei* (3:3) states: חֶסֶד וֶאֱמֶת אַל־יַעַזְבֻךָ קָשְׁרֵם עַל־גַּרְגְּרוֹתֶיךָ כָּתְבֵם עַל־לוּחַ לִבֶּךָ, *Kindness and truth will not forsake you. Bind them upon your neck; inscribe them on the tablet of your heart. Malbim* (ibid.) notes that most ethical aspects of the Torah are encompassed in the words חֶסֶד — the principles governing man's relationship with his fellow man — and אֱמֶת — the principles of faith taught by the Torah. However, to fully acquire these characteristics, one must first verbalize them constantly until they are customary aspects of one's language (this is alluded to in the verse's instruction to bind them *upon your neck* — as the neck houses the vocal cords which produce voice) and inscribe them on one's heart. "For the heart is the ruling power of a person, and is always ready to cast its nets of evil inclinations and desires upon a person's spirit, so that they may attack and destroy his wisdom. He should etch the principles of wisdom on the tablet of his heart as an indelible script, and read it all his life, thereby learning to keep his distance from these evil inclinations."

It is instructive and no simple coincidence that one of the preeminent theological and *mussar* treatises is named חוֹבוֹת הַלְּבָבוֹת, *Duties of the Heart;* it was written by *R' Bachya ben Yosef Ibn Pekudah* in Arabic, in the early 12th century. His lengthy introduction, itself a masterpiece, delineates the categories of wisdom in the world, and characterizes the major principles through which one investigates and obtains wisdom. It is replete with many references to "the heart" that are found both in the Written and Oral Law. He sets out to prove that an understanding of the "duties of the heart" is necessary, and that "these duties are in force continuously, throughout our lives, without interruption, and we have no excuse for neglecting them." He continues by explaining (very apologetically and self-effacingly) that he undertook to write a book that details these duties, to serve as a handbook of proper thought and behavior. In his own words: "I aimed to make the book one of permanent value . . . a lamp to illuminate one's path, and to show the way in which a person should go. I said to myself that I would compose a book that would deal with the subject of 'Duties of the Heart' . . . to serve as a guide to the customs of the ancient Sages and the discipline of the pious; awaken men from their senseless sleep . . . recall to men the knowledge of God and of His law . . .; encourage the observant; stir up the negligent, set the eager on the right road . . . and show the way to those who have gone astray."

Several passages later, he instructs the reader: "When, my brother, you have read this book and understood its contents, take it as a reminder of your duties and shortcomings . . . Read my book repeatedly; develop its thoughts. Bring it close to your mind and heart."

HALACHAH OF THE DAY

The next of the thirty-nine labors forbidden on Shabbos is צוֹבֵעַ, *coloring* or *dyeing*. This *melachah* was performed as part of construction of the Mishkan, with the dyeing of wool and hides for the Mishkan's various curtains and coverings. It is the fourth of the thirteen *melachos* involved in the preparation of wool.

The definition of the *melachah* of *dyeing* is the improvement or beautification of an object through dyeing, coloring, or painting.

We may better understand the underlying concept of this *melachah* by contrasting it with the *melachah* of כּוֹתֵב, *writing*. One could argue that since the formation of written letters involves the coloring of the surface upon which the lettering is being written, all writing should be a violation of *dyeing*. This, however, is not the case. The object of writing is the creation of characters or symbols. The coloration being applied to the writing surface is merely a medium used for the formation of these characters. The color is in no way the object of the writing exercise. By contrast, the purpose of dyeing is the beautification of the surface being dyed or otherwise colored. It is this beautification that is prohibited under the prohibition against dyeing.

The Biblical prohibition of dyeing applies only when the color one applies is intended to remain permanently. There is some debate among the *poskim* regarding the definition of "permanent." Some *poskim* say that the color is considered permanent if it will remain until the end of Shabbos. Others maintain that the color must remain for a significant amount of time in order to be considered permanent. We follow the more stringent view; thus, if one applies color that is intended to last until the end of Shabbos, it is considered permanent and he has violated the Biblical prohibition of dyeing. If the color will fade in a few hours, it is not considered to be permanent, and therefore coloring something in this manner is not a violation of the Biblical law. Furthermore, even when the color will not fade by itself, but it can be easily removed (i.e., by hand), it is considered to be temporary. Nonetheless, although one does not violate the Biblical

prohibition when color is applied in a temporary manner, it is prohibited by Rabbinic law.

The act of coloring human skin is prohibited by Rabbinic law, though it is permitted under Biblical law. The *poskim* explain that since it is impossible to permanently color human skin, it is permitted under Biblical law; nonetheless, it is prohibited by Rabbinic decree.

A CLOSER LOOK AT THE SIDDUR

Let us continue our discussion of the requests that are found in the central blessing of each Shabbos *Shemoneh Esrei.*

After asking Hashem to *satiate us with Your goodness*, we continue by asking, שַׂמְּחֵנוּ בִּישׁוּעָתֶךָ, *Gladden us with Your salvation.* This, of course, is a plea for the ultimate redemption, when Hashem's majesty will be fully revealed to all, and we will live in a time "that is always Sabbath and rest eternally" (this is the description of the World to Come that is found in an extra prayer appended to the end of *Bircas HaMazon* [Grace After Meals] on the Sabbath). It is singularly appropriate to pray for redemption on the Sabbath, in line with the famous Midrash that states that if all of Israel were to properly observe two consecutive Sabbaths (and according to some texts, even a single Sabbath), the redemption would arrive immediately.

Eitz Yosef connects this request to the previous one, commenting that the *good* for which we pray is not only the material beneficence of this world, but the true good that we will experience *after* the redemption. He notes further that with respect to salvation, we ask that we merit to experience שִׂמְחָה, *joy,* because it is only in the World to Come that we will be able to attain the level of true joy.

Following this request, we ask: וְטַהֵר לִבֵּנוּ לְעָבְדְּךָ בֶּאֱמֶת, *and purify our hearts, so we may serve You with truth.* Although, as we have discussed many times in our studies, the decision to be righteous or evil is man's alone, this does not mean that we cannot ask Hashem for assistance in fortifying our will to do good. Indeed, the Gemara in *Yoma* (38b) states explicitly: בָּא לְטַהֵר מְסַיְּיעִין אוֹתוֹ, *If one comes to purify himself, he is given assistance [from Heaven].* Purity of heart is a difficult level to achieve, as it requires that a person remove from within himself the many mundane distractions or leanings that may influence his thoughts and actions. On the Sabbath, when we are at least somewhat removed from the physical, we ask Hashem to give us the strength we need to carry this focus into the workweek as well, so that we can concentrate on serving Him properly.

We will continue our analysis of this blessing next week.

QUESTION OF THE DAY:

What additional miracle occurred after the plague of hail?

For the answer, see below.

ANSWERS TO QUESTIONS OF THE DAY

Sunday:

Before the Covenant Between the Parts (בְּרִית בֵּין הַבְּתָרִים), Hashem said to Avraham, *I am HASHEM Who brought you out of Ur Kasdim* (*Bereishis* 15:7).

Monday:

Since Moshe had expressed concern that he could not speak clearly (see v. 12), Hashem told him to take Aharon as his spokesperson (*Rashi*).

Tuesday:

Ibn Ezra suggests that Aharon received the first position first either because he was older, or because he had become a prophet before Moshe.

Wednesday:

Rashi states that after each of the first five plagues, Pharaoh hardened his heart *himself.* Only after that did Hashem harden his heart.

Thursday:

They died so that the Egyptians would not benefit by being able to eat them.

Friday:

Ramban explains that wild animals have a tendency to roam, and therefore it would be natural for them to attack Goshen as well. Thus, the fact that they did not highlighted the miraculous nature of the protection.

Shabbos:

When the plague ended, the hail that had not yet reached the ground stopped in midair, and did not fall (see *Rashi* to 9:33).

פרשת בא

Parashas Bo

פרשת בא

SUNDAY

PARASHAS BO

A TORAH THOUGHT FOR THE DAY

וַיֹּאמֶר ה׳ אֶל־מֹשֶׁה נְטֵה יָדְךָ עַל־הַשָּׁמַיִם
וִיהִי חֹשֶׁךְ עַל־אֶרֶץ מִצְרָיִם וְיָמֵשׁ חֹשֶׁךְ

HASHEM said to Moshe,
"Stretch forth your hand toward the heavens,
and there shall be darkness upon the land of Egypt,
and the darkness will become darker" (*Shemos* 10:21).

R*ashi* explains this verse as follows: The darkness by day during the plague will be darker than the darkness of a normal night, and the darkness of the night during the plague will be even darker than the darkness that will prevail by day.

Although *Rashi* here is discussing only the level of darkness during the plague, noting that it was a stronger level of darkness, it seems quite clear from all the commentaries that this plague was a unique, totally different type of darkness. *Rashi* himself cites the Midrash on the words וְיָמֵשׁ חֹשֶׁךְ stating that the darkness had substance and was actually tangible. Furthermore, the verse states (v. 23) that for the three final days of the plague, no Egyptian was able to move from the position in which he found himself. This was a result of the darkness intensifying and becoming even denser. What, indeed, was the nature of this darkness that was brought upon the Egyptians for six days?

Sforno explains the words וְיָמֵשׁ חֹשֶׁךְ as meaning: the regular darkness of night shall be removed. The darkness that reigns every night is only an absence of light (see further on this point in *A Closer Look at the Siddur*), and it was designed so that light of any sort can overcome it. The darkness of this plague, however, had a thickness to it that did not allow any light to penetrate. It would not allow a candle to be lit or a ray of light to pierce through.

The Midrash gives an interesting description of this darkness: it had a thickness similar to the thickness of a coin (a *dinar*). This is hard to understand — how does one measure the thickness of darkness? The *Torah Temimah,* among others, addresses this problem and offers a novel interpretation. He suggests that this plague was not a visible darkness all around Egypt. It was a membrane that grew in front of each Egyptian's eyes, similar to a cataract. This, he says, can be measured by the thickness of a coin. What he does not explain, however, is how such a membrane would render them incapable of moving around for the final three days of this plague; and it is obvious from the verse that this inability was a direct result of the darkness.

The *HaKesav VeHaKabbalah* follows in this vein, stating that from the Torah's words: וִיהִי חֹשֶׁךְ, *and there shall be darkness,* we see that this darkness was a new creation, and not merely an absence of light, as regular darkness is. [He explains that it is for this reason that when the Torah tells us the story of Creation, Hashem said, "Let there be light," but did *not* say, "Let there be darkness." Regular darkness is not a creation, but simply the absence of light.] Around every Egyptian there was something tangible, as if a shade had been pulled over his eyes. He goes on to explain that in the last three days of the plague, Hashem sent frightful angels, whose appearance paralyzed the Egyptians with fear, so they could not even move.

Ralbag states that the darkness was so thick that it went into the Egyptians' nostrils and mouths, making it hard for them to breathe and causing severe pain. The *Me'am Loez* says that it was a miracle they even survived the duration of this painful plague.

MISHNAH OF THE DAY: SHABBOS 16:6

The following Mishnah deals with how one may react to others who set about extinguishing a fire for him:

עוֹבֵד כּוֹכָבִים שֶׁבָּא לְכַבּוֹת — ***An idolater who comes to extinguish*** a fire that has broken out in a Jew's home on the Sabbath, **אֵין אוֹמְרִים לוֹ כַּבֵּה** — ***they may not say to him, "Extinguish*** it,"[1] **וְאַל תְּכַבֶּה** — ***nor*** do they have to say to him, ***"Do not extinguish*** it,"[2] **מִפְּנֵי שֶׁאֵין שְׁבִיתָתוֹ עֲלֵיהֶן** — ***because his resting is not their responsibility.***[3] **אֲבָל קָטָן שֶׁבָּא לְכַבּוֹת** — ***However, a*** Jewish ***minor who comes to extinguish*** the

NOTES

1. I.e., a Jew may not encourage the non-Jew — even though the non-Jew came forward for this purpose (*Mishnah Berurah* 334:63) — for the Rabbis decreed that a Jew may not instruct a non-Jew to perform a forbidden labor on the Sabbath (*Rav; Rashi*).

2. I.e., neither is a Jew obligated to object to the non-Jew's extinguishing the fire on his behalf (*Rav; Rashi*).

3. While the Torah requires a Jew to ensure his own Sabbath observance, the Sabbath observance of his children, that of his fellow Jews and even that of his Canaanite slaves (see *Exodus* 20:9-10 and *Rashi* ad loc.; see *Sotah* 37b with *Rashi*), he is not required to ensure that free non-Jews rest on the Sabbath (*Rav; Rashi*). This is the case even if the non-Jew's labor is for the good of the Jew, as long as it is not being performed at the Jew's behest (see *Tiferes Yisrael*).

fire, אֵין שׁוֹמְעִין לוֹ — ***they may not listen to him,*** i.e., they may not allow him to do so, מִפְּנֵי שֶׁשְּׁבִיתָתוֹ עֲלֵיהֶן — ***because his resting is their responsibility.*** [4]

NOTES

4. Although there generally is no requirement to prevent a minor from violating any of the Torah's commandments, that holds true only where the minor is doing so for his own benefit or pleasure — e.g., if he eats nonkosher food. However, if he does so on behalf of an adult — as in our case — the adult is required to make him desist (see *Shulchan Aruch* 343:1).

GEMS FROM THE GEMARA

The Gemara (121a) cites an incident that illustrates the halachah taught in the Mishnah: "The Rabbis taught in a Baraisa: There was once an incident in which a fire broke out [on the Sabbath] in the courtyard of Yosef ben Simai in the town of Shichin. The men of the [Roman] governor of Tzippori came to extinguish the fire, because [Yosef ben Simai] was the treasurer of the king. However, Yosef ben Simai did not allow the governor's men to extinguish the fire, on account of the honor of the Sabbath. A miracle occurred on his behalf, and rain began to fall, extinguishing the flames. That night [after the conclusion of the Sabbath], Yosef ben Simai sent every member of [the garrison that had been sent to assist him] two *selaim,* and to the lieutenant among them fifty *selaim,* as a mark of his gratitude for their having offered to help him.

"When the Sages heard that Yosef ben Simai had refused to allow the non-Jewish soldiers to extinguish the fire, they said: He did not need to do this, for we have learned in the Mishnah: *An idolater who comes to extinguish, they may not say to him, 'Extinguish it,' nor [do they have to say to him], 'Do not extinguish it!'* "

[*Rashba* (to 122a) explains that Yosef ben Simai thought that just as in other similar circumstances, Rabbinic decree prohibits one from allowing the non-Jews to perform *melachah* on a Jew's behalf on the Sabbath, so too one is not permitted to allow non-Jews to act on his behalf even when it comes to saving property from a fire. However, the Sages subsequently informed him that this is not the case; while normally one may not allow non-Jews to work on his behalf, the Sages did not extend their decree to the case of a fire. *Maharsha,* however, notes that the Gemara does not say that Yosef ben Simai forbade the soldiers to extinguish the fire because it was *forbidden* to do so on the Sabbath;

rather, it says that he did so because of the *honor* of the Sabbath. He therefore explains that Yosef ben Simai was stringent upon himself, and voluntarily held back from allowing his property to be saved. He did this so others would not suspect him of having instructed the soldiers to do so (which would have been forbidden), as such suspicion would be a disgrace to the honor of the Sabbath.]

A MUSSAR THOUGHT FOR THE DAY

In *A Torah Thought for the Day,* we discussed the severity of the plague of darkness. We know that all of the plagues were clearly designated for the Egyptians and none of them entered the land of Goshen; this plague was no exception. Nevertheless, the Torah stresses: וּלְכָל־בְּנֵי יִשְׂרָאֵל הָיָה אוֹר בְּמוֹשְׁבֹתָם, *for all the Bnei Yisrael, there was light in their dwellings* (10:23). *Ohr HaChaim* explains this to mean that even in the homes of the Egyptians, where darkness was predominant, for the Jew who entered there was light. As *Rashi* cites from the Midrash, the Jews searched the Egyptian homes for hidden treasures that they would later take with them upon leaving Egypt.

Targum Yonasan says on this verse that the light that did penetrate the darkness in Egypt was the light of Torah and mitzvos, as the verse states (*Mishlei* 6:23): כִּי נֵר מִצְוָה וְתוֹרָה אוֹר, *For a commandment is a candle, and the Torah is light.*

Rav Shmuel Rozovsky explains this important message. Even in the darkest moments, with the worst imaginable conditions weighing down a person with such density that his every movement is torture — when it seems that no light can penetrate such thick barriers — there is one light that *can* prevail. That is the light of Torah and mitzvos, which can illuminate any situation. Even in Egypt, engulfed in total darkness, in a time of turmoil and chaos, those who clung to the words of Hashem were able to find their way.

A remarkable story was often told by the Ponevezher Rav. A certain Rav in a small Russian town was known for his great love of and dedication to Torah study. Once, when he was learning late at night, some Russian soldiers who were keeping surveillance spotted a ray of light coming from his house, and it aroused their suspicions. Upon entering and investigating, they saw an old rabbi bent over a worn, yellow-paged Talmud, and immediately suspected him of spying and reading coded

information. The verdict was quick to come: "Put him to death!" As it was customary to grant a last wish, they asked him what his request would be before taking leave of this world. He responded, "I beg of you, give me a half-hour to finish understanding the words of the Talmud; I will soon be meeting all the great Rabbis whose words are discussed here, and I must prepare myself." The wish was granted, and the ensuing delay caused his life to be saved, as the soldiers were called away before the sentence could be carried out.

The Ponevezher Rav would say that only true love for Torah could override the darkness that had surrounded this Rav, and that is what saved him.

HALACHAH OF THE DAY

We will now discuss some of the activities that fall under the prohibition of *dyeing.*

It is a violation of the *melachah* of *dyeing* to dye any material at all on Shabbos. This includes, but is not limited to, the dyeing of fabrics, leather, hair, or wigs.

One may not apply paint to any surface or substance on Shabbos. The application of paint is forbidden even if one is repainting a surface with a coat of the same color of paint that had been previously applied to that surface.

One may not add color to a preexisting picture on Shabbos. Even if the picture has already been colored, the addition of more color is forbidden. This is true even if the fresh color is being added only to make the existing color a darker shade.

It is not only the *use* of paint that is forbidden on Shabbos; the production of paint is forbidden as well. Hence, one may not create a new color by mixing different paints together.

At the outset of our discussion of this *melachah,* we defined the labor of *dyeing* as the *improvement* of an item through the addition of coloration. In accordance with this definition, some authorities rule that if the coloration of an object has a negative effect rather than a positive one, this coloration would not be prohibited under this *melachah.* A prime example of such a case would be the use of a cloth to clean blood from a wound. While the cloth will become colored through such use, this coloration is certainly not seen as an improvement. Rather, quite the opposite is true — the cloth is now seen as an unclean item which must be laundered. According to these authorities, this type of coloring is not included in the prohibition of *dyeing*.

Other *poskim* maintain that while it is true that this form of coloring is not in keeping with the concept of the *melachah*, this only exempts such acts from being a violation of Biblical law. They remain, however, prohibited by Rabbinic decree. According to this view, one would be forbidden to use a cloth to wipe away blood on Shabbos, for by touching the cloth to the blood, one is dyeing the cloth red.

We do not have a final ruling in this dispute. For this reason, in practice it is best to follow the more stringent view and to avoid staining a cloth even where the staining is undesired. We will discuss this question further tomorrow.

A CLOSER LOOK AT THE SIDDUR

The first blessing that we say before *Krias Shema* during *Shacharis* reads: יוֹצֵר אוֹר וּבוֹרֵא חֹשֶׁךְ עֹשֶׂה שָׁלוֹם וּבוֹרֵא אֶת הַכֹּל, *Who forms light and creates darkness, makes peace and creates all.* [This wording is based on a verse in *Yeshayah* (45:7).]

The *Gra* establishes from this verse that darkness is also a creation in its own right, not only an absence of light. If so, he asks, why does light overpower the creation of darkness? He answers that Hashem created the nature of light with the ability to overpower the weaker creation of darkness. On the other hand, during the plague of darkness in Egypt, he gave instruction to the darkness to prevail and push away the light.

This would also seem to be the view of *Rabbeinu Yonah* (to *Berachos* 5b), who explains why we mention Hashem's power over both the light and the darkness during *Shacharis* and during *Maariv.* Would it not make sense to mention only light during the day and only darkness at night? He cites an incident where a certain heretic claimed that the Creator of light did not create the night, and vice-versa. He was disproved by this verse in *Yeshayah,* which states explicitly that Hashem created light and He also created darkness, clearly indicating that both were His creations. From *Rabbeinu Yonah's* words it is also obvious that darkness is a creation in itself.

Now, in *A Torah Thought for the Day,* we mentioned the opinion of *Sforno,* who holds that regular darkness is not a creation, but only an

absence of light. This *berachah* and its source, the verse in *Yeshayah,* would seemingly dispute that. However, *Ramban,* who also seems to hold the opinion that regular darkness is just an absence of light [except the darkness in Egypt which was a special creation — see *Ramban* to *Shemos* 10:23], is not bothered by the words בּוֹרֵא חֹשֶׁךְ. He states (*Shemos* 4:11) that one responsible for the removal of any power can be called the creator of the resulting vacuum, and he brings this verse as his proof.

[It is interesting to note that even according to the opinions stating that darkness is a creation, this is true only of the darkness of nighttime. The darkness found inside a house without any windows is clearly only an absence of light. This is obvious from the *Yerushalmi* in *Pesachim* that relates a story of people who were living in a cave for a prolonged period of time, and who observed that the candles they lit by day were dimmer than those they lit at night. The *Netziv* explains this phenomenon: Since the creation of darkness rules at night, the light of a candle is a greater contrast to the ruling aspect, and therefore a stronger light. By daytime, however, the candle will not shine as strongly, even if all daylight is blocked out. This is because by day, the darkness is only an absence of light. The strength of a candle is amplified only when it is lit under the influence of the *creation* of darkness, which occurs only at nighttime.

QUESTION OF THE DAY:

Why did Hashem include the paralysis of the Egyptians in the plague of darkness?

For the answer, see page 166.

A TORAH THOUGHT FOR THE DAY

פרשת
בא

MONDAY

PARASHAS
BO

וּשְׁמַרְתֶּם אֶת־הַמַּצּוֹת כִּי בְּעֶצֶם הַיּוֹם הַזֶּה
הוֹצֵאתִי אֶת־צִבְאוֹתֵיכֶם מֵאֶרֶץ מִצְרָיִם

You shall guard the matzos,
for on this very day I have taken your legions
out of the land of Egypt (*Shemos* 12:17).

R*ashi* quotes the *Mechilta*: "Do not read the words only as 'matzos,' but rather (also) as 'mitzvos.'" Thus, the verse is teaching: Just as you do not allow the matzos to become leavened, so too do not allow the commandments to become leavened, by leaving the opportunities for their performance unattended; rather, if a mitzvah comes to your hand, do it immediately.

The same concept is also learned from Avraham Avinu. The Torah tells us (*Bereishis* 22:3) that Avraham woke up early to perform the mitzvah of *milah;* we learn from this that זְרִיזִין מַקְדִּימִין לְמִצְוֹת, *the zealous are early to perform mitzvos* (see *Pesachim* 4a).

Meiri explains that both sources for this principle are necessary. With respect to Avraham, the Torah wished to tell us of his great love for the mitzvah; but we would not know that such conduct is mandatory. Therefore, the Torah repeats the directive here.

According to *Radvaz,* this halachah, which requires us to do a mitzvah immediately and not to procrastinate, is so important that it takes precedence over doing a mitzvah in the most perfect way (מִצְוָה מִן הַמּוּבְחָר). [See *Chasam Sofer* to *Megillah* 6b.]

On the other hand, some authorities are of the opinion that it is preferable to delay performance of a mitzvah if this will allow it to be performed in a perfect fashion. [For example, they rule that it is preferable to delay the recital of *Kiddush Levanah,* the Sanctification of the New Moon, until Motza'ei Shabbos, so that one will perform the mitzvah while attired in his Shabbos finery (*Terumas HaDeshen*).]

It is related that *Reb Leibele Eiger* (the grandson of Rav Akiva Eiger), who was a well-known *mohel,* needed quite some time to prepare himself for the mitzvah, and often could not perform the *milah* early in the day. Some argued that this delay in performing the *milah* early in the morning was indefensible. *Rav Tzadok HaKohen* came to Reb Leibele's defense, stating in a letter that when a *bris milah* is performed with the perfection of Reb Leibele Eiger, this is far more important than doing it without delay. He cited the aforementioned *Terumas HaDeshen* as proof of this.

MISHNAH OF THE DAY: SHABBOS 16:7

The following Mishnah continues to consider how a fire may be prevented from spreading on the Sabbath and then discusses similar preventive measures that do not involve fire:

כּוֹפִין קְעָרָה עַל גַּבֵּי הַנֵּר — ***We may invert a bowl over a lamp,*** בִּשְׁבִיל שֶׁלֹּא תֶּאֱחוֹז בַּקּוֹרָה — ***in order that it*** [i.e., the flame] ***not catch onto the beam*** that is on top of the lamp;[1] וְעַל צוֹאָה שֶׁל קָטָן — ***and*** we also may invert a bowl ***over the feces of a child,***[2] וְעַל עַקְרָב שֶׁלֹּא תִּישַּׁךְ — ***or over a scorpion so that it not sting.*** אָמַר רַבִּי יְהוּדָה — ***R' Yehudah said:*** מַעֲשֶׂה בָּא לִפְנֵי רַבָּן יוֹחָנָן בֶּן זַכַּאי בַּעֲרָב — ***An incident*** of a person who inverted a bowl over a scorpion on the Sabbath ***came before Rabban Yochanan ben Zakkai in Arav,***[3] וְאָמַר חוֹשְׁשַׁנִי לוֹ מֵחַטָּאת — ***and he said, "I fear for him*** that he is liable ***to a chatas,"*** for violating the Biblically forbidden labor of trapping.[4]

NOTES

1. However, this is permitted only if by doing so one does not extinguish the lamp (*Rav; Rashi*). That is, one must cover the lamp in such a way that the air supply is not completely cut off, so that the flame is not smothered (*Shaar HaTziyun* 277:26).

2. The Mishnah literally reads: *over the feces of a child.* The implication is that one may only cover it with a bowl but not remove it, since it is *muktzeh.* However, this implication is misleading. Since the waste of a child is generally found in a place frequented by people, one *is* permitted to remove it, under the special exemption to the ban of *muktzeh* accorded for the removal of repulsive objects. Therefore, the Mishnah must be understood to mean that we may invert a bowl over feces *because* of a child; and the Mishnah is referring to the feces of a bird, which is generally found only in trash heaps. Since these places are not frequented by people who would find it repulsive, it may not be moved away. However, since children have a predilection for playing there, the droppings may be covered with a bowl to prevent the children from becoming soiled (*Rav* as explained by *Tos. Yom Tov*).

3. I.e., an incident once occurred in the city of Arav, a Galilean city where Rabban Yochanan ben Zakkai lived for eighteen years, involving one who inverted a bowl over a scorpion (*Meleches Shlomo* from *Yerushalmi*).

4. In the case considered by the Tanna Kamma, the scorpion was chasing a person. Since the situation was life-threatening, it was permissible to perform the Biblically forbidden labor of trapping. On the other hand, R' Yochanan ben Zakkai's incident involved a scorpion that was not chasing anyone. Thus, there was no immediate threat to life that would allow the performance of a forbidden labor. R' Yochanan ben Zakkai was therefore afraid that the fellow had become liable to a *chatas* (see *Rashi*).

GEMS FROM THE GEMARA

The Gemara (121b) records a discussion regarding a Baraisa that addresses the topic of whether it is permitted to kill dangerous creatures on the Sabbath:

A teacher of Baraisos taught the following in the presence of Rava bar Rav Huna: "If one kills snakes or scorpions on the Sabbath, the spirit of pious ones is not pleased with him, for he has killed a creature on the Sabbath unnecessarily." [*Rashi* explains that the Baraisa deals with a situation where the snakes and scorpions are not actually attacking anyone. When these creatures are attacking, the danger that they pose is deemed to be life-threatening, and all agree that they may be killed, even on the Sabbath.]

Rava bar Rav Huna said to the teacher of Baraisos, "And those pious ones, who are displeased with the one who kills the snakes or scorpions on the Sabbath, the spirit of the Sages is not pleased with *them*!" [Rava bar Rav Huna held that a person who kills snakes or scorpions on the Sabbath has acted correctly. For though these creatures were not posing a direct threat at the time they were killed, had they been left alive, they would ultimately have posed a danger when aroused to attack. Thus, in his opinion, it is permitted to kill them at any time (see *Rashi*).]

However, notes the Gemara, the opinion of Rav Huna disagrees with the sentiment just expressed here by his son, Rava bar Rav Huna. This is seen in the following incident: Rav Huna once saw a certain person who was killing a bee on the Sabbath. Rav Huna criticized him, saying, "Have you finished them all off!?" — i.e., what have you accomplished by killing this single bee? There are still so many left! Thus, we see that Rav Huna himself did not allow the killing of bees that are not attacking on the Sabbath — even though they are in the category of potentially dangerous creatures (*Rashi*). Thus, he did not accord with the view of his son.

[*Tosafos* maintain that Rav Huna would in theory permit killing the bees, except that he forbids doing so because it is too public a display of Sabbath desecration. From *Tosafos* it emerges that *trapping* the bees, which is not deemed such an obvious desecration, would be permitted according to Rav Huna.]

QUESTION OF THE DAY:

What do we learn from the verse: וּשְׁמַרְתֶּם אֶת־הַמַּצּוֹת, with respect to the preparation of matzah?

For the answer, see page 166.

פרשת
בא

MONDAY

PARASHAS BO

A MUSSAR THOUGHT FOR THE DAY

The trait of *zerizus,* alacrity, is fundamental in serving Hashem (see *A Mussar Thought for the Day* to *Parashas Noach,* Shabbos). It is interesting that this key element was taught to us in the Torah only in a roundabout manner, by means of a hint concealed inside the command to guard the matzos (see *A Torah Thought for the Day*). What did the Torah want to teach us in combining this lesson with the laws of matzah? Why did it not state clearly that one should perform mitzvos with *zerizus*?

The *Nachalas Eliezer* offers a powerful insight regarding this important trait and its derivation from the commandment not to allow the matzos to become leavened. In order to allow dough to become leaven, one need not do much; in fact, just leaving it alone and sitting by idly will allow it to rise and become *chametz* (leavened). The same is true of performing mitzvos; if a person does not take an active role and deal with a mitzvah that comes his way, he may miss the opportunity to do it at all. To think that the mitzvah is not running away is a mistake. If one grabs the mitzvah, he will merit reward in the World to Come; if not, it will just rush by him and be lost.

Another important lesson can be learned here. One might think that the *middah* of *zerizus* is either an inborn character trait possessed by some, or an elevated level of observance to be acquired by those who would like to enhance their mitzvah performance and raise it to an exalted level. One could surmise that a mitzvah done without *zerizus* and one performed with *zerizus* are the same, as far as the mitzvos themselves are concerned. But the Torah comes to dispute this way of thinking. We are aware that the halachic difference between *chametz* and matzah is hardly noticeable in appearance or texture. A split second of waiting can change a dough from being matzah, fit for eating on Pesach, to *chametz,* for which one who consumes it on Pesach can incur the punishment of *kares* (Divinely imposed premature death). The two doughs may be similar in appearance and taste alike, but it is the *zerizus* that separates them. The same thing is true of mitzvos. A mitzvah performed with *zerizus* and a mitzvah performed without *zerizus* may seem similar, but they are actually worlds apart.

HALACHAH OF THE DAY

As we learned yesterday, in general we follow the more stringent ruling that forbids the staining of a cloth with a colored substance even if the coloration is undesirable. However, in cases where it is not possible to follow this ruling, we may rely on the more lenient view. Therefore, if one must clean a wound and has nothing else available to him, he may use a cloth to wipe away the blood.

All authorities agree that this question applies only to re-usable items such as garments, towels, or cloth napkins. Disposable items such as paper towels, tissues, gauze pads, or Band-aids, which will be discarded after their use, may definitely be "colored" by soiling them.

Another situation which may at times involve the prohibition against *dyeing* on Shabbos is the coloration of foods. Whether or not coloring foods is restricted by this *melachah* depends primarily on the purpose of the coloration. Let us explain:

If the ingredient that lends color to the food is being added solely as a flavoring agent, and any resulting color change is merely an incidental effect of its introduction into the food, one may add the ingredient despite its effect on the color. As we explained above, *dyeing* is defined as the improvement of an object through the addition of color. Since in this case the purpose of the coloring agent is not to improve the appearance of the food, but rather its taste, there is no violation of the *melachah.*

Food that is not meant for consumption, but rather for decorative use, may not be colored on Shabbos. For example, a decorative table centerpiece using decanters of colored water may not be prepared on Shabbos.

The *poskim* rule that one may not color food in order to make it more appealing to a potential buyer.

The commonly accepted ruling is that just as one may add flavoring to solid foods despite any resultant coloration of the food, one may also add flavoring to beverages even if the beverage will become colored. For this reason, one may add instant coffee or tea to water on Shabbos, even though these items color the water.

A CLOSER LOOK AT THE SIDDUR

There is a great debate between the Rabbinic authorities (such as the *Noda BiYehudah* and the *Divrei Chaim*) whether one should recite preparatory prayers (the prayers that usually begin with the words: לְשֵׁם יִחוּד קֻדְשָׁא בְּרִיךְ הוּא, *for the sake of the unification of the Holy One . . .*). One of the reasons given for refraining from saying them is that we are not on the level of greatness required to undertake such holy tasks as the

unification of Hashem's Name — indeed, we are not even capable of properly understanding what this concept means. It is better, then, for us not to recite prayers that we do not comprehend,

However, it seems that all would agree that the part of many of these prayers that contains a declaration of intent and readiness to perform the mitzvah (הִנְנִי מוּכָן וּמְזוּמָן, *Behold. I am ready and prepared . . .*), may — and should — be said. *Chayei Adam* (68:25) states that reciting such formulas is a proper method of preparing oneself to do Hashem's commandments.

The verse that we discussed today (in *A Torah Thought for the Day* and *A Mussar Thought for the Day*), which teaches us that we must always perform mitzvos with alacrity, also teaches us another important lesson. The word וּשְׁמַרְתֶּם, *and you shall guard,* can also mean *and you shall anticipate,* as in the verse stated regarding Yaakov's reaction to Yosef's dreams (*Bereishis* 37:11): וְאָבִיו שָׁמַר אֶת־הַדָּבָר, *and his father waited for the matter.* When one recites הִנְנִי מוּכָן וּמְזוּמָן, *I am ready and prepared . . .,* it shows that he is not performing the mitzvah suddenly and abruptly, and saying this will cause him to perform the mitzvah with more care. *Chayei Adam* writes that when he himself performed a mitzvah without proper preparation, he found that the mitzvah was lacking and incomplete.

The Mishnah in *Berachos* tells us that the righteous people of old used to prepare for a full hour before starting each *Shemoneh Esrei.* One cannot just casually stroll into the King's presence without first preparing by attaining the proper frame of mind. Indeed, this is why we preface the *Shemoneh Esrei* prayer of *Minchah* by reciting *Ashrei* — so that we will be prepared and ready to pray to Hashem.

A TORAH THOUGHT FOR THE DAY

וַיִּקְרָא מֹשֶׁה לְכָל־זִקְנֵי יִשְׂרָאֵל וַיֹּאמֶר אֲלֵהֶם מִשְׁכוּ וּקְחוּ לָכֶם צֹאן לְמִשְׁפְּחֹתֵיכֶם וְשַׁחֲטוּ הַפָּסַח

Moshe called to all the elders of Israel and said to them: "Draw forth and take for yourselves one of the flock for your families, and slaughter the pesach-offering" (Shemos 12:21).

Many commentaries discuss the meaning of the two verbs used in Moshe's instruction to the elders: מִשְׁכוּ וּקְחוּ, which literally mean *draw forth and take* the sheep or goat for the *korban pesach.* Now, a person commanded to *take* something will clearly *draw* it toward himself, and vice versa; thus, had Moshe simply told them to *draw forth* the animal *for yourselves,* it would have been understood that it must be taken. What is the Torah telling us by employing this double phraseology?

Rashi explains by saying that these two directives are in fact speaking to different types of people. A person who already owns an animal appropriate to be used for his *korban pesach* is directed to *draw* it toward him, i.e., to take it out from among his flock and begin preparing it for use as an offering by inspecting it to ensure that it is blemish-free. The commandment to *take* an animal is directed to someone who does not own any animals. This person is not absolved from bringing a *korban pesach,* but must *take* a sheep or goat — by purchasing it — to offer and eat on Pesach night.

R' Aharon Leib Shteinman asks why this specific commandment to *take* (i.e., "buy") the *korban pesach* is necessary. Seemingly, it is obvious that if someone must perform a mitzvah and does not have the materials necessary to carry it out, he must purchase these items! Why, then, did Moshe have to stress to the Jewish people that they were to buy an animal if necessary? R' Shteinman answers that while it is true that money must often be spent to buy objects to use as mitzvos, the Gemara (*Kesubos* 50a) states that a person is not required to pay a price for these items that exceeds 20 percent of his assets. However, this rule is true only in regard to expenses that are not inherently mitzvos, but are only ways to acquire an object that will later be used for a mitzvah — such as purchasing a *lulav* and *esrog* before Succos to use during the holiday. If, however, paying the money *intrinsically* fulfills a mitzvah — such as repaying a debt — a person must pay whatever it costs to ensure that the mitzvah is fulfilled. The reason for this is that the money one is spending is not an ancillary preparation for the mitzvah that may be waived if it is difficult to pay for it; rather, spending this money — at any sum — is what the Torah is commanding to be done. This is the reason, explains R' Shteinman, for Moshe's specific directive telling the people to purchase an animal for the *korban pesach.* Although a person who did not own any animals would clearly have to go to the market and buy one, too high a price would exempt such a person from making this preparation for the mitzvah (by purchasing an animal) and consequently from offering the *korban.* Thus, to ensure that every Jew would fulfill the mitzvah of *korban pesach,* included in Moshe's commandment to the Bnei Yisrael was the directive to buy an animal, telling them that no matter what the price, a *korban pesach* must be bought and offered.

Mechilta (see also *Shemos Rabbah* §16) offers a different explanation of the apparent redundancy, explaining that while both *draw forth* and *take* were said to all the Jewish people, two separate actions were in fact being commanded. The commandment *take* is referring to the obligation to select a *korban pesach.* Telling the Jews to *draw forth,* however, was not referring to the animal that they would soon select, but was instructing them to withdraw *their hands* from the idols that they had worshiped while in Egypt. Thus, Moshe was saying that a prerequisite for offering the *korban pesach* was being free of idol worship.

R' Zundel Kroizer, in his *Ohr HaChamah,* points out that *Rashi* in fact mentions *Mechilta's* explanation of מִשְׁכוּ וּקְחוּ earlier in the chapter (in his comments to 12:6). Why, then, does *Rashi* offer a different reading of these words when he is actually explaining the verse? R' Kroizer answers this question by explaining that the two interpretations of מִשְׁכוּ וּקְחוּ are in fact related. The reason that it was imperative for every Jew to offer the *korban pesach* — as R' Shteinman explained, at any cost — was that it would help free them from the idol worship to which they had become so attached during their stay in Egypt, and only then would they be worthy of redemption. This was accomplished through the mitzvah of *korban pesach,* because the animal used for this *korban* was the lamb, which was the Egyptian deity; commanding the Jews to publicly slaughter this deity, explain R' Kroizer and *Malbim,* ensured that their *yetzer hara* to worship this idol would finally be broken. [See further in *A Mussar Thought for the Day* regarding this point.] Accordingly, it was imperative that every Jew, in every circumstance, offer this *korban.*

[Although Moshe's characterization of the obligation of every Jew to offer a *korban pesach* as absolute was speaking specifically about the first *korban pesach,* offered in Egypt, subsequent *korban pesachs* that were offered every year also were requirements that (once the time appropriate for fulfillment had arrived) could not be neglected, even in order to perform another, pressing mitzvah. For further discussion of this, see *A Taste of Lomdus.*]

MISHNAH OF THE DAY: SHABBOS 16:8

The following Mishnah teaches us that if a non-Jew performs any *melachah* for a Jew on the Sabbath, no Jew is permitted to derive any benefit from that labor on the Sabbath. This is true even if the Jew did not instruct the non-Jew to do the *melachah.* However, if the non-Jew performs the *melachah* for himself, a Jew may derive benefit from it (*Rambam, Hil. Shabbos* 6:2):

עוֹבֵד כּוֹכָבִים שֶׁהִדְלִיק אֶת הַנֵּר — If ***an idolater lit a lamp*** for his own use, **מִשְׁתַּמֵּשׁ לְאוֹרוֹ יִשְׂרָאֵל** — ***a Jew may use its light;***[1] **וְאִם בִּשְׁבִיל יִשְׂרָאֵל אָסוּר** — ***but if*** a non-Jew lit the lamp ***for a Jew,*** even if the non-Jew did so without being asked, a Jew ***may not*** use it.[2] **מִילֵּא מַיִם לְהַשְׁקוֹת בְּהֶמְתּוֹ** — If a non-Jew ***drew water*** from a well that was in a private domain ***to give it to drink to his own animal*** that was standing in a public domain,[3] **מַשְׁקֶה אַחֲרָיו יִשְׂרָאֵל** — then ***a Jew may water*** his animal ***after him;*** **וְאִם בִּשְׁבִיל יִשְׂרָאֵל אָסוּר** — ***but if*** the non-Jew drew the water ***for a Jew,*** a Jew ***may not*** use it.[4] **עָשָׂה עוֹבֵד כּוֹכָבִים כֶּבֶשׁ לֵירֵד בּוֹ** — If

NOTES

1. Since the lamp was lit by the non-Jew for his own use, and not for the use of a Jew, a Jew may make use of its light on the Sabbath (*Meiri*).

We are not concerned that if the Jew is permitted to derive benefit from the light, he may forget and light a lamp himself (*Tosafos* to 122a).

2. I.e., no Jew may use it (*Rosh*). This is a Rabbinic decree (*Rashi*).

3. The non-Jew is thus performing the forbidden labor of הוֹצָאָה — transferring something from a private domain to a public domain (see *Rashi*).

4. I.e., the Jew may not give this water to his animal to drink. The Rabbis enacted this prohibition as a precautionary measure, lest the Jew *ask* the non-Jew to draw water for him, thus violating the Rabbinic injunction against telling a non-Jew to perform forbidden *melachah* on the Sabbath (*Tos.*).

[Clearly, a Jew may not give this water to his animal to drink, but may he himself drink it, or use it to wash his hands, etc.? *Tosafos* record a dispute concerning this question: *Rabbeinu Tam* contends that the Jew may use the water himself, since he could have climbed down into the well and drunk the water there. Hence, the non-Jew's action did not benefit him substantially. *Ri* and other Rishonim, however, do not accept this reasoning (see *Orach Chaim* 325:10).

an idolater made for himself ***a gangplank upon which to disembark*** from a ship,[5] **יוֹרֵד אַחֲרָיו יִשְׂרָאֵל** — ***a Jew may disembark after him;*** **וְאִם בִּשְׁבִיל יִשְׂרָאֵל אָסוּר** — ***but if*** the non-Jew made the gangplank ***for a Jew,*** a Jew ***may not*** use it.[6] **מַעֲשֶׂה בְּרַבָּן גַּמְלִיאֵל וּזְקֵנִים שֶׁהָיוּ בָּאִין בִּסְפִינָה** — ***It once happened that Rabban Gamliel and the Elders were coming on a ship*** that arrived at port on the Sabbath, **וְעָשָׂה עוֹבֵד כּוֹכָבִים כֶּבֶשׁ לֵירֵד בּוֹ** — ***and an idolater made*** for himself ***a gangplank on which to disembark,*** **וְיָרְדוּ בוֹ רַבָּן גַּמְלִיאֵל וּזְקֵנִים** — ***and Rabban Gamliel and the Elders disembarked on it.***[7]

NOTES

5. A gangplank is needed to disembark from a large ship (*Rashi*).

6. No Jew may derive benefit from a non-Jew's "forbidden" *melachah* for the duration of the Sabbath during which it was performed. Furthermore, in all of these three cases, the prohibition extends *after* the Sabbath for as long as it takes to duplicate the particular benefit. For example, in the case of the water drawn by a non-Jew on a Jew's behalf, no use may be made of this water until enough time has passed after the Sabbath to draw the same amount of water. The Sages applied this decree (known as בִּכְדֵי שֶׁיַּעֲשׂוּ) to many items produced in violation of the Sabbath (see *Rashi*).

7. Although disembarking on the Sabbath is prohibited if the ship traveled beyond its 2,000-*amah techum* (see Mishnah *Eruvin* 4:11), one may leave the ship if it reaches within 2,000 *amos* of the shore before the onset of the Sabbath. Rabban Gamliel determined that this was the case by looking through a telescope calibrated to resolve images up to a distance of 2,000 *amos* (*Tosefta* 14:13; see also *Eruvin* 43b with *Rashi*).

GEMS FROM THE GEMARA

The Gemara (122a) raises a difficulty with our Mishnah, based on a qualifying statement that appears in a Baraisa. For we were taught a Baraisa that states in its conclusion: "Regarding what circumstances are these leniencies (i.e., that a Jew may benefit from *melachah* that a non-Jew performed for his own benefit on the Sabbath) stated? When the non-Jew does not know the Jew. However, if the non-Jew knows the Jew, the Jew may not benefit from the non-Jew's *melachah.*"

The Gemara contends that this qualification would seem to be contradicted by the incident cited at the end of the Mishnah, in which a non-Jewish passenger on a ship constructed a gangplank on the Sabbath to disembark from the ship, and Rabban Gamliel and the Elders descended on the Sabbath using the gangplank. Now, in this incident, the non-Jew who built the gangplank knew the Jew (Rabban Gamliel), since they had been traveling on the ship together! How, then, could Rabban Gamliel and the Elders disembark on the gangplank, which was built by the non-Jew on the Sabbath?

The Gemara presents two answers. Abaye says that Rabban Gamliel was not in the non-Jew's presence when the latter constructed the gangplank; hence, it was clear that the non-Jew had no intent to benefit him. Rava says that even if Rabban Gamliel *was* in the non-Jew's presence when the gangplank was constructed, its use would still be permitted, based on the principle that "a lamp [provides light] for one, and the [same] lamp [provides light] for one hundred." That is, the same gangplank that serves one passenger can serve one hundred passengers, and so no extra effort was expended by the non-Jew on Rabban Gamliel's behalf.

Subsequently (122b), the Gemara relates a story: Shmuel once visited the house of Avin Toran. A certain non-Jew came and lit a lamp. Shmuel turned his face away so as not to benefit from the light. However, once he saw that the non-Jew who lit the lamp brought a document and was reading it by the light, Shmuel said to himself, "He lit with himself in mind." Thereupon, Shmuel turned his face back toward the lamp.

[We assume that a non-Jew lit a lamp for a Jew only when his intent is unclear. Where there is a definite indication that he lit it for himself or another non-Jew, a Jew is permitted to use the light, in accordance with the principle of "a lamp for one, a lamp for one hundred" (*Rosh*).]

A MUSSAR THOUGHT FOR THE DAY

We explained in *A Torah Thought for the Day* that the Midrash teaches that one of the purposes of the mitzvah of *korban pesach* was to help the Jews draw back from idolatrous practices. By openly slaughtering the animal that was the Egyptian deity, and seeing that the Egyptians, although undoubtedly furious, were powerless to stop them, the Jewish people would finally overcome their passion for *avodah zarah,* idol worship, and now, focused only on Hashem, would merit leaving Egypt.

R' Yechezkel Levenstein, in his *Ohr Yechezkel* (*Emunah,* p. 277), makes a fascinating observation. At the time that the Jewish people were commanded to begin preparing an animal for use as a *korban pesach,* a few days before the Exodus, they had already witnessed — for a period of over a year, in each of the first nine plagues — open miracles that, one after another, openly defied nature. After seeing these clear indications of Hashem's omnipotence over and over again, why did the Jews need to perform the mitzvah of *korban pesach* in order to defeat their desire to worship idols and to finally achieve the cognizance of Hashem necessary for their leaving Egypt? How could they have continued to wish to serve idols after seeing Hashem's overt hand?

R' Yechezkel Levenstein explains that it is clear from this that *emunah* — belief in Hashem, His power, and His constant hand in every area of a person's life — can be completely acquired only by actively doing something to strengthen this trait. While it was true that the Jewish people had seen miracles that made it clear to them that Hashem was the only force in creation, these miracles had been *seen,* not actively lived. Since the people themselves had not done anything to internalize these powerful messages, clear indications of Hashem's omnipotence, they — like much of what a person sees over the course of a lifetime — would soon be forgotten. The reason for this is simple: when a person sees something out of the ordinary that he has never seen before, this experience does not naturally overcome his inherent perspectives and feelings. No matter how powerful these new messages are, they are foreign to the character, actions, and feelings that have directed him for years. After the initial amazement has worn off, the person will revert back to who he really is, namely, the same person he was before.

The only way a person can use what he sees in the world to strengthen his *emunah* and begin to see Hashem's guiding hand in areas of his personal life as well, continues R' Levenstein, is by actively doing something that reflects this *emunah* perspective. In this way, the person is no longer a bystander who has gained a momentary glimpse of appreciating Hashem's ways; rather, by using this new understanding as an initiative to change *himself,* he has started to undo his previous tendencies of not being mindful of Hashem's role in everyday life. Now, this person will not just be an observer of Hashem's involvement in the world; he will begin to live it.

It was for this reason that the Jewish people had to publicly slaughter the Egyptian deity to finally break their desire for idolatry. Although they had seen miraculous wonders, it was only through action clearly and tangibly showing their appreciation of Hashem's power and control that they were able to inculcate within themselves a lifestyle of *emunah,* and thus merit to leave Egypt.

HALACHAH OF THE DAY

Let us now discuss some manifestations of the *melachah* of *dyeing*:

The use of most cosmetics is forbidden on Shabbos due to the restrictions of this *melachah.* One may not apply any type of nail polish — even clear polish — on Shabbos. The use of eye makeup such as mascara and eyeliner is likewise forbidden. Lipstick may not be used on Shabbos. As we shall see further, the use of lipstick may involve the violation of another *melachah* other than *dyeing.*

One may not use a cream of any sort for the purpose of covering a skin blemish on Shabbos. Since the application of the cream on the blemish in essence changes the color of the skin in order to hide the flaw, this may not be done on Shabbos.

One may remove cosmetics — even those that may not be applied — on Shabbos. However, one may not use a cream in order to remove the cosmetics because the application of the cream involves violation of the *melachah* of *smoothing.* Additionally, when removing the cosmetics, it is preferable to use a disposable item such as a tissue or cotton ball. As we explained above, the use of a towel or cloth may violate the *melachah* of *dyeing,* since the cloth will take some color from the cosmetics.

The use of photochromic lenses (lenses which darken when exposed to sunlight) is permitted on Shabbos.

There is a dispute among the *poskim* regarding the use of deodorizing blocks commonly placed in either the water tanks or the bowls of toilets, which color the water as it flows into the bowls. While some *poskim* forbid their use because they color the water in the bowl, others permit their use on Shabbos. Therefore, it is best to remove them prior to the onset of Shabbos. If they were not removed before Shabbos, they may be removed on Shabbos. If this is not possible for whatever reason, one may rely on those *poskim* who permit their use on Shabbos.

Polishing shoes violates the *melachah* of *dyeing.* Even if the shoes had been polished prior to Shabbos, one may not add more polish to the shoes. Furthermore, shining shoes that have already been polished is also forbidden.

If a colored liquid spills, it should preferably be cleaned up with a disposable napkin or towel. If no disposable item is available, one may use a cloth; however, one should try not to use a cloth of the same color as the spilled liquid. If no cloth of another color is available, this one may be used.

This concludes our discussion of the *melachah* of *dyeing.*

פרשת בא

TUESDAY

PARASHAS BO

A CLOSER LOOK AT THE SIDDUR

In *A Mussar Thought for the Day* we cited *R' Yechezkel Levenstein,* who points out that the Jews had seen the open miracles of the first nine plagues during their final year in Egypt, which made Hashem's total mastery of creation blatantly obvious. Of course, explains R' Yechezkel (in a different volume of his *Ohr Yechezkel — Darchei HaAvodah* p. 63), we do not need open miracles to make us cognizant of Hashem's existence and involvement in the world. A person has to look no further than his own body — with its flawless design that works for decades without need for repairs, and is encased in a protective packaging made of flesh and bone — to realize that there is a Creator. Another way to clearly see Hashem's involvement in the world is to contemplate the miracle of rain. Water evaporates from the seas and is carried by the clouds to the places that need precipitation. It then falls to the earth as rain, enabling plants to grow, which in turn allows animals and humans to survive. Furthermore, this process has been flawlessly continuing for thousands of years. Indeed, every single part of the natural world strongly proclaims the One Who created it. [See *Chovos HaLevavos, Shaar HaBechinah,* and the Steipler Gaon's *Chayei Olam,* for an awe-inspiring description of the simple wonders through which we may recognize Hashem during every day of our lives.]

Moreover, continues R' Yechezkel, Hashem's involvement in the world is clear when a person looks at world history and realizes that the Jewish people's survival is the greatest proof of Hashem's protection. It is also noteworthy that no other nation has ever managed to settle and thrive in Eretz Yisrael. If a person, instead of just looking at daily developments — each one of which may be explained through happenstance — sees the greater picture, he cannot help but be awed by Hashem's greatness. As a result, he will be moved to find ways to become closer to Him.

However, as we explained in *A Mussar Thought for the Day,* simply seeing the most obvious miracles did not strengthen the Jewish people's *emunah,* their tangible awareness of Hashem; their active involvement in offering the *korban pesach* was necessary to incorporate this perspective into their lives. Sadly, we are no different, and the wonders that we see on a daily basis largely do not affect us. How many of us really are amazed every time that we breathe or feel our heart beat? How can we use the many demonstrations of Divine involvement that Hashem offers us on a daily basis to become spiritually refined people? R' Yechezkel Levenstein suggests another way for a person to consciously work on inculcating deeper awareness of Hashem into the way he instinctively sees the world — by thinking about what we say during *Pesukei D'Zimrah,* the verses of praise that we say each morning.

Included in the praises of Hashem that we say during this part of *Shacharis* are many of the "natural phenomena" that we often overlook. For example, we praise Hashem, הַמְכַסֶּה שָׁמַיִם בְּעָבִים הַמֵּכִין לָאָרֶץ מָטָר הַמַּצְמִיחַ הָרִים חָצִיר. נוֹתֵן לִבְהֵמָה לַחְמָהּ לִבְנֵי עֹרֵב אֲשֶׁר יִקְרָאוּ, *Who covers the heavens with clouds, Who prepares rain for the earth, Who makes mountains sprout with grass. He gives to an animal its food, to young ravens that cry out* (*Tehillim* 147:8-9). In the same paragraph, we also speak of Hashem's constant care for the Jewish people in Eretz Yisrael: שַׁבְּחִי יְרוּשָׁלַיִם אֶת־ה׳ הַלְלִי אֱלֹהַיִךְ צִיּוֹן. כִּי־חִזַּק בְּרִיחֵי שְׁעָרָיִךְ בֵּרַךְ בָּנַיִךְ בְּקִרְבֵּךְ. הַשָּׂם־גְּבוּלֵךְ שָׁלוֹם חֵלֶב חִטִּים יַשְׂבִּיעֵךְ, *Praise* H*ASHEM*, *O Jerusalem, laud your God, O Zion, for He has strengthened the bars on your gates and blessed your children in your midst. It is He Who makes your borders peaceful, and with the cream of the wheat He satiates you* (ibid. vs. 12-14). Earlier in *Pesukei D'Zimrah,* we mention Hashem's kindness in simply allowing us to live in Eretz Yisrael: אֲשֶׁר כָּרַת אֶת־אַבְרָהָם וּשְׁבוּעָתוֹ לְיִצְחָק וַיַּעֲמִידֶהָ לְיַעֲקֹב לְחֹק לְיִשְׂרָאֵל בְּרִית עוֹלָם לֵאמֹר, לְךָ אֶתֵּן אֶרֶץ־כְּנָעַן, חֶבֶל נַחֲלַתְכֶם, *that He covenanted with Avraham, and [gave] His oath to Yitzchak; then He established it for Yaakov as a statue, for Yisrael as an everlasting covenant, saying, "To you I shall give the land of Canaan, the lot of your heritage"* (*Divrei HaYamim I* 16:16-18). Simply concentrating on the meaning of these and other parts of the prayers will reinforce our cognizance of Hashem's presence on a daily basis.

QUESTION OF THE DAY:

Why was the command to ready the pesach-offering stated to the "elders" of the Jews, if the command applied to everyone?

For the answer, see page 166.

פרשת בא

WEDNESDAY

PARASHAS BO

A TORAH THOUGHT FOR THE DAY

וְאַתֶּם לֹא תֵצְאוּ אִישׁ מִפֶּתַח־בֵּיתוֹ עַד־בֹּקֶר

And as for you, no man shall leave the entrance of his house until morning (*Shemos* 12:22)

Rashi states that we derive from this verse that once the Destroyer (i.e., the *Malach HaMavess,* the Angel of Death) has been given permission to destroy, it does not distinguish between a righteous person and an evil one. Apparently, *Rashi* means to say that since on that night all the first-born of Egypt were to be killed, and the Angel of Death would be roaming the city, the Jews were to stay indoors, where they would be protected.

However, there is a difficulty with this understanding. When, in an earlier verse (12:12), Hashem speaks of the plague that He will visit upon the Egyptian firstborn, He states: וְעָבַרְתִּי בְאֶרֶץ־מִצְרַיִם בַּלַּיְלָה הַזֶּה, *And I will pass through Egypt on this night.* In the *Haggadah Shel Pesach,* it is derived from this verse that the plague of the slaying of the firstborn was carried out by Hashem *Himself* — in the words of the Haggadah: אֲנִי וְלֹא מַלְאָךְ, אֲנִי וְלֹא שָׂלִיחַ . . . אֲנִי הוּא וְלֹא אַחֵר, *I, and not an angel; I, and not a messenger . . . it was I, and no other.* This seems to contradict *Rashi's* implication that the Destroyer would be carrying out the plague. Furthermore, if the plague was performed by Hashem Himself, what reason was there for the Jews to remain indoors? Surely Hashem will always distinguish between the righteous and the wicked!

Some commentators suggest that *Rashi's* mention of the Destroyer does not refer to his role in the plague of the firstborn; rather, it refers to the fact that on this night, as on most others, there were people (including Jews) whose time to die had arrived. Normally, these souls would have been taken by the Destroyer on that night. However, Hashem wished to distinguish between the *righteous* (i.e., the Jews) and the *wicked* (the Egyptians) on that night; thus, He desired that *no* Jew, even one whose time had come to die, should die at that time. Accordingly, the Jews were told to stay indoors, so that any Jew whose end had come should not be taken by the Angel of Death.

R' Moshe Feinstein advances a novel approach. He suggests that in truth, the reason the Jews were told to stay indoors had nothing to do with any danger. Rather, Hashem wished them to remain inside so it would be abundantly clear that they were not leaving Egypt at the behest of Pharaoh (who would indeed urge them to leave immediately once the plague occurred), but rather as the result of Hashem's command to that effect. Thus, they were told that when Pharaoh would appear, commanding them to get out of Egypt, they were to ignore him completely, and not even stir from their houses until morning, when Hashem wished them to leave.

The Jews, however, were not told the reason they were to stay indoors. They *assumed* that this restriction was due to the danger of the proximity of the Angel of Death — and, R' Moshe explains, it was from *their assumption* that *Rashi* learns that the Destroyer does not distinguish between the righteous and the wicked when he is given free reign. But in truth, they were never in any danger at all, because the Destroyer never came to Egypt that night — the plague was executed by Hashem Himself, as is stated in the Haggadah.

MISHNAH OF THE DAY: SHABBOS 17:1

This chapter considers the laws of *muktzeh.* The following Mishnah begins with a rule concerning the *muktzeh* status of utensils that have doors — for example, movable cabinets. (For some general information on the subject of *muktzeh,* see *Gems from the Gemara* to our Mishnah and to the next three Mishnahs.)

כָּל הַכֵּלִים נִיטָּלִין בְּשַׁבָּת — ***All utensils may be taken on the Sabbath,***[1] **וְדַלְתוֹתֵיהֶן עִמָּהֶן** — ***and their doors*** may be taken ***with them.***[2] **אַף עַל פִּי שֶׁנִּתְפָּרְקוּ** — ***Even though they were detached*** already before the onset of the Sabbath, **בְּשַׁבָּת** — they may nevertheless be taken ***on the Sabbath,***[3] **שֶׁאֵינָן דּוֹמִין לְדַלְתוֹת הַבַּיִת** — ***for they are not like the doors of houses,*** which if detached may *not* be moved, **לְפִי שֶׁאֵינָן מִן הַמּוּכָן** — ***since*** house doors ***are not prepared*** for Sabbath use.[4]

NOTES

1. I.e., all utensils that are normally used for activities that are permissible on the Sabbath — e.g., non-*muktzeh* utensils — may be handled and moved about on the Sabbath (*Tos. Yom Tov* from *Ran; Tiferes Yisrael*). [Utensils that are normally used for activities that are forbidden on the Sabbath are discussed below (Mishnah 4).]

2. I.e., doors or lids of these utensils that have become detached may also be moved on the Sabbath. Since these doors were originally parts of permissible utensils, they are not *muktzeh,* and may be moved (*Rav; Rashi*).

3. [If the doors became detached on the Sabbath, they may certainly be moved, since at the onset of the Sabbath the doors were still part of the utensil.]

4. I.e., not designed to be moved. The doors of buildings are not designed to be *moved* about, but rather to be *swiveled* on a hinge while remaining attached to the doorframe. They are, therefore, considered parts of *structures* rather than *utensils.* Since they are not utensils, they may not be moved upon becoming detached from the house. The doors of utensils, on the other hand, *are* designed to be moved together with the utensils to which they are attached. They are, therefore, considered "prepared" to be moved and are not *muktzeh* (*Rav; Rashi*). [Any object designed not to be moved is automatically *muktzeh.*]

פרשת
בא

WEDNESDAY

PARASHAS BO

GEMS FROM THE GEMARA

The Gemara (123b) states that "originally" [i.e., when the original enactment prohibiting the handling of certain items as *muktzeh* was formulated] they used to say that there are only three utensils that may be handled on the Sabbath — the knife used to cut a cake of pressed figs; the spoon used to skim off the foam from the top of a cooking pot; and the small table-knife that was used for cutting bread, meat and other foods. [Handling these was permitted because their use was constantly necessary (*Rashi*).] At three subsequent times, parts of the original enactment were repealed. This resulted in progressively more lenient laws of *muktzeh.* The final version of the law of *muktzeh* appears below, in Mishnah 4: *All* utensils may be moved on the Sabbath, with the exception of a large saw and the large, sharp peg of a plow (and similar utensils that fall into a specific category of *muktzeh,* about which we will learn in that Mishnah). All other utensils may be handled. Some may be handled at will, while others may be handled only under certain specific conditions, as we will learn.

The Gemara later states that the original enactment of *muktzeh* that is stated by our Mishnah was promulgated in the days of Nechemiah, son of Chachaliah. The reason that Nechemiah made the enactment is found in this verse (*Nechemiah* 13:15): *In those days I saw in Judea* [*people*] *treading wine presses on the Sabbath, and hauling the sheaves* [*of grain*]. Nechemiah enacted the laws of *muktzeh* to counter the flagrant violations of the Sabbath that he discovered upon his arrival in Jerusalem. As the people became more meticulous in their Sabbath observance, the Sages saw that the need for the almost total ban on handling utensils was no longer necessary, and they were able to relax these [originally very stringent] safeguards. In each new stage, the *muktzeh* laws were made more lenient, until they arrived at the present-day levels.

We will discuss various categories of *muktzeh,* and when and how some of them may be permissibly handled on the Sabbath, in our next few selections from the Gemara.

QUESTION OF THE DAY:

Where do we find that even Moshe remained indoors for the entire night of the Plague of the Firstborn?

For the answer, see page 166.

A MUSSAR THOUGHT FOR THE DAY

פרשת בא

WEDNESDAY

PARASHAS BO

The Torah tells us that when midnight of the 14th of Nissan arrived, on the last night of the Jews' exile in Egypt, Hashem slew all the Egyptian firstborn, as the last of the Ten Plagues. The Torah then records Pharaoh's reaction, stating (*Shemos* 12:30): וַיָּקָם פַּרְעֹה לַיְלָה, *And Pharaoh arose at night. Rashi* adds a single word of explanation to this verse — the word מִמִּטָּתוֹ, *from his bed.* That is, the Torah does not mean that Pharaoh arose from his throne to rush to find Moshe and Aharon; rather, he arose from his sleeping chambers.

R' Gershon Weiss would often use this *Rashi* as an object lesson, pointing out how blind it is possible for a person to become when he is ensnared in the clutches of the *yetzer hara.* Consider: Pharaoh had been visited by Moshe before and after each of the preceding nine plagues, and every single thing Moshe had predicted had come to pass exactly as he had stated. Pharaoh had already witnessed the destruction of his economy, his country and his subjects. And, during the very last time that he was confronted by Moshe, he had pronounced that on this night all of the firstborn would die. Thus, Pharaoh had every reason to believe that there would be a mass slaughter that night. Moreover, the Midrash tells us that earlier on that day, the firstborn of Egypt, fearing for their lives, had banded together in a desperate attempt to overthrow the king and free the Jews so that they would not die (as *they* believed Moshe implicitly). The Midrash relates that the revolt was led by Pharaoh's own firstborn, who was killed in the fighting, along with many others. But that is not all. Pharaoh *himself* was a firstborn. Thus, he himself should have expected to die that night. [Although he was spared on this night, so he would be able to receive his final punishment later, at the *Yam Suf,* he had no way of knowing that this would be his fate.] And what did he do in preparation? *He went to sleep*!! How, R' Gershon would ask, is it possible that Pharaoh could even *consider* going to bed during what he every reason to believe were the last few hours of his life?

From this, we see how blind Pharaoh had become. In spite of all the proof staring him in the face, in spite of the many miracles performed openly, he was able to convince himself that this time, somehow, things would not happen as Moshe had predicted. This is the power of the *yetzer hara.*

HALACHAH OF THE DAY

The *melachah* of *spinning* is the twisting together of individual fibers in order to combine them and form a long thread. Spinning may also be performed in order to combine several threads into one thicker thread. Both of these activities took place as part of the construction of the Mishkan. Woolen fibers were first twisted together in order to form threads of the three colors primarily used in the Mishkan — blue wool, purple wool, and red wool. These individual threads were then spun together with a linen thread in order to create one unified, thick four-ply thread.

Any act of spinning performed on Shabbos, whether it is done using an implement made specifically for such a purpose, or by hand, is a violation of this *melachah.*

The next four *melachos* are all parts of the weaving process. Textiles were woven for use in the Mishkan, both for the coverings and hangings used in the Mishkan complex, as well as for production of the Kohanim's clothing. In order to properly understand these *melachos,* we will describe the weaving process, and introduce each forbidden labor in its place in the process.

Woven cloth consists of two series of parallel threads that crisscross each other at right angles. Every second horizontal thread passes over the first vertical thread, under the second, over the third, under the fourth, etc., until it has passed through all the vertical threads. Each remaining horizontal thread passes under the first vertical thread, over the second, under the third, etc.

In the weaving process, the vertical threads (called the שְׁתִי, or *warp* threads) are fixed in place, while a single thread (called the עֵרֶב, or *weft* thread) is passed over and under them, first from right to left, and then back from left to right. With each pass of the weft thread through the arranged warp threads, the woven cloth grows ever longer.

In order to assure an even weave, the warp must be kept taut while the weft passes through it. This is accomplished by wrapping the warp threads around a beam called the warp beam, and then stretching them to a second beam called the cloth beam. The cloth beam derives its name from the fact that it is around this beam that the final product — the woven cloth — will become wrapped. The act of fixing the warp threads to the warp beam and then to the cloth beam is the first of the weaving labors forbidden on Shabbos, and is known as the melachah of מֵיסֵךְ, *dressing the loom.*

A CLOSER LOOK AT THE SIDDUR

This week, we continue our discussion of the tenth of the Thirteen Fundamental Principles (י״ג עיקרים) enumerated by *Rambam,* which states:

> אֲנִי מַאֲמִין בֶּאֱמוּנָה שְׁלֵמָה שֶׁהַבּוֹרֵא יִתְבָּרַךְ שְׁמוֹ יוֹדֵעַ כָּל מַעֲשֵׂה בְנֵי אָדָם וְכָל מַחְשְׁבוֹתָם שֶׁנֶּאֱמַר ״הַיֹּצֵר יַחַד לִבָּם הַמֵּבִין אֶל־כָּל־מַעֲשֵׂיהֶם״.
> *I believe with complete faith that the Creator, Blessed be His Name, knows all the deeds of human beings, and all of their thoughts, as it is stated: "He Who fashions all their hearts together, Who comprehends all of their deeds."*

Last week, we addressed the question of how Hashem can know everything, and yet we ourselves can have free choice. With that question laid to rest, we must explore another question: Why is it so important for us to believe that Hashem knows all of our thoughts and deeds?

On the simplest level, of course, we are required to believe that Hashem is all-powerful, and that there is nothing beyond His capabilities. But there are deeper reasons as to why this belief is fundamental. If a person were to believe that Hashem is unaware of his actions, there would be no reason for him not to give in to his desires and evil inclinations. He could reason: No one will ever know. Why should I refrain from sinning? Thus, we must always remember, as the Mishnah in *Avos* (2:1) states: דַּע מַה לְמַעְלָה מִמְּךָ – עַיִן רוֹאָה, וְאֹזֶן שׁוֹמַעַת, וְכָל מַעֲשֶׂיךָ בְּסֵפֶר נִכְתָּבִים, *Know what is above you — an Eye that sees, an Ear that hears, and a Book in which all your deeds are recorded.* Most people will not give in to their sinful desires when others are watching. And Hashem is always watching! One who holds this thought in mind will be protected from sin.

Moreover, Hashem knows not only our deeds, but even our thoughts. One can fool his fellow man, but Hashem cannot be fooled. He knows our true motives, and our hidden hypocrisies. This realization, properly utilized, can serve as the greatest deterrent to sin.

However, there is also a positive aspect to the knowledge that Hashem knows all. Often, a sinner who truly wishes to repent is reluctant to do so, because he is discouraged by the fact that his friends and acquaintances will not take his new determination seriously. They will dismiss it as an act, or as a new fad, refusing to accept the possibility that a person can actually change for the better. Such a person must hold fast to the comforting knowledge that Hashem does know what is in his heart, and will treasure the true feelings of remorse and new resolve that reside there, regardless of what people may say or think. This can be a powerful aid to one who wishes to do *teshuvah.*

This concludes our discussion of the tenth of the Thirteen Fundamental Principles.

A TASTE OF LOMDUS

T*osafos* (*Pesachim 3b*) state that a person who does not own property is exempt from performing the mitzvah of *korban pesach. Ohr Chodosh* and *Chida* (*Chaim Shaal* §84) explain that this exemption is based on the Gemara's statement in *Pesachim* (8b) that a person without land is absolved from *aliyah l'regel,* making a festival pilgrimage to the *Beis HaMikdash.* Since, explains the Gemara, the Torah promises (*Shemos* 34:24): וְלֹא־יַחְמֹד אִישׁ אֶת־אַרְצְךָ בַּעֲלֹתְךָ לֵרָאוֹת אֶת־פְּנֵי ה׳ אֱלֹהֶיךָ שָׁלֹשׁ פְּעָמִים בַּשָּׁנָה, *and no man (enemy) shall covet your land when you go up to appear before HASHEM, your God, three times a year,* this mitzvah is clearly directed at a person who owns land, and a person without land is permitted to remain at home during these times. Accordingly, conclude *Ohr Chodosh* and *Chida, Tosafos* understand that if the Torah excuses a person without land from making the festival pilgrimage, he will not be in Yerushalayim for Pesach, and this implicitly excuses him from offering a *korban pesach* as well.

R' Dovid Deitsch (cited in *Teshuvos Chasam Sofer, Orach Chaim* §224) asks a powerful question on *Tosafos'* assertion that a person without land is exempt from *korban pesach.* The Gemara (*Shabbos* 131a-b) explains that (according to the minority view of R' Eliezer that is mentioned in the Mishnah there) preparations for many mitzvos may be performed on Shabbos, even though this will involve actions that are normally forbidden *melachos.* Thus, for example, according to R' Eliezer a *mohel* would be allowed to sharpen his *milah* knife on Shabbos, a *succah* may be built on Shabbos, and water can be heated in order to cleanse the baby as is needed after the *bris.*

The Gemara then qualifies R' Eliezer's permit, stating that this allowance does not apply to all mitzvos. Attempting to identify which mitzvos are not included, the Gemara concludes that R' Eliezer would not allow preparations for the mitzvos of *tzitzis* and *mezuzah* to be done on Shabbos, for attaching *tzitzis* to a four-cornered garment involves forbidden *tying,* and affixing a *mezuzah* to a house transgresses the

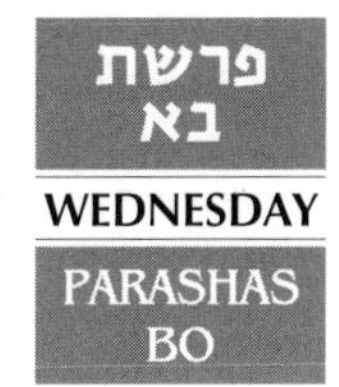

melachah of *building.* Although R' Eliezer allows these preparations with regard to other mitzvos — for example, he permits building a *succah,* or tying together the Four Species into a bundle, on Shabbos — the Gemara explains that R' Eliezer permits these actions only because the mitzvah cannot be circumvented. R' Eliezer is telling us that when faced with a conflict between Shabbos and a mitzvah, Shabbos is pushed aside. When dealing with *tzitzis* and *mezuzah,* however, there does not have to be a conflict between Shabbos and the need to perform the mitzvah, since the person can relinquish his ownership of the garment or building, and exempt himself from the obligations of *tzitzis* and *mezuzah* — and hence the need to tie or to build. If the conflict can be avoided, even R' Eliezer agrees that there is no permit to do *melachah* on Shabbos.

The Mishnah in *Pesachim* (65b), continues R' Dovid Deitsch, teaches that many aspects of the *korban pesach* offering, such as slaughtering the animal and burning its fats, may be performed on Shabbos. Although these actions are normally forbidden on Shabbos, a *korban pesach* must always be offered at the appropriate time — the afternoon of the 14th of Nissan — even if this date falls on Shabbos.

R' Dovid Deitsch concludes his question: Since the Gemara in *Shabbos* explains that a person can relinquish his ownership of his garment or building and avoid the mitzvah of *tzitzis* or *mezuzah* in order not to desecrate Shabbos, why is the same not true in regard to the *korban pesach*? According to *Tosafos,* a person faced with slaughtering a *korban pesach* on Shabbos is able to avoid this conflict in halachah by renouncing ownership of his land, thus exempting himself from bringing a *korban pesach.* Since, by this means, the conflict can be avoided, *korban pesach* should be like *tzitzis* and *mezuzah,* and should not override Shabbos! According to *Tosafos,* how can a *korban pesach* ever be offered on Shabbos?

The Baltimore Rosh Yeshivah, *R' Yaakov Yitzchak Ruderman,* provides an answer to this question by explaining the precise nature of the obligation to offer the *korban pesach.* The Gemara in *Zevachim* (100a) states that although a Kohen is normally commanded to become *tamei* (ritually impure) to attend to the burial of one of his close relatives, he is not allowed to do so on the *afternoon* of Erev Pesach — the reason being that the *korban pesach* requires a person to be *tahor* (pure). The *morning* of Erev Pesach, however, is different. Even though becoming *tamei* on the *morning* of the 14th will also disqualify a person from offering the *korban pesach* in a few hours and eating it at night, if it is still before noon the time for offering the *korban* has not yet begun, and

the current mitzvah of becoming *tamei* for a relative must be carried out. However, once the time of the actual obligation of the *korban pesach* begins in the afternoon, nothing may be done that will prevent this mitzvah from being fulfilled.

We see from this Gemara, explains R' Ruderman, that a person on Erev Pesach afternoon has no right to do anything that will prevent him from offering the *korban pesach,* for this is a mitzvah that he is already obligated to fulfill. The only reason why the Gemara in *Shabbos* was able to offer the suggestion of averting the need to fulfill the mitzvos of *tzitzis* and *mezuzah* is because these commandments are not based on preexisting obligations; rather, since every second that a person wears a garment without *tzitzis* he enjoys the option of either attaching *tzitzis* or removing the garment, he is able, and accordingly required, to avoid the conflict between Shabbos and *tzitzis* at any time by renouncing his ownership of this garment in order to alleviate the need to perform the *melachah* of tying on Shabbos. The obligation of *korban pesach,* however, once it is incurred when a person is present in Yerushalayim on Erev Pesach afternoon, can no longer be avoided in any way (such as by renouncing his property). Thus, it may be performed even on Shabbos.

A TORAH THOUGHT FOR THE DAY

וַיֹּאמֶר ה׳ אֶל־מֹשֶׁה וְאַהֲרֹן זֹאת חֻקַּת הַפָּסַח
כָּל־בֶּן־נֵכָר לֹא־יֹאכַל בּוֹ

HASHEM said to Moshe and Aharon,
"This is the statute of the pesach-offering:
any stranger may not eat from it" (*Shemos* 12:43).

Rashi states that this prohibition applies to one whose deeds have become alien to his Father in Heaven. Both a non-Jew and a Jew who is an apostate are included in the prohibition.

The Gemara in *Pesachim* (3b) relates an interesting episode pertaining to this prohibition. There was a non-Jew who once boasted to Rav Yehudah ben Beseira, who lived in Netzivin: "The Torah states that 'a stranger may not eat from the *pesach,*' and 'any uncircumcised male may not eat from the *pesach,*' and I managed to eat from the best portion of the *pesach*-offering!" Rav Yehudah, who understood that the non-Jew had fooled the Kohanim in the *Beis HaMikdash* and passed himself off as a Jew, thought of an idea that would reveal the man's malicious intent. [Rav Yehudah did not have the power to stop the non-Jew (see *Rashi* there), and he was ill and could not make the trip to Yerushalayim (*Tosafos*).] Rav Yehudah asked the non-Jew, "Have they ever given you a portion from the *alya* (the fatty part of the tail, which is the choicest part of the meat)?" When the non-Jew answered that they had not, Rav Yehudah instructed him to go up to Yerushalayim the next year, and demand a portion from the *alya.* [The non-Jew was not aware that this portion of the *pesach* is not consumed; rather, it is burned on the Altar along with the other *emurim* (sacrificial parts).]

When the non-Jew came to Yerushalayim the next year and requested the *alya,* they asked him, "Who told you to ask for that portion?" The non-Jew told them that Rav Yehudah had instructed him to do so. Realizing that Rav Yehudah would never have done such a thing without a purpose, they investigated more closely. The non-Jew's true identity was then uncovered, and he was executed.

After this, the Kohanim sent a message to Rav Yehudah: "Although you are living in the distant town of Netzivin, your nets (meaning your influence) are spread out in Yerushalayim!"

Minchas Chinuch (§14) asks: Why was the non-Jew put to death? This prohibition is not included in the seven mitzvos that must be observed by non-Jews (the *Sheva Mitzvos Bnei Noach*). It is the Jew who is commanded not to share the *pesach* with non-Jews.

Rav Elchanan Wasserman (in *Kovetz Shiurim*) answers that the non-Jew was guilty of stealing, an offense that, when committed by a non-Jew, is punishable by death. The law is that one can eat of a *korban pesach* only if he registered beforehand upon that particular *pesach.* If a non-Jew registers under false pretenses, he is stealing from the rest of the registered group.

The *Netziv* says that the non-Jew was guilty of entering the *Mikdash* while being *tamei,* impure. The Gemara in *Sanhedrin* (81a) states: A Kohen who enters the *azarah* in an impure state may be executed by his fellow Kohanim. Here, too, the Kohanim exercised this authority that was given to them. [For another possible explanation, see *Me'il Shmuel.*]

MISHNAH OF THE DAY: SHABBOS 17:2

The following Mishnah lists specific uses for which certain utensils that are otherwise *muktzeh* may be moved:

נוֹטֵל אָדָם קוּרְנָס — ***A person may take a hammer*** **לְפַצֵּעַ בּוֹ אֶת הָאֱגוֹזִין** — ***to crack open nuts with it;***[1] **קַרְדּוֹם לַחְתּוֹךְ בּוֹ אֶת הַדְּבֵילָה** — ***a hatchet to cut a cake of pressed figs with it;***[2] **מְגֵירָה לָגוֹר בָּהּ אֶת הַגְּבִינָה** — ***a saw to slice cheese with it;***[3] **מַגְרֵיפָה לִגְרוֹף בָּהּ אֶת הַגְּרוֹגְרוֹת** — ***a shovel to scoop up dried figs*** from the bottom of a barrel ***with it;*** **אֶת הָרַחַת וְאֶת הַמַּלְגֵּז לָתֵת עָלָיו לַקָּטָן** — ***a winnowing shovel or a pitchfork to put*** food ***on it for a child;***[4] **אֶת הַכּוּשׁ וְאֶת הַכַּרְכַּר לִתְחוֹב בּוֹ** — ***a spindle or weaver's reed***[5] ***to spear*** fruit ***with***

NOTES

1. Our Mishnah refers to an ordinary hammer, and permits using it for this purpose even though the hammer is a כְּלִי שֶׁמְּלַאכְתּוֹ לְאִיסּוּר, *a utensil used primarily for work prohibited on the Sabbath.* Our Mishnah thus teaches that a utensil that is normally used for an activity prohibited on the Sabbath is a unique category of *muktzeh.* Whereas most categories of *muktzeh* may never be moved directly, under certain conditions a utensil that is normally used for an activity prohibited on the Sabbath may be moved. In this case and in the subsequent cases, our Mishnah teaches that such a utensil may be moved לְצֹרֶךְ גּוּפוֹ, *to make use of it,* for any activity permissible on the Sabbath — for example, using the hammer to crack nuts (Gemara 123a).

2. After figs were dried, they were pressed into a circular cake. This cake was thick and hard, and a hatchet was required to cut it (*Rav; Rashi*).

3. Since a saw has a serrated edge, it cuts through a thick cheese quickly (*Rav; Rashi*).

4. I.e., to pass food to a child who is on the opposite side of a stream, and is unable to cross over (*Tiferes Yisrael*).

5. A weaver's reed was used in the weaving process to arrange the threads one beside the other. It resembled a sackmaker's needle (*Rav; Tiferes Yisrael*).

it;[6] מַחַט שֶׁל יָד לִיטּוֹל בּוֹ אֶת הַקּוֹץ — ***a hand-needle*** normally used for sewing ***to remove a splinter with it;***[7] וְשֶׁל סַקָּאִים לִפְתּוֹחַ בּוֹ אֶת הַדֶּלֶת — ***or a sackmaker's*** needle[8] ***to open a door with it.***[9]

NOTES

6. The spindle or reed would be used to pick up mulberries, or any other soft fruit, in order to eat them without soiling one's hands (*Rav; Rashi; Tiferes Yisrael*).

7. I.e., a thorn or splinter embedded in one's skin. [Although it might cause bleeding, a person is nevertheless permitted to remove the thorn on the Sabbath. Since he does not intend to make his skin bleed, the Rabbis permitted removing the thorn to alleviate his pain (*Tos. R' Akiva Eiger*). This is similar to the rule that one may lance a boil to remove the pus as long as he does not intend to make an opening for the air to enter (*Rav; Tiferes Yisrael*).]

8. A large needle used for sewing sacks (*Rav; Rashi*).

9. Someone who lost his key would use such a needle as a lock pick (*Rav; Rashi*).

GEMS FROM THE GEMARA

◆§ The Categories of Muktzeh — Part 1

The basic definition of *muktzeh* is any item which was not "prepared" for use before the Sabbath. This preparation, however, need not be active. Any object which, in the normal course of events, stands to be used on the Sabbath is considered "prepared," and consequently may be נִטָּל, *taken,* on the Sabbath — i.e., it may be handled and moved about. Only objects which, for one reason or another, do not stand to be used are deemed *muktzeh.*

There are several reasons for classifying objects as *muktzeh,* and various categories into which these objects may be placed. *Beis Yosef* (to *Orach Chaim* §308) classifies the various types of *muktzeh,* some of which appear in the Mishnahs of our chapter (as noted in each classification), and some of which are expounded elsewhere (the list will be continued in *Gems from the Gemara* to the next two Mishnahs).

(1) כְּלִי שֶׁמְּלַאכְתּוֹ לְאִיסּוּר, *a utensil used primarily for work prohibited on the Sabbath* (this type of *muktzeh* is discussed in Mishnahs 2 and 3). This category includes any utensil (such as a hammer) whose primary use (building) is forbidden on the Sabbath, but which is also occasionally used for permissible activities, such as cracking nuts. Since the items in this category are not easily damaged, the owner does not object to their being used for these secondary purposes.

(2) מֻקְצֶה מֵחֲמַת חֶסְרוֹן כִּיס, *set aside for fear of monetary loss* (this type of *muktzeh* is discussed in Mishnah 4). This category includes any utensil whose use for non-primary purposes is objected to by the owner, for fear it will become damaged. Examples are the large saw and plow blade mentioned in Mishnah 4, a slaughterer's knife, or a barber's razor. Though the owner certainly uses these for their primary functions, those functions are prohibited on the Sabbath. Since these blades must be kept perfectly sharp, the owner objects to their being used for any secondary, permissible function (e.g., as a table knife) for fear of damaging the cutting edge.

We will continue our listing of the types of *muktzeh* tomorrow.

A MUSSAR THOUGHT FOR THE DAY

One may wonder why there are so many mitzvos pertaining to the *korban pesach* in particular [e.g., not to take the *korban* outside, not to break its bones, not to leave it over, to eat it only roasted, not cooked in water, etc.] and to the Yom Tov of Pesach in general [such as *chametz,* matzah, and *maror*]. Every mitzvah in the Torah has its unique message and lesson. We know that the primary reason for all the Pesach-related mitzvos is זֵכֶר לִיצִיאַת מִצְרָיִם, to remember all the miracles Hashem performed while taking us out of Egypt; but why do we need so many mitzvos for this reminder?

The *Sefer HaChinuch,* one of the Rishonim who offers reasons for all the mitzvos, addresses this very question. He answers it with a concept that is a basic *mussar* teaching: חִיצוֹנִיּוּת מְעוֹרֶרֶת הַפְּנִימִיּוּת, *external behavior,* when constantly repeated, *will* ultimately *influence* one's *inner character,* for better or for worse. For example, if a good-natured person would be appointed by the king to be in charge of killing criminals, as time would go by he would become accustomed to his new job. Eventually, the value of life would be cheapened in his eyes, and he would become evil.

The same holds true in the opposite situation. If an ill-natured person, who constantly thinks about how to commit evil, will decide to perform good deeds, it will not take long for him to change his mean-spirited character and intentions, and become a better person.

Rav Moshe Chaim Luzzato, in *Mesillas Yesharim,* uses this concept when he discusses how practicing the *middah* of *zerizus* (alacrity) will help cure a person of laziness. He says with certainty that it is tested and proven that if one performs actions, even without inner feelings of appreciation for what he is doing, eventually his bad *middos* will be broken and he will become a better person.

When the Jews left Egypt, the Jewish nation was born. At this time, when Hashem was bringing us under His wings to become His chosen nation, it was important to provide us with many mitzvos surrounding this seminal event, to drive the message home again and again. We were thus provided with many opportunities to develop our character and become deserving of being Hashem's nation.

This important lesson repeats itself every year, and each year (although we unfortunately cannot offer the *korban pesach* at this time) we relive the experience of becoming the chosen nation. By performing all the mitzvos of the Seder night, we recommit ourselves to the responsibility that this entails, and express the hope that we will soon be able to offer the *pesach* in the rebuilt *Beis HaMikdash.*

HALACHAH OF THE DAY

The task of manually weaving long bolts of cloth for use in the manufacture of clothing and other textiles is a prohibitively long and arduous one. A large bolt of cloth may contain one hundred or more warp threads per inch. A method which would enable the weft thread to make a complete pass through all the warp threads in one motion would speed the process of weaving considerably. Additionally, if a method could be found to allow the use of an exceptionally long weft thread, the amount of knots in the final product could be reduced. This would increase the beauty of the product, as well as avoid tangling caused by the knots. In order to accomplish this, it was necessary to find a way to alternately raise all the even warp threads above the odd ones, and then all the odd threads above the even ones. Once this was done, a spool holding the weft thread wrapped around it could be passed first under all the even threads and above the odd threads, and then under the odd threads while traveling over the even ones. If the space between the raised and lowered threads could be made large enough, the spool could hold a weft thread of a sufficient length to avoid the use of knots.

All of these objectives are met through the use of the mechanized loom. In the weaving loom, two frames, called harnesses, are positioned between the warp beam and the cloth beam. Each of these harnesses contains a number of taut vertical threads equal to half the number of the warp threads found on the loom. At the center of each of these vertical threads there is a loop, or an eye, called a heddle. All of the even-numbered warp threads pass through the heddles of one frame, while all the odd-numbered warp threads pass through the heddles of the second frame.

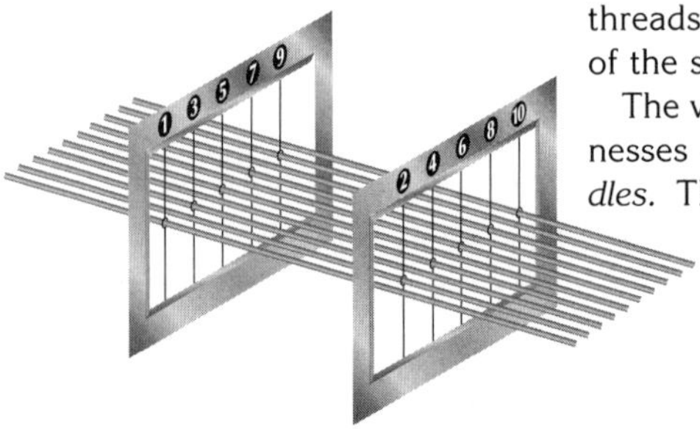

The vertical threads of the harnesses are known as נִירִין, *heddles.* The loops at their center are known as בָּתֵּי נִירִין, *heddle eyes.* Thus we arrive at the second of the labors of weaving forbidden on Shabbos — עוֹשֶׂה שְׁתֵּי בָּתֵּי נִירִין, the *setting of two heddle eyes.* Placing two warp threads through two heddle eyes on Shabbos is a violation of this *melachah.*

A CLOSER LOOK AT THE SIDDUR

The Gemara in *Menachos* (43b) tells us that a person is obligated to make 100 blessings every day, for the verse states (*Devarim* 10:12): וְעַתָּה יִשְׂרָאֵל מָה ה׳ אֱלֹהֶיךָ שֹׁאֵל מֵעִמָּךְ, *Now, Israel, what (mah) does HASHEM, your God, ask of you?* The numerical value of the word *mah* is 100; thus, the verse is expounded to be saying: "100 (blessings each day) is what Hashem asks of you."

One may ask: What is the significance of the number 100? *Tur* states that Dovid HaMelech instituted this requirement because of a plague that struck during his reign. Every day, 100 people would die, and no one could find the cause. It was revealed to Dovid through *ruach hakodesh* (Divine inspiration) that it was because the Jews were deficient in their blessings. When David implemented this requirement, the epidemic subsided.

The connection between the epidemic and the blessings is unclear, except for the numerical equivalence. *Rabbi Avigdor Miller* explains, however, that there is a deeper connection: When there is death and destruction, it is because Hashem's Name is being forgotten. The verse

states (*Shemos* 20:21): בְּכָל־הַמָּקוֹם אֲשֶׁר אַזְכִּיר אֶת־שְׁמִי אָבוֹא אֵלֶיךָ וּבֵרַכְתִּיךָ, *wherever you will mention My Name, I will come and bless you.* Just the mere mention of Hashem's Name is a call for blessing. If someone gets into the habit of repeating something, even an insignificant expression, that is what he will think about and be connected to; as we discussed in *A Mussar Thought for the Day,* external acts influence internal thoughts. Thus, if one makes 100 blessings a day, he has connected himself to Hashem 100 times, and asked for Hashem's abundant blessing 100 times. This brings great protection from any harm.

It is interesting to note that the simple meaning of the verse in *Devarim* is that all Hashem asks from us is to fear Hashem; however, the Gemara expounds מָה to refer to 100 blessings. *Imrei Emes* explains that the simple meaning of the verse and the exposition are connected, for reciting 100 blessings every day is like receiving 100 injections of *yiras Shamayim,* fear of Heaven. A blessing, when recited properly with the right intention, concentrating on Hashem's Name, will automatically instill true *yiras Shamayim* in a person. Thus, a wonderful and [relatively] easy way to acquire *yiras Shamayim* is to make the required 100 blessings every day.

QUESTION OF THE DAY:

How can there be a prohibition for a non-Jew to eat of the pesach, if this is not one of the seven mitzvos given to all people (Sheva Mitzvos Bnei Noach)?

For the answer, see page 166.

פרשת בא

FRIDAY

PARASHAS BO

A TORAH THOUGHT FOR THE DAY

וְהִגַּדְתָּ לְבִנְךָ בַּיּוֹם הַהוּא לֵאמֹר בַּעֲבוּר זֶה עָשָׂה ה׳ לִי בְּצֵאתִי מִמִּצְרָיִם

And you shall tell your son ***on that day, saying****: "It is on account of this that* HASHEM *did for me when I left Egypt"* (*Shemos* 13:8).

O*hr HaChaim* asks several question on this verse. Among them, why is the father instructed to tell his son the story of the Exodus from Egypt on that "day," when we know that the mitzvah of סִיפּוּר יְצִיאַת מִצְרַיִם, *telling the story of the Exodus from Egypt,* is performed only "when matzah and *maror* are lying in front of you," which is only on Pesach *night*? Second, why is the word לֵאמֹר, *saying,* added, after the verse has already stated: וְהִגַּדְתָּ לְבִנְךָ, *And you shall tell your son* etc.?

Ohr HaChaim answers that this verse is referring to a great miracle that took place on the night of Pesach, the night preceding the actual Exodus. He quotes a *Zohar HaKadosh* that states, based on a verse in *Tehillim*: לַיְלָה כַּיּוֹם יָאִיר, *the night [of Yetzias Mitzrayim] was illuminated like daytime.* The *Zohar* explains that this is meant literally: The sun came out, and was shining in the middle of the night as if it were a bright summer day.

Thus, this verse, by mentioning "day" and adding the word לֵאמֹר, is hinting to us that we must also *say* to our sons that there was a miracle of *day* — meaning the miracle of the night turning into daylight. One should mention this miracle as well when speaking about the Exodus. [See *A Mussar Thought for the Day,* today, for the important lesson to be gleaned from this miracle.]

Rav Shternbuch, in his Haggadah *Tuv Taam,* takes issue with this, asking why this important detail is omitted from the Haggadah, if according to the *Ohr HaChaim* the verse itself makes reference to it. *Gra,* however, writes that the mitzvos of the Seder are all performed at night (rather than during the day, when most mitzvos are performed), because the night of Pesach had the status of day due to this miracle. [In fact, *Gra* explains that the opening question of the *Mah Nishtanah* — "Why is this night different from all other nights?" — is inquiring as to why the mitzvos of the Seder are performed at night rather than during the day.] In addition, we find that this night is the only night when *Hallel* is recited; and the Midrash relates that the Jews who were not yet circumcised underwent *milah* on that night, although *milah* is usually performed only by day. *Mirkeves HaMishneh* suggests that this was due to the aforementioned miracle, which gave this night the status of day.

MISHNAH OF THE DAY: SHABBOS 17:3

פרשת בא

FRIDAY

PARASHAS BO

The following Mishnah presents another case in which a כְּלִי שֶׁמְּלַאכְתּוֹ לְאִיסּוּר, *a utensil used primarily for work prohibited on the Sabbath,* may be moved לְצֹרֶךְ גּוּפוֹ, *to make use of it,* for any activity permissible on the Sabbath:

קָנֶה שֶׁל זֵיתִים — ***A cane*** that is used ***for*** turning ***olives,***[1] **אִם יֵשׁ קֶשֶׁר בְּרֹאשׁוֹ מְקַבֵּל טוּמְאָה** — ***if there is a knot at its end, it is susceptible to tumah,***[2] **וְאִם לַאו אֵין מְקַבֵּל טוּמְאָה** — ***but if not, it is not susceptible to tumah.***[3] **בֵּין כָּךְ וּבֵין כָּךְ נִיטָּל בַּשַּׁבָּת** — ***In either case, it may be taken on the Sabbath.***[4]

NOTES

1. A cane made for testing harvested olives in their storage vat, to ascertain whether they are ready to be pressed (*Rav; Rashi*). The cane is inserted into the olives and removed. One examines the oil adhering to the end of the cane to determine whether the olives are ready to be pressed or not (*Tiferes Yisrael*).

2. I.e., if the cane has at its tip a natural knot which creates even a slight indentation, it meets the criterion for a non-metallic utensil to be susceptible to *tumah* — e.g., that it must also be a receptacle (*Rav; Rashi*). Since oil can collect on its tip, the cane is treated as a receptacle, and is in consequence susceptible to *tumah* (*Rav; Rambam Commentary*).

3. I.e., if there is no knot or bowl at the end of the cane in which oil can collect, it is not susceptible to *tumah* (*Rav*). Moreover, even if the cane is hollow, without a knot at its end, any oil collected will spill as soon as the cane is turned over. Hence, it is not treated as a receptacle, and therefore is not susceptible to *tumah* (*Rav; Meiri*).

4. Even though it is not considered a utensil with regard to the laws of *tumah,* it is nevertheless considered a utensil with regard to the laws of *muktzeh,* and may be moved on the Sabbath to be used for some permissible activity or if one needs to make use of its place (*Rambam, Hil. Shabbos* 25:7). This is the case even though the cane is used to extract oil from the olives, which is forbidden on the Sabbath, because the cane is *a forbidden-use utensil* (see Mishnahs 7:2 and 22:1). Since the laws of *muktzeh* do not require that a utensil have a receptacle, the cane remains a utensil with respect to the laws of *muktzeh* because it can be used to turn over the olives — regardless of whether it can also hold oil. On the other hand, since the laws of *tumah* do require a utensil to have a receptacle, the cane is deemed a proper utensil in regard to *tumah* only if it is capable of holding oil (*Tos. Yom Tov; Tiferes Yisrael*).

QUESTION OF THE DAY:

If the verse says that we must tell our sons about the Exodus "on that day," why do we do this during the Seder "at night"?

For the answer, see page 166.

GEMS FROM THE GEMARA

◆§ The Categories of Muktzeh — Part 2

(3) מֻקְצֶה מֵחֲמַת גופו — something that is *set aside because of its intrinsic properties* (this type of *muktzeh* is discussed in Mishnah 5). This category includes anything which is neither a utensil nor a food edible to humans or animals. Examples of this classification include stones, money, reeds, wood, earth, sand, a corpse, living animals, figs or raisins that are in the process of being dried, and anything else not fit for use on the Sabbath. [There are cases where objects of this classification can be rendered usable, through being designated and/or prepared for use before the Sabbath. For example, if one designated a large stone and uses it as a seat before the Sabbath, it is no longer considered *muktzeh,* and may be moved on the Sabbath.]

(4) נוֹלָד — literally: *just born* (this type of *muktzeh* is discussed in Mishnah 5). *Nolad* is any otherwise non-*muktzeh* object which has first achieved its presently useful state on this Sabbath. [An example of this category would be snow that fell on the Sabbath.] Since it was not in a usable state prior to the Sabbath, it cannot be said to have been "prepared" for use at the onset of the Sabbath. Consequently, it is *muktzeh.*

As is the case regarding many aspects of the *muktzeh* laws, the scope of the prohibition of *nolad* is subject to a dispute between R' Yehudah and R' Shimon. R' Shimon limits the prohibition of *nolad* to only those items whose present form and function is radically different from their pre-Sabbath one (*Tos.* to *Beitzah* 2a, *Eruvin* 46a). R' Yehudah, however, prohibits even certain items whose *function* has changed on the Sabbath, though their form has not (Gemara 124b). [According to many authorities, the halachah with regard to the laws of the Sabbath follows the opinion of R' Shimon. With regard to Yom Tov, it follows the opinion of R' Yehudah (*Shulchan Aruch* and *Rama, Orach Chaim* 495:4; see *Mishnah Berurah* 495:17).]

We will conclude our listing of the various types of *muktzeh* tomorrow.

A MUSSAR THOUGHT FOR THE DAY

In *A Torah Thought for the Day,* we discussed the great miracle that took place on the Jews' final night in Egypt, when the darkness of light was interrupted by a sudden brightness like that of day. We know that the Exodus included many miracles, and Bnei Yisrael had much for which to thank Hashem (we list each of them separately in the joyful song of *Dayeinu*). What was the purpose of this additional miracle, and what lesson are we supposed to derive from it?

Rav Chaim Volozhin says: It is important to always remember that there is no evil or harm that comes from Hashem. Every punishment for a wicked man is meted out not as Hashem's revenge, but rather for the person's benefit, to cleanse his soul and prepare him for some portion in the World to Come. In the dark bitter days of *galus,* when one says in the morning, "If only it would be evening," and in the evening, "If only it would be morning" (see *Devarim* 28:67), one must proceed without asking questions. As we say every day in *Krias Shema,* ה׳ אֱלֹהֵינוּ ה׳ אֶחָד, *HASHEM is our God, HASHEM is One.* After the ultimate redemption from our *galus* (exile), when it will be clear to all how everything was caused by His loving hand, and how all the pain and suffering of *galus* was meant for our good, it will be proclaimed by all that Hashem is One. Hashem wants us to understand how all our trials and tribulations were for our benefit, and how it was His loving hand that watched over us in every situation.

This was the purpose of the sudden light at the end of the Egyptian *galus.* All of a sudden there was a break in the darkness, a light at the end of the tunnel, so to speak. Everything suddenly became clear to the Jews. They saw with clarity the purpose of the exile. They understood with certainty the necessity for all the hard work and toil, how it had prepared them to become true servants of Hashem. As they ate the *korban pesach* and saw clearly how Hashem passed over their houses, killing only the Egyptian firstborn, this gave them not only an appreciation for the redemption but an understanding of the purpose of the *galus* itself.

We too are in *galus,* and we live through many dark situations, and witness many incidents that we fail to understand. We must look forward to and anticipate the days about which the prophet *Yeshayahu* says (60:1): קוּמִי אוֹרִי כִּי־בָא אוֹרֵךְ וּכְבוֹד ה׳ עָלַיִךְ זָרָח, *Arise! Shine! For your light has arrived and the glory of HASHEM has shined upon you.* May we merit to see that light speedily, in our days.

HALACHAH OF THE DAY

Let us continue with our explanation of the weaving process using a mechanized loom. As we described yesterday, the loom has two frames placed between the two beams carrying the warp threads. Half of the warp threads travel through the heddle eyes of one frame, and the remaining warp threads travel through the heddle eyes of the second frame. By alternately raising first one frame and then the other, the weaver raises all the even warp threads above the odd ones, and then vice versa. When the even threads are raised, a space, called a shed, is created between the raised even threads and the lower odd ones. The weft wrapped around its spool may easily be passed through this space in one quick motion. When the odd threads are then raised, the weft spool may be passed back again. Each time the weft spool traverses the width of the loom, another line of woven cloth is completed.

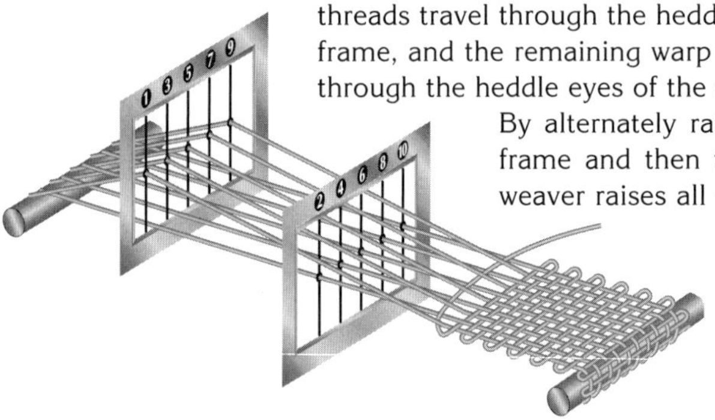

We have now arrived at the the third forbidden *melachah* involved in the weaving process, namely, the actual weaving itself. Passing the weft thread twice through the warp — once in each direction — thereby creating two lines of woven cloth, is a violation of the *melachah* of אוֹרֵג, *weaving.*

One example of a common application of this *melachah* would be attempting to repair an article of clothing which was damaged on Shabbos. Often when a garment gets caught on a sharp item, the result is that a thread gets pulled out of the weave (this is often called a "pull"). This can result in two problems. First, there is a thread sticking out of the garment. Second, the pull creates an unsightly area of fabric bunched together at the site of the pull. In order to effect a quick repair, one is tempted to hold the fabric on the two sides of the gathered area and pull them apart. This can realign the weave and may even cause the pulled thread to be reinserted into the garment. Such a repair may not be performed on Shabbos.

The final *melachah* of the weaving process is the *melachah* of פּוֹצֵעַ,

removing threads. The exact definition of this *melachah* is a matter of dispute among the Rishonim. According to some Rishonim, פּוֹצֵעַ refers to repairs that are made to the fabric during the weaving process. According to others, this *melachah* speaks of the final step in the weaving process — the removal of the end product from the loom.

On a practical level, removing a thread from the weave of a fabric is a violation of the *melachah* of פּוֹצֵעַ. Therefore, one should take great care not to pull threads from any garment or other fabric on Shabbos. Even a loose thread that is dangling from an article of clothing, rag, or other fabric, may not be removed on Shabbos.

A CLOSER LOOK AT THE SIDDUR

The Gemara in *Berachos* (12a) states: Whoever does not say the prayer of אֱמֶת וְיַצִּיב (*True and certain . . .*) during *Shacharis* and the prayer אֱמֶת וֶאֱמוּנָה (*True and faithful . . .*) during *Maariv* has not fulfilled his obligation properly.

These two prayers are recited after *Krias Shema* of *Shacharis* and *Maariv* respectively. Although they begin differently, they both end with the same blessing: בָּרוּךְ אַתָּה ה׳ גָּאַל יִשְׂרָאֵל, *Blessed are You,* HASHEM, *the Redeemer of Israel,* and both are called "the blessing of redemption." Why, then, do they begin differently?

Beis HaLevi cites a Midrash on the verse לֵיל שִׁמֻּרִים הוּא לַה׳, *It is a "night" of keepings for* HASHEM (*Shemos* 12:42). The Midrash states that while the redemption from Egypt took place at night (although, as we discussed at length in *A Torah Thought for the Day* and *A Mussar Thought for the Day,* the night was illuminated by the sun, it was still nighttime), the ultimate redemption will take place during the day. *Beis HaLevi* explains that when a redemption occurs during the night, it is a sign that this is only a temporary relief from *galus.* However, when the redemption takes place by day, it signifies that exile is over forever.

He goes on to say that at midnight in Egypt, when the *galus* came to an end, there was still an outstanding account to be settled. Not all of the 400 years that Avraham's children had to spend in exile had actually passed while they were in Egypt, and this balance was held in abeyance, to be satisfied at some later time, in another *galus.* In essence, then, this redemption was incomplete. [Note that in earlier studies, we cited the

view of other commentators that the decree of 400 years was satisfied fully by counting from the birth of Yitzchak.]

Although we are now in *galus,* we must always remember that Hashem has not forsaken us, and that He will eventually bring the גְאוּלָה שְׁלֵמָה, *complete redemption.* This redemption, which we anticipate every day, will take place during the day.

It is for this reason that our approach to the blessing of redemption changes from the day prayers to the night prayers. By *Shacharis,* which is the prayer of day, we say אֱמֶת וְיַצִּיב, *it is true and certain, established,* etc. We use many expressions of certainty because the redemption of day will be permanent and everlasting. *Maariv,* however, is the prayer of night, which is the symbol of *galus.* The redemption of the night is only temporary, and therefore we say אֱמֶת וֶאֱמוּנָה, for we are *faithful,* since we realize that every redemption serves to strengthen us; and we believe that Hashem will continue to be with us until we merit the final, true redemption.

וְהָיָה לְאוֹת עַל־יָדְכָה וּלְטוֹטָפֹת בֵּין עֵינֶיךָ
כִּי בְּחֹזֶק יָד הוֹצִיאָנוּ ה׳ מִמִּצְרָיִם

And it shall be a sign upon your arm and as tefillin between your eyes, for with a strong hand HASHEM *removed us from Egypt* (*Shemos* 13:16).

Although the Torah does not specifically state how many passages are inserted into the *tefillin,* there is an allusion to this in the verse. The word טוֹטָפֹת is a combination of two words from two different languages — *tat* in the Kaspi language means two, and *pas* in the Afriki language also means two. This gives us the sum total of four passages for *tefillin.* For the *tefillin* that are worn on the head (*tefillin shel rosh*), they are written on four separate pieces of parchment and inserted into four separate compartments (בָּתִּים); for the *tefillin* worn on the arm (*tefillin shel yad*), they are written on a single piece of parchment and inserted into a single compartment. Two of the passages appear at the end of this *parashah* (13:1-10 and vs. 11-16), while the other two passages are written in *Sefer Devarim* — the passage of *Shema* (*Devarim* 6:5-9) and the passage of *Vehayah Im Shamo'a* (ibid. 11:13-21).

What is not clear, however, is what the Bnei Yisrael wore in their *tefillin* for all the forty years that they spent in the Wilderness, for only two of those passages were given to them in Egypt, while the other two were not told to them until the end of the forty years. Did they wear *tefillin* with only two passages? Or did they not wear *tefillin* at all?

Panim Yafos (to *Parashas Ki Savo*) suggests that perhaps they did not wear *tefillin* until the end of the forty years because of the missing two passages that were not given until then. Without all four passages, the mitzvah is incomplete, and one would not be allowed to wear incomplete *tefillin* [as this would violate the prohibition to subtract from the Torah's commandments (known as *bal tigra*)].

The *Mabit,* in his work *Beis Elokim* (*Yesodos* §37), says that to assume that the Bnei Yisrael could not fulfill any mitzvah until the end of the forty years in the Wilderness is hard to comprehend. He suggests that all the mitzvos were given at Mt. Sinai, including the passages of *tefillin;* although they are recorded in the Torah in *Sefer Devarim,* the Jews were in possession of them beforehand. In his view, the Jews were able to wear *tefillin* from the time that the Torah was given.

Rashba in *Menachos* (34a) seems to go even further. He explains that in Egypt, when the Jews were commanded to don *tefillin* (in our verse),

they were given all four passages; the Torah, however, records only two of them at this time.

The *Daas Zekeinim MiBaalei HaTosafos* at the end of *Parashas Shelach* cites a Midrash: Why is the *parashah* of *tzitzis* written in the Torah next to the *parashah* of the *mekosheish eitzim* (the person who gathered wood on the Sabbath, thereby desecrating it)? Because Moshe attempted to find some justification for this lapse, stating that perhaps the sin came about because (since *tefillin* are not worn on Shabbos) they were lacking the "sign" of *tefillin* to safeguard them to keep all the mitzvos. Hashem said in reply, "I will grant you a mitzvah that *is* worn on Shabbos — the mitzvah of *tzitzis.* Thus, there will always be a reminder of Me." It is clear from Moshe's words that Bnei Yisrael wore *tefillin* during the years in the Wilderness.

[Incidentally, the *Daas Zekeinim* in *Parashas Beshalach* (14:29) says that when Moshe asked the water to split right and left at the time of *Krias Yam Suf* (the Splitting of the Reed Sea), he said, "Let the water to the left make way for Bnei Yisrael, who *will* wear *tefillin* on their left hand." From his use of the future tense it would seem that the Jews were not yet wearing *tefillin* at that time. It is possible, of course, that in the few days between the command and the confrontation at the *Yam Suf,* there had been no time to make *tefillin,* or perhaps they did not wear them because it was still during the festival.]

MISHNAH OF THE DAY: SHABBOS 17:4

The following Mishnah continues the consideration of the *muktzeh* status of various utensils:

רַבִּי יוֹסֵי אוֹמֵר — ***R' Yose says:*** **כָּל הַכֵּלִים נִיטָּלִין** — ***All utensils may be taken*** on the Sabbath,[1] **חוּץ מִן הַמַּסָּר הַגָּדוֹל וְיָתֵד שֶׁל מַחֲרֵישָׁה** — ***except for a large saw*** of the type used for sawing beams, ***and*** the large, sharp ***peg of a plow*** that cuts into the ground to make furrows.[2]

NOTES

1. [This statement by R' Yose is reiterated and expanded below. Here it serves to preface the introduction of the new category of *muktzeh* about which we are now to learn.]

2. Since people are careful not to use these implements for anything other than their designated purposes, they set them aside before the Sabbath (when their designated uses are forbidden). They are therefore *muktzeh,* and may not be moved even for a permissible use or for use of their place (*Rav; Rashi*). [This category of *muktzeh* — viz., utensils that are set aside by their owners because of potential monetary loss — is called מוּקְצֶה מֵחֲמַת חֶסְרוֹן כִּיס — *muktzeh on account of monetary loss.* The two items listed here are examples of such utensils.]

כָּל הַכֵּלִים — ***All utensils***[3] נִיטָּלִין לְצוֹרֶךְ — ***may be taken*** either ***out of necessity,***[4] וְשֶׁלֹּא לְצוֹרֶךְ — ***or not out of necessity.***[5] רַבִּי נְחֶמְיָה אוֹמֵר — ***R' Nechemyah says:*** אֵין נִיטָּלִין אֶלָּא לְצוֹרֶךְ — ***They may not be taken except out of necessity.***[6]

NOTES

3. I.e., utensils (such as cups and plates) that are normally used for purposes that are permissible.

4. I.e., such a utensil may be moved when necessary on the Sabbath, either (1) לְצֹרֶךְ גופו, *to make use of it;* or, (2) לְצֹרֶךְ מְקוֹמוֹ, *to make use of its place,* i.e., to remove it from where it is in order to make some other use of that place.

5. Moreover, such utensils may be moved even when they will not be used and their place will not be used; for example, to prevent them from being damaged by the elements or stolen. [This is known as מֵחַמָּה לְצֵל — lit., *from sun to shade.*] Utensils that are normally used for forbidden purposes (*forbidden-use utensils*) may also be moved, but only for a necessity of the Sabbath (i.e., one of the situations described in the previous two Mishnahs). Such utensils may *not* be moved "from sun to shade" (*Rav* from Gemara 124a).

6. I.e., even utensils that are normally used for permissible purposes may be moved only for their designated purpose — viz., a knife may be moved in order to use it for cutting, but not in order to use it to prop up a bowl, etc. (*Rav* from Gemara 146a).

GEMS FROM THE GEMARA

◆§ The Categories of Muktzeh — Part 3

(5) בָּסִיס לְדָבָר הָאָסוּר, *a base to a muktzeh object* (this type of *muktzeh* is discussed in Mishnah 6). This group comprises all otherwise non-*muktzeh* articles upon which an item of *muktzeh* is placed before the Sabbath — e.g., a barrel upon which a stone is lying, or a pillow upon which money is lying. Even after the *muktzeh* has been removed (e.g., by a non-Jew), the base remains *muktzeh* until the end of that Sabbath. This rule applies only to utensils that served as a base to a *muktzeh* object at the onset of the Sabbath — i.e., at twilight.

Other categories of *muktzeh* that are not considered in our chapter include:

(6) מְחֻבָּר וּמְחֻסַּר צֵידָה, something that is *attached* [*to the ground*] *or lacking capture.* Included in this category is any animal that was not trapped [this is relevant primarily to Yom Tov, when animals may be slaughtered and their meat cooked, but when they may not be trapped]; and any growing item, such as a fruit, vegetable, or wood

that had not been reaped as of twilight on the eve of the Sabbath.

(7) מֻקְצֶה לְמִצְוָתוֹ, something that is *set aside because of its mitzvah.* Such items as the wood of a *succah* and its ornaments fall into this classification. As long as the mitzvah for which these materials have been designated is still in effect, they may not be used for any other purpose. [This category of *muktzeh* is different than the preceding ones, in that it is not a function of a time period — viz., the Sabbath or a holiday — and in that it does not prohibit moving the *muktzeh* item, but rather prohibits using it for some other purpose.]

Our Mishnah seems to permit one to freely move utensils that are normally used for permissible purposes. However, there must be some purpose for the movement — such as removing it either from the sun to the shade to prevent it from spoiling, or moving it to a safe place to prevent it from being stolen or broken. One may not move even a permissible utensil for no purpose. Books of Scripture and foods do not fall into this category, and may be moved about even for no purpose whatsoever (*Shulchan Aruch* 308:4).

A MUSSAR THOUGHT FOR THE DAY

One is commanded to wear *tefillin* on top of his head positioned between the eyes, and on his left upper arm, opposite his heart. In the prayer that many recite prior to donning *tefillin,* we state the reason that these specific places were chosen. The idea is that a person must subjugate all his desires, thoughts, senses, and potential to the service of Hashem.

Let us expound on this a bit. The two places that were chosen — the head and the hand — embody the power and ability of man, i.e., his intellect and the ability to carry out his ideas. The intent of this placement of the *tefillin,* then, is to remind a person that Hashem is really the source of any idea or accomplishment.

When the Torah states (*Devarim* 8:18): כִּי הוּא הַנֹּתֵן לְךָ כֹּחַ לַעֲשׂוֹת חָיִל, *for He is the One Who has given you strength to accomplish, Targum Onkelos* translates: Hashem is the One Who gave you the idea to purchase all of your possessions and acquire your wealth. This is the lesson of the head *tefillin* — our intellect is a gift from Hashem. The hand *tefillin* remind us of Hashem's strong hand, and bid us to remember always that His is the only absolute power, and we are but insignificant pawns in

Hashem's world. For this reason, *Rabbeinu Bachya* explains, we place the *tefillin* on the weaker hand, the left one, to emphasize our inability to accomplish without the help of Hashem's hand.

R' Menachem Yurowitz would often say that this is also the reason why the head *tefillin* has four compartments, while the hand *tefillin* has only one. As we explained above, the purpose of the *tefillin* is to remind us that we are, first and foremost, servants of Hashem, and that we must therefore subjugate our thoughts and deeds to Him. Thus, the head, which is the repository of four of the person's five senses (sight, hearing, smell and taste), has four compartments, to remind us that every one of these four senses should be wholly dedicated to Hashem's service. The hand, which controls only the single sense of touch, has a single compartment, reminding us that all our deeds should be intended to further Hashem's Glory in this world.

HALACHAH OF THE DAY

T*ying* a knot is another of the thirty-nine *melachos* forbidden on Shabbos. In the time of the Mishkan, knots were tied to hold down the curtains surrounding the Mishkan courtyard, and to enlarge the nets used to catch the *chilazon,* a sea creature whose blood was used in the production of the blue *techeiles* dye. This dye was necessary for production of the Mishkan's curtains, and for the garments of the Kohanim.

The definition of *tying* with respect to the laws of Shabbos is the act of fastening a pliable material, such as rope, thread, ribbon or soft plastic, with a knot. This includes knotting two strands together; for example: tying several handkerchiefs together to form a rope; knotting two ends of a single strand, as one does with shoelaces; or knotting a single strand onto itself, as when knotting the end of a *tzitzis* string to prevent it from unraveling.

This *melachah* also applies to tying knots in clothing, tying up bags (such as garbage bags) and tying recreational items, such as balloons.

In order to be considered a "knot" in the eyes of halachah, the knot must have the ability to remain in place and not unravel without manipulation. Thus, to tie together two strands of rope using a single knot is not seen as an act of tying; since such a knot has the tendency to loosen and become untied without any pressure, it cannot be considered a viable knot. On the other hand, a double knot is halachically considered to be a knot, as is a single knot in the center of a single strand of rope.

Another activity that is halachically similar to tying a knot is twisting thin strings together to form a thicker string or rope. Since the strands are held firmly together, twisting them is considered similar to tying. [In our discussion of the *melachah* of *spinning,* we mentioned that the twisting of existing strings to create a thick rope is an act of *spinning.* Whether such twisting is classified as *spinning* or *tying* is the subject of a dispute among the Rishonim.]

The Talmud states that knots fall into three categories — those that are Biblically prohibited, those that are Rabbinically prohibited, and those that are permitted. There is a major dispute as to what criteria define each of these categories.

According to one view, a knot is forbidden under Biblical law only if its creation is a מַעֲשֵׂה אוּמָן, the *work of a professional,* and the knot is a קֶשֶׁר שֶׁל קַיָּימָא, a *permanent knot.* If it meets only one of these conditions, it is forbidden only by Rabbinic decree. If none of these criteria are met, it is permitted to make this type of knot on Shabbos.

According to another view, the deciding factor is the duration for which the knot was meant to remain tied. A truly permanent knot (i.e., one meant to last indefinitely) is Biblically prohibited. A knot that is somewhat permanent (i.e., meant to remain knotted for more than a day, but not indefinitely) is forbidden by Rabbinic decree. A temporary knot (i.e., one meant to be untied within twenty-four hours) is permitted.

A CLOSER LOOK AT THE SIDDUR

Let us continue our study of the central blessing of the Friday night *Shemoneh Esrei.*

After concluding the list of requests that we have previously discussed, we say: וְהַנְחִילֵנוּ ה׳ אֱלֹהֵינוּ בְּאַהֲבָה וּבְרָצוֹן שַׁבַּת קָדְשֶׁךָ, *And grant us as an inheritance,* H*ASHEM*, *our God, with love and with favor, Your Holy Sabbath.* There are two points that must be clarified here. First, why is it necessary that the Sabbath be given to us as *an inheritance*? Second, why do we ask that this be done specifically *with love and favor*? (These words do not appear on festivals, when we ask Hashem to do this *with joy and rejoicing.*)

Shiras David explains that it is not a simple matter to rest properly on the Sabbath. As we have discussed previously, the *complete rest* that is the desired accomplishment of the Sabbath involves spiritual growth

and a close connection to Hashem that will sustain us throughout the coming week. For this to be accomplished, we require Divine assistance. It is not enough for us to *experience* the Sabbath, we must *internalize* it — we must make it into part of ourselves. This is the meaning of making the Sabbath an inheritance.

Abudraham explains that the *love* mentioned in this prayer refers to the special love that Hashem showed us when He gave the Jews the mitzvah of the Sabbath in Marah, even before the rest of the mitzvos of the Torah were given (see *Shemos* 15:25 with *Rashi*); and the *favor* refers to the fact that Hashem allows us to bring sacrifices to Him even on the Sabbath, so that He will continue to regard us with favor. [This does not explain why the word *favor* is not said on festivals, as the sacrifices that override the Sabbath may be offered on festivals as well. Others, however, note that the Sabbath is unique in that it alone among the holy days does not call for a special sin-offering of a goat; rather, we are asked only to offer two sheep as *olos,* which are not sin-offerings. This, too, shows that Hashem regards the Jews with special favor on the Sabbath. For yet another explanation, see *Torah Temimah* (to *Shemos* ibid.).]

QUESTION OF THE DAY:

What do we learn from the fact that the word יָדְכָה, your hand, is spelled in this unusual way, instead of the more common יָדְךָ?

For the answer, see page 166.

ANSWERS TO QUESTIONS OF THE DAY

Sunday:

This was done in order to enable the Jews to search out the valuables of the Egyptians (see *Rashi* to 10:22) without fear of being caught (*Gur Aryeh*).

Monday:

We learn that one must work the dough constantly while shaping it, thus guarding it from becoming *chametz* (*Rashi*); we also learn that the matzah we eat on Pesach night must have been baked for the sake of the mitzvah (see *Pesachim* 38a-b).

Tuesday:

Ohr HaChaim suggests that since the Torah had not yet been given and the Jews were not accustomed to obeying such commands, Moshe told the elders to visit each family separately and tell them of the mitzvah, so they would accept it more readily.

Wednesday:

The Torah tells us that Pharaoh ran out, calling for Moshe and Aharon. *Ohr HaChaim* (to 12:31) states that Moshe explained to Pharaoh that he could not come out to speak to him because of Hashem's command.

Thursday:

The mitzvah does not forbid the non-Jew from eating; it forbids the Jew from supplying the meat to the non-Jew (*Rambam, Hil. Korban Pesach* Ch. 9).

Friday:

This question is found in the *Hagaddah Shel Pesach.* So is the answer — the words בַּעֲבוּר זֶה, *because of this,* found in the answer of the father, refer to the *korban pesach* and the matzah *and maror.* Thus, the answer must be given when these items are before him, which is at night.

Shabbos:

We learn that *tefillin* are placed on the weaker arm (יָדְכָה is expounded to be read יַד כֵּהָה, *the weaker hand*).

פרשת בשלח

Parashas Beshalach

A TORAH THOUGHT FOR THE DAY

וַיֹּאמֶר מֹשֶׁה אֶל־הָעָם אַל־תִּירָאוּ הִתְיַצְּבוּ
וּרְאוּ אֶת־יְשׁוּעַת ה׳ אֲשֶׁר־יַעֲשֶׂה לָכֶם הַיּוֹם
כִּי אֲשֶׁר רְאִיתֶם אֶת־מִצְרַיִם הַיּוֹם לֹא תֹסִפוּ לִרְאֹתָם
עוֹד עַד־עוֹלָם. ה׳ יִלָּחֵם לָכֶם וְאַתֶּם תַּחֲרִשׁוּן.
וַיֹּאמֶר ה׳ אֶל־מֹשֶׁה מַה־תִּצְעַק
אֵלָי דַּבֵּר אֶל־בְּנֵי־יִשְׂרָאֵל וְיִסָּעוּ

And Moshe said to the people, "Do not fear! Stand fast and see the salvation of HASHEM that He will perform for you today; for as you have seen Egypt today, you shall not see them ever again. HASHEM will do battle on your behalf, and you shall remain silent." HASHEM said to Moshe, "Why do you cry out to Me? Speak to the Children of Israel and let them journey forth!" (*Shemos* 14:13-15).

The *Mechilta* (and *Targum Yonasan* as well) explains that there were four separate groups of Jews, each one with its own unique opinion as to how to deal with the imminent danger that they were facing. One group said, "Let us jump into the water and die that way, rather than fall into the hands of the wicked Egyptians." Another, braver group said, "Let us confront the Egyptians, and do battle with them!" A third group suggested, "Let us surrender to the Egyptians, and return to be servants in Egypt." The last group offered no coherent plan of action, but attempted to disorient the Egyptians, making all types of noises and screaming wildly at them. They thought this would cause the Egyptians to become confused and retreat.

The Midrash explains that Moshe had a specific message from Hashem for each of these groups. To the first group that was ready to surrender, he said, "Stand fast, and you will see the salvation of Hashem." The group that wanted to return to Egypt received the message, "for as you have seen Egypt today, you shall not see them again." To the group that wanted to do battle with the Egyptians, Moshe said, "Hashem will do battle on your behalf." And finally, to the group that was making a chaotic scene to chase the Egyptians away, the message was clear, "You shall remain silent!"

According to this Midrash, all four groups were inaccurate in their assessment and their planned reaction to the situation. Even the group that wished to jump into the sea wanted to do so out of hopelessness — they were told to wait until they would see the salvation of Hashem, Who would split the sea to save them. We will see in tomorrow's *Torah Thought for the Day,* however, that according to the *Gra* there was a group that followed Nachshon ben Aminadav to jump into the sea as a sacrifice for the sake of Hashem's Name, and it was in this merit that the sea actually split.

MISHNAH OF THE DAY: SHABBOS 17:5

The following Mishnah considers the *muktzeh* status of broken utensils on the Sabbath:

כָּל הַכֵּלִים הַנִּיטָּלִין בְּשַׁבָּת — ***All utensils that may be taken on the Sabbath,*** **שִׁבְרֵיהֶן נִיטָּלִין עִמָּהֶן** — ***their fragments may*** also ***be taken with them,***[1] **וּבִלְבַד שֶׁיְּהוּ עוֹשִׂין מֵעֵין מְלָאכָה** — ***provided they can*** still be used to ***perform some sort of task.***[2] **שִׁבְרֵי עֲרֵיבָה לְכַסּוֹת בָּהֶן אֶת פִּי הֶחָבִית** — For example, ***fragments of a mixing bowl*** may be taken if they are fit ***to cover the mouth of a cask with them,*** **שִׁבְרֵי זְכוּכִית לְכַסּוֹת בָּהֶן אֶת פִּי הַפַּךְ** — and ***fragments of a glass*** may be taken if they are fit ***to cover the mouth of a flask with them.***[3] **רַבִּי יְהוּדָה אוֹמֵר** — ***R' Yehudah says:*** **בִּלְבַד שֶׁיְּהוּ עוֹשִׂין מֵעֵין מְלַאכְתָּן** — Fragments may be taken ***only if they can*** still be used to ***perform a semblance of their***

NOTES

1. I.e., if any of these utensils broke, their fragments may be moved about on the Sabbath, whether they broke on or before the Sabbath (*Tiferes Yisrael* from Gemara 124b). [Although the word עִמָּהֶן, *with them,* implies that the fragments may be moved only together with the remaining original utensils, in fact, fragments that meet our Mishnah's criterion may be moved by themselves. Indeed, in some editions the word עִמָּהֶן is omitted (see above, Mishnah 1 — neither of the reasons cited there for including the word in that Mishnah apply here). *Meleches Shlomo* approves of the word's omission here.]

2. I.e., any sort of task, even one that is unrelated to the original function of the utensil (*Rav; Rashi* from Gemara ibid.). Since these fragments are still functional, they do not lose their previous designation as utensils. Consequently, they are not *muktzeh* (*Ritva*). [Fragments of utensils that are no longer useful fit into the category of מוּקְצֶה מֵחֲמַת גופו, *inherently muktzeh.* Such fragments are like sticks and stones, and may not be moved for any purpose (*Mishnah Berurah* 308:28).]

3. [In Mishnaic times, it was common to use pieces of broken utensils as covers for casks and jugs. A shard fit for such use was therefore considered functional.] Fragments of a wooden mixing bowl must be large enough to cover a cask in order to retain their non-*muktzeh* classification, because smaller pieces are generally used as firewood (*Ran*).

former ***task.***[4] שִׁבְרֵי עֲרֵיבָה לָצוּק לְתוֹכָן מִקְפָּה — For example, ***fragments of a mixing bowl*** may be taken if they are fit ***to pour porridge into them,*** וְשֶׁל זְכוּכִית לָצוּק לְתוֹכָן שֶׁמֶן — ***and*** fragments ***of a glass*** may be taken if they are fit ***to pour oil into them.***

NOTES

4. The dispute between the Tanna Kamma and R' Yehudah only concerns utensils that broke *on* the Sabbath. R' Yehudah maintains that the continued designation of the broken shards and pieces as utensils can be based only on their continued use as something for which the original utensil was used. Otherwise, they must be regarded as newly made utensils, which are *muktzeh* under the categorization of נוֹלָד, *newly made* [lit., *born*] on the Sabbath. On the other hand, the Tanna Kamma maintains that as long as the fragments are fit for any use at all, they may be considered as remnants of the original utensil. Even R' Yehudah agrees, however, that if the utensils broke *before* the Sabbath, they may be moved as long as they serve some purpose. Since they were designated for their new function before the Sabbath, they are not *nolad* (*Rav* from Gemara ibid.).

GEMS FROM THE GEMARA

Our Mishnah considers whether shards are *muktzeh* (and therefore forbidden to be handled) on the Sabbath. The Gemara (124b) cites a related discussion, in which Rav Nachman says in the name of Shmuel: A small earthenware shard may be moved about inside a courtyard, but it may not be handled in a *karmelis.* [As we have learned, a *karmelis* is an area that resembles a public domain in certain respects and a private domain in others. With respect to a *karmelis,* it is Rabbinically prohibited: (a) to transfer items from or into it, from either a private or a public domain; and (b) to carry something four *amos* within the *karmelis* itself.] Shmuel is of the opinion that a shard is not useful in a *karmelis,* and therefore it is not considered a utensil there.

Rav Nachman then states his own opinion, that one may handle a shard even in a *karmelis,* but it may not be moved in a public domain (for there, one will certainly have no use for it). Rava, however, goes even further, and maintains that one may move the shard even in a public domain. [Rava holds that since the shard is considered a utensil when it is found inside a courtyard, it retains this classification even when found in a location where it is not useful (*Rashi*).]

The Gemara notes that Rava followed his own reasoning, for Rava was once walking on the avenue of Riska (a public domain in the city of Mechoza), and his shoes became soiled with mud. His servant came

along, took a shard that had been lying in the public domain, and began to wipe the mud off Rava's shoes. [If the mud is wet, this can be done permissibly, as we have learned in our studies in *Halachah of the Day.*] The Rabbis who had been accompanying Rava shouted at the servant to stop, but Rava remarked, "Not only did these Rabbis not learn what is permitted and what is forbidden, they even teach others their erroneous views! If the shard were in a courtyard, would it not be fit to be used to cover a utensil? Here too, in the public domain, it is fit for me to use to scrape mud off my shoes." [Although it is rarely needed for this purpose in the public domain and would not qualify as a utensil on its basis, it is nevertheless treated as a utensil due to its status as a utensil inside a courtyard (*Rashi*).]

A MUSSAR THOUGHT FOR THE DAY

We discussed in *A Torah Thought for the Day* how the four very different opinions of four groups of Jews were each addressed by Hashem through Moshe. Each group had its own outlook concerning how best to tackle the imminent danger of the approaching Egyptians. There is an important lesson to be learned here: The Torah has the proper formula for every individual problem, although no two people are the same and no two problems are identical.

The Mishnah says in the beginning of the sixth chapter of *Avos* that if someone studies Torah with the proper intention, he will enjoy the sound counsel and advice that the Torah has to offer. This has been proven by countless Torah sages in all generations, who were able to offer advice on the most complex and involved issues, without having any formal background or education in those various esoteric areas of knowledge. It was only through their understanding of the Torah that they were elevated to see and understand what most people would not be able to comprehend.

However, the ability to use the Torah to illuminate one's path is not limited to the scholar. While there are some branches of secular knowledge that are incomprehensible to all but a learned few, the Torah is written for every Jew, and has a message for every individual mind-set and character. This is alluded to in the tradition that the Torah contains 600,000 letters, representing the number of Jewish adult males who left Egypt and received the Torah. Thus, the Torah has a letter for every Jew, as it were. Everyone can find and derive proper guidance with regard to his life decisions, big and small, from the Torah. Those who study Torah for its own sake (לִשְׁמָהּ) merit the clarity to be able to divine from the Torah what is right and wrong, and how to proceed in even the most complicated situation. And those who do not attain this level can seek Torah guidance from Torah sages, who can interpret any situation through the lens of the Torah.

[Incidentally, the *Nefesh HaChaim* writes that when the original light — created during the six days of Creation, which gave Adam the ability to see from one end of the world to the other — was concealed and put away for the days of Mashiach, it was hidden within the Torah. This gives the Torah the ability to enlighten murky and confusing situations.]

HALACHAH OF THE DAY

As we mentioned yesterday, there are two differing opinions as to what criteria determine whether knots are the type that one is Biblically prohibited to tie (and untie) on Shabbos, or the type that are prohibited only by Rabbinic decree. According to one view, only knots that are both *professional* and *permanent* are Biblically prohibited, while the other view maintains that the only significant criterion is the duration for which the knot is tied.

A practical difference between these two opinions would be as follows: May one tie a professional knot on Shabbos with the intent to untie it within twenty-four hours? According to the first opinion, since the knot is professional but not permanent, it is not Biblically prohibited, and would be forbidden only by Rabbinic decree. According to the opposing view, however, since this is only a temporary knot, it may be tied on Shabbos. A second difference between these two opinions would be the tying of a non-professional knot that is intended to remain in place for more than twenty-four hours, but not indefinitely. According to the first opinion, since this knot is both not professional and not truly permanent, it may be tied on Shabbos. According to the second opinion, since this knot is a somewhat permanent knot (as it is intended to last more than twenty-four hours) it is forbidden by Rabbinic decree.

The *Rama* states that there is no final decision concerning this dispute, and therefore, we must adhere to the stringencies that emerge from each view. Thus, it is forbidden to tie any permanent knot, whether it is professional or not. It is also prohibited to tie any professional knot, whether or not it is permanent. Also, tying any knot with the intent to leave it in place for more than twenty-four hours is prohibited.

At this point, it is necessary for us to define the two above-mentioned criteria — *professional* and *permanent.*

In the course of describing knots that may not be tied on Shabbos, the Talmud cites as examples knots that were commonly tied by various types of tradesmen engaged in their trades. However, since it is unclear to us precisely how these knots mentioned by the Sages were tied, it is difficult for us to comprehend the Sages' criteria for determining which knots reach the threshold of being considered professional knots. As a result of this ambiguity, the *poskim* rule that any tight double knot must be viewed as a professional knot with regard to the restrictions of this *melachah.* Similarly, a single knot tied securely in a single strand of rope should also be considered a professional knot. However, a single knot, even when combined with a bow, that is tied with two strands of rope, or with the two ends of one strand — as is the case with shoelaces — is considered to be only an ordinary, non-professional knot.

A CLOSER LOOK AT THE SIDDUR

We discussed the four groups at the *Yam Suf,* and the fact that each of them failed in responding correctly to the danger. However, *Rashi* tells us what was really the intent of this last and final encounter with Pharaoh. On the verse (14:10): וְהִנֵּה מִצְרַיִם נֹסֵעַ אַחֲרֵיהֶם וַיִּירְאוּ מְאֹד וַיִּצְעֲקוּ בְנֵי־יִשְׂרָאֵל אֶל־ה׳, *... and behold, Egypt was journeying after them, and they were very frightened; the Children of Israel called out to HASHEM, Rashi* comments: They adopted the craft of their forefathers — that is, prayer. When faced with mortal danger, Jews from time immemorial have always turned to Hashem in prayer.

The Midrash goes even further, stating that when the Torah says in the beginning of that same verse, וּפַרְעֹה הִקְרִיב, *And Pharaoh brought himself close,* it should have said instead, *and Pharaoh drew [them] close,* for in truth, by his pursuit of the Jews, Pharaoh brought them close to their Father in Heaven.

This Midrash gives us a new insight into the purpose of pain and suffering. Praying to Hashem to remove the pain is not the only objective. Rather, Hashem will sometimes send us pain so that we will call out

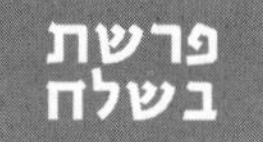

to Him and feel close to Him. In a similar vein, we find that the Matriarchs were barren, although the Divine plan called for all of them to bear children. And why was this? Because Hashem desires the prayers of the righteous (see *Yevamos* 64b).

Hashem calls out to Bnei Yisrael in *Shir HaShirim* (2:14): הַרְאִינִי אֶת־מַרְאַיִךְ, *Show Me your prayerful gaze,* which means: Show Me to whom you turn when you are in trouble; let Me hear your supplicating voice in prayer. According to one opinion in the Midrash, this is referring to the time when Bnei Yisrael were standing at the *Yam Suf* and the Egyptians were chasing them.

Thus, in truth Pharaoh served as a vehicle to bring us closer to Hashem. This explains the continuation of the Midrash: Pharaoh's chase achieved greater results than hundreds of prayers and fast days. As mentioned, the goal of prayer is to create within us a feeling of total dependence on Hashem; this was most definitely accomplished through Pharaoh's pursuit.

QUESTION OF THE DAY:

Why did Moshe stress that the Egyptians would never be seen again by the Jews as they appeared now?

For the answer, see page 220.

A TORAH THOUGHT FOR THE DAY

פרשת בשלח

MONDAY

PARASHAS BESHALACH

וַיָּשָׁב הַיָּם לִפְנוֹת בֹּקֶר לְאֵיתָנוֹ וּמִצְרַיִם נָסִים לִקְרָאתוֹ

And toward morning the water went back to its power as the Egyptians were fleeing toward it (*Shemos* 14:27).

The *Midrash Rabbah* rearranges the letters of the word לְאֵיתָנוֹ to read לתנאוי, meaning *to its original condition.* This refers to a condition that was made on the third day of Creation. When Hashem commanded the waters of the world to separate themselves from the land, he informed the waters of the *Yam Suf* that the time would come when they would be obligated to split in order for the Jews to pass through them. Thus, the sea was fulfilling an old command when it split for the Jews.

If so, that the splitting of the sea was all arranged in advance, why does the Midrash tell us that the angel placed in charge of the *Yam Suf* did not wish to allow it to split (the Midrash states that it refused to listen to Moshe, claiming seniority based on the fact that man had been created on the sixth day of Creation, later than the sea), until Hashem supported Moshe's claim? If a previous condition was already in place, why did the sea not split immediately?

Furthermore, asks the *Ohr HaChaim,* we find many instances in the Talmud where the great Sages had the power to perform miracles, such as splitting the waters of rivers. [One such example is the miracle wrought by R' Pinchas ben Yair, as related in *Chullin* 7a.] Why, then, was it not possible for Moshe to cause the waters of the *Yam Suf* to split without preconditions and arguments with angels?

Ohr HaChaim explains that this "condition" was not based on a special agreement made between Hashem and the water specifically regarding this point in history. Rather, it was part of a broader agreement that Hashem had made with the entire universe at the time of Creation: the entire world would be dominated by, and subservient to, the power of Torah and its scholars. Only with this precondition was the world created. That is why the Gemara tells us many times that צַדִּיק גּוֹזֵר וְהַקָּדוֹשׁ בָּרוּךְ הוּא מְקַיֵּים, *a righteous one decrees, and Hashem fulfills [his request].*

This condition would be in effect, however, only after the Torah was given, as in the case of R' Pinchas ben Yair (indeed, the water actually *feared* Rav Pinchas ben Yair, as the Gemara in *Chullin* states). Since the splitting of the *Yam Suf* occurred prior to the Giving of the Torah, the water did not feel compelled to obey Moshe's command until, as the Midrash relates, Hashem "stood on his right side." This is a reference to the power of Torah, which was given with Hashem's right hand, as the verse states in *Devarim* (33:2): מִימִינוֹ אֵשׁ דָּת לָמוֹ, *From His right hand, He presented a fire of law to them.* When the sea saw that Hashem would award the Torah to Moshe, it yielded and split.

MISHNAH OF THE DAY: SHABBOS 17:6

The following Mishnah considers *muktzeh* objects that are paired with non-*muktzeh* objects and are used in tandem with them:

הָאֶבֶן שֶׁבַּקֵּירוּיָה — ***A stone that is in a gourd-shell,***[1] אִם מְמַלְּאִין בָּהּ וְאֵינָהּ נוֹפֶלֶת — ***if*** water ***can be drawn with it*** [the gourd-shell] ***without it*** [the stone] ***falling out,***[2] מְמַלְּאִין בָּהּ — ***we may draw*** water ***with it*** on the Sabbath;[3] וְאִם לַאו אֵין מְמַלְּאִין בָּהּ — ***but if not, we may not draw*** *water* ***with it.***[4] זְמוֹרָה שֶׁהִיא קְשׁוּרָה בְּטְפִיחַ — ***A vine that is tied to a pitcher,***[5] מְמַלְּאִין בָּהּ בְּשַׁבָּת — ***we may draw*** water ***with it on the Sabbath.***[6]

NOTES

1. Dry gourd-shells, or dry pumpkin-shells, were used as buckets to draw water. Since a shell is light, it will not sink into the water (and is thus useless as a bucket) unless a stone is placed in it to weigh it down (*Rav; Rashi*).

2. If the gourd-shell can be used to draw water without the stone falling out, then the stone is obviously attached to the gourd-shell securely (*Rav; Rashi*).

3. I.e., we need not refrain from using the gourd-shell because of the attached stone (which, by itself, is *muktzeh*). Since the stone is securely attached to the gourd-shell, it is treated as a part of the gourd-shell. The stone therefore shares the gourd-shell's status as a utensil, and it is permissible to move the gourd-shell (*Rav; Rashi*).

4. I.e., if the stone is not fastened securely enough to the gourd-shell to prevent it from falling out when submerged, it is forbidden to draw water with this gourd-shell. Since the stone is not considered part of the gourd-shell, it remains *muktzeh,* as are all other stones. The gourd-shell, therefore, may also not be moved, since it serves as a בָּסִיס לְדָבָר הָאָסוּר, *a base for a prohibited object* — the stone (*Rav; Rashi*).

5. A branch from a grapevine was tied to a pitcher, to facilitate its being lowered into a well or cistern to draw water (*Rav; Rashi*).

6. As in the Mishnah's first case, by tying the branch to the pitcher, one has made it part of the utensil (*Rav; Rashi*).

GEMS FROM THE GEMARA

The Gemara (125b) cites a dispute: Rabbah in the name of R' Ami in the name of R' Yochanan holds that if one wishes to use a stone as the cover for a cask on the Sabbath, a significant act of preparation is required before the Sabbath to render the stone into a utensil and thus remove its *muktzeh* status (such as shaping or smoothing the stone, or making it into part of a utensil). Rav Yosef in the name of R' Assi in the name of R' Yochanan holds, however, that no significant act of preparation is required; merely *placing* the stone on the cask suffices.

The Gemara then cites another instance of this dispute, in which R' Ami and R' Assi each follow their own reasoning as found in our case. When Rav Dimi came to Babylonia, he said in the name of R' Chanina, and others say that Rav Zeira said it in the name of R' Chanina: Rebbi (R' Yehuda HaNasi) once went to a certain place before the Sabbath, and found a row of stones that had been prepared for building (and were therefore *muktzeh*). He said to his students: "Go out and have intent that those stones be designated as utensils, so that we may sit on them tomorrow during the lecture" — and Rebbi did not require them to perform any act of preparation.

On the other hand, R' Yochanan maintained that Rebbi *did* indeed require them to perform an act. And what was it? R' Ami said that Rebbi told the *talmidim* to perform the act of positioning the stones properly, so it would not be necessary to move them on the Sabbath. [R' Ami holds that a minimal act of preparation is insufficient to turn a stone into a utensil. Since it was not possible for the students to do a significant preparatory act to the stones, Rebbi told them to position the stones properly so that the students would be able to sit upon them the next day without needing to move them (*Rashi*). Even *muktzeh* items may be touched if they are not moved.]

On the other hand, R' Assi said that Rebbi told them: Go out and wipe the stones clean, so that we will be *allowed* to move them on the Sabbath. Thus, R' Assi holds that even a minimal act such as wiping a stone clean is sufficient to give it the classification of a utensil, whereas R' Ami holds that such a minor act is insufficient. Thus, each sage follows the same reasoning that he offered in the case of a stone that was placed on top of a cask as a cover.

A MUSSAR THOUGHT FOR THE DAY

We mentioned in *A Torah Thought for the Day* that when Hashem created the universe, He programmed into its very fabric that it must always be subservient to the power of Torah. The concept of nature being subservient to Torah is so basic that it can even have an impact upon halachic decisions. The *Yerushalmi* (*Nedarim* 23b) states that certain laws pertain to a girl only when she reaches the age of 3 years and one day. Apparently these laws do not apply to a girl younger than 3 because of biological and developmental considerations. Thus, once the girl is 36 months old, the laws should apply. But what happens if her birthday is slated to be in Nissan, and the Sages find reason to add a month to the year, making it a leap year? In such a case, even those laws that may be biologically related to being 3 years old do not go into effect until her birthday, although, in actuality, more than 36 months will have passed since she was born. Thus, we see that the pronouncement of a leap year by the Sages has the power to delay even the physical effects of age upon the girl. Why is this so? Because the very power of nature is subservient to the law of the Torah.

This idea is alluded to in a verse in *Tehillim* (57:3): אֶקְרָא לֵאלֹהִים עֶלְיוֹן לָאֵל גֹּמֵר עָלָי, *I will call upon God, Most High, to the God Who fulfills for me.* This refers to the Torah scholar, who can dictate and make changes even in matters that are affected by nature.

Nefesh HaChaim expounds on this idea, and connects it to the phrase אִיסְתַּכֵּל בְּאוֹרַיְיתָא וּבָרָא עָלְמָא, *[Hashem] looked into the Torah and created the world.* This means that the Torah was the basic blueprint for the world, for the world was created for the purpose of allowing man to fulfill the precepts of the Torah. *Rav Elchanan Wasserman* once said in illustration of this principle: "It is not because we have parents that the Torah commands us to honor them. Rather, because there is a mitzvah in the Torah to honor our parents, Hashem created the system of parents and children."

Since the Torah is the master plan for the world, we can easily understand why the Sages and Torah scholars have the ability to affect the entire universe with their words and actions.

The *Chofetz Chaim* explains that this is why the Torah is referred to as *Toras Chaim,* a Torah of life. Since the Torah was the blueprint for all of Creation, it emerges that the Torah is really the source of all life, and everything that is connected to life.

HALACHAH OF THE DAY

The second criterion which we must now define is that of permanence. A knot is seen as being truly permanent if it is tied with the intent that it will be left undisturbed and in place indefinitely. [This does not mean that there is no *possibility* that the knot will be untied at a later date; it merely means that the knot is tied with the *intent* that it remain tied.] It is important to understand that this "intent" is not determined by the one tying the knot, but rather by the practice of most individuals who tie this sort of knot. To illustrate this point, let us take the following example. If one ties a set of *tzitzis* strings to a *tallis* with the intent to remove them the next day, is this considered a permanent knot? While it is true that the intent of this individual was to create only a temporary knot, the common practice is to tie *tzitzis* strings to a *tallis* and leave them there indefinitely. This sort of tying is therefore viewed by halachah as being permanent.

The prohibition against tying a permanent knot applies even if the benefit derived from the knot is only short-lived. For example, if one ties a knot in a garbage bag, the knot serves him only from the time that he ties it until the time of garbage collection. Nevertheless, since the knot is one that usually will remain tied permanently, it is considered to be a permanent one.

It is forbidden by Rabbinic decree to tie any knot with intent to leave it intact longer than twenty-four hours. In contrast to our explanation above of the truly permanent knot, this rule *is* dependent upon the intent of the person tying the knot. This Rabbinic prohibition applies only when the individual tying the knot either has specific intent for the knot to remain in place for more than twenty-four hours, or when it is his practice to *always* leave that particular item tied for longer than twenty-four hours. For example, if one is in the habit of tying his shoes and then leaving them tied for several days, so that he typically slips his feet in and out of them while they are tied, tying his shoes would be considered tying a knot intended for more than twenty-four hours and would be forbidden Rabbinically on Shabbos.

One may tie a knot without specific intent if he sometimes does untie that particular type of knot within twenty-four hours. For example, a person who on occasion keeps his shoes tied for longer than twenty-four hours, and sometimes unties his shoes within twenty-four hours of tying them, may tie his shoes with a single knot and bow with no specific intent as to the duration of the knot.

A CLOSER LOOK AT THE SIDDUR

In *Hallel,* we recite the verse (*Tehillim* 114:3): הַיָּם רָאָה וַיָּנֹס הַיַּרְדֵּן יִסֹּב לְאָחוֹר, *The sea saw and fled, the Jordan turned backward.*

The verse thus tells us that the sea (that is, the *Yam Suf,* Sea of Reeds), "fled," and split, allowing the Jews to pass through. The Jordan River, too, split when Yehoshua led the Bnei Yisrael into Eretz Yisrael (see *Yehoshua* 4:19).

The question arises: Why, concerning the *Yam Suf,* does the prayer use the language of "fleeing," implying that the sea wished to remain, but it fled in fear, while in the case of the Jordan, the verse simply states that the Jordan turned back, allowing the Bnei Yisrael to pass without incident, without "fleeing"?

This question, in turn, leads us to a bigger question: Why do we dedicate so much attention to commemorate the miracle of the splitting of the *Yam Suf* (indeed, the entire Torah reading of the seventh day of Pesach commemorates this miracle, and we also mention the song of the *Yam Suf* [the *shirah* of *Az Yashir*] every day during *Shacharis),* while the miracle of splitting the Jordan is hardly mentioned, and few even know on which day it occurred?

In fact, it is remarkable that we find the Sages almost going out of their way *not* to establish a memorial for the miracle of the splitting of the Jordan. It is stated in *Shulchan Aruch* (*Orach Chaim* §430) that the Shabbos before Pesach is called *Shabbos HaGadol* because of the miracle that occurred in Egypt while preparing the Pesach sacrifice, four days before Pesach. [During the year that the Jews left Egypt, the 10th day of Nissan fell on Shabbos.] The *Taz* asks: Why, then, is the appellation of *Gadol* not fixed upon the tenth of Nissan of every year, whether it is Shabbos or not? He answers in the name of *Rav Moshe Charif*: Since the 10th day of Nissan was the day when the Jordan was split, people might think that the reason behind this special day was the miracle of the splitting of the Jordan. To avoid confusion, the Sages established the Shabbos before Pesach as *Shabbos HaGadol,* as it is obvious that the Jews did not go through the Jordan on Shabbos. This *Taz* seemingly makes the question even stronger: What is so bad about remembering the miracle of the splitting of the Jordan?

A solution can be offered according to the *Ohr HaChaim* that we mentioned in *A Torah Thought for the Day.* A miracle that changes nature, that occurs after the Giving of the Torah, is not such a novelty, as the universe is just fulfilling its original condition to be subservient to

פרשת בשלח

MONDAY

PARASHAS BESHALACH

the will of the Torah. *Krias Yam Suf,* however, happened prior to receiving the Torah, and was therefore a greater miracle. Thus, it was deserving of greater commemoration. Also, *Krias Yam Suf* required that the sea be "chased away," as it were [הַיָּם רָאָה וַיָּנֹס]. The Jordan, however, just turned back [הַיַּרְדֵּן יִסֹּב לְאָחוֹר], for it could be expected to do so — since the Bnei Yisrael, following the *Aron Hashem,* which contained the Torah, were fulfilling the will of Hashem by entering Eretz Yisrael. In this situation, it was only natural that the sea would turn aside and allow them to pass.

QUESTION OF THE DAY:

Where else do we find that Hashem made a stipulation at the time of Creation?

For the answer, see page 220.

פרשת בשלח

TUESDAY

PARASHAS BESHALACH

A TORAH THOUGHT FOR THE DAY

וּבְנֵי יִשְׂרָאֵל הָלְכוּ בַיַּבָּשָׁה בְּתוֹךְ הַיָּם
וְהַמַּיִם לָהֶם חֹמָה מִימִינָם וּמִשְּׂמֹאלָם

The Children of Israel went on dry land in the midst of the sea; the water was a wall for them, on their right and on their left (*Shemos* 14:29).

The *Mechilta* to this verse states that the Jews deserved to drown in the *Yam Suf,* as it says: *they went on dry land in the midst of the sea.* At first glance, this *Mechilta* is difficult to understand. Where in this verse did the *Mechilta* see such a strong condemnation of the Jews?

The *Gra* raises another question. The Midrash says that the word חֹמָה, *wall,* is written without a 'ו' in this verse, and can be read as חֵמָה, *anger.* This means that there was anger even at the Jews. The Midrash relates that the guardian angel of Egypt complained that the Jews, too, were sinners and should also die. *Gra* asks: A bit earlier in the passage, we find a similar verse (v. 22), which states as follows: וַיָּבֹאוּ בְנֵי־יִשְׂרָאֵל בְּתוֹךְ הַיָּם בַּיַּבָּשָׁה וְהַמַּיִם לָהֶם חוֹמָה מִימִינָם וּמִשְּׂמֹאלָם, *The Children of Israel came into the sea on dry land; and the water was a wall for them on their right and on their left.* The word חוֹמָה in this verse is spelled with a 'ו', and thus cannot be read as חֵמָה, *anger.* What sin took place between verses 22 and 29 that caused this anger? Furthermore, verse 22 states that they *came into the sea on dry land,* whereas in our verse the order is reversed: *they went on dry land in the midst of the sea.* What is the reason for this discrepancy?

Gra explains that there were actually two disparate groups of Jews at the sea [see yesterday's *Torah Thought for the Day,* where we learned that according to *Targum Yonasan,* there were four groups]. There was the group headed by Nachshon, the son of Aminadav, who were ready to sacrifice their lives and jump into the sea in order to sanctify Hashem's Name. According to the *Alshich,* it was because of this group that the Jews merited to be saved, for their willingness to sacrifice themselves served to counteract the complaint of the angel of Egypt.

This group was the one that went into the sea, and when they were up to their necks in the water, the water split, and they were able to walk through dry land. It is this first group that is being discussed in verse 22; they are the ones who *came into the sea on dry land,* because they were already *in* the sea when it split. Of course, this verse spells out the word חוֹמָה with a 'ו', as there was no reason for Hashem to be angry at them.

The other group, however, who were not ready to sacrifice themselves, waited until the sea had turned into dry land, and only then did they go *on dry land [which was located] in the midst of the sea.* Regarding them, the expression of anger is hinted at in the word חֵמָה, for their worthiness was indeed called into question by the angel of Egypt; it was only the merit of Nachshon's group that saved them.

MISHNAH OF THE DAY: SHABBOS 17:7

In the following Mishnah, the issue is not *muktzeh,* but rather the Rabbinic prohibition to perform activities that appear to be in violation of the Biblically forbidden *melachah* of *building* (see *Rashba; Ritva*): פְּקַק הַחַלּוֹן — Regarding ***a window shutter,***[1] רַבִּי אֱלִיעֶזֶר אוֹמֵר — ***R' Eliezer says:*** בִּזְמַן שֶׁהוּא קָשׁוּר וְתָלוּי — ***When it is tied*** to the building by a rope, ***and*** the rope is so short that the shutter is ***suspended*** in midair and does not reach the ground, פּוֹקְקִין בּוֹ — ***we may shutter*** the window ***with it*** on the Sabbath;[2] וְאִם לָאו — ***but if*** the shutter is ***not*** suspended in this manner, אֵין פּוֹקְקִין בּוֹ — ***we may not shutter*** the window ***with it.***[3] וַחֲכָמִים אוֹמְרִים — ***But the Sages say:*** בֵּין כָּךְ וּבֵין כָּךְ פּוֹקְקִין בּוֹ — ***In either case, we may shutter*** the window ***with it.***[4]

NOTES

1. I.e., a board, curtain, or anything else used to close a window (*Rav*).

2. Since it is attached to the window and never rests on the ground, it is regarded as part of the building. Therefore, when one covers the window with the shutter, he cannot be regarded as adding in any way to the building.

3. Since it rests on the ground, when one picks it up to shut the window, he appears to be adding to the structure, in violation of the *melachah* of בּוֹנֶה, *building* (*Rav; Rashi*). Since it appears as if he is building, this act is prohibited by Rabbinic decree. However, when the shutter is suspended, it is clearly evident that the shutter is already a part of the structure, and putting it in the window is merely a matter of returning it to its former position (*Ritva*).

4. The Sages hold that by placing the shutter in the window temporarily — even if it is not tied to the building at all — one does not appear to be performing the forbidden labor of *building,* and therefore this is not prohibited, even by Rabbinic decree (Gemara 126a).

QUESTION OF THE DAY:

Why does the Torah repeat that the Jews crossed over dry land "after" it states that the Egyptians drowned?

For the answer, see page 220.

GEMS FROM THE GEMARA

The dispute in our Mishnah is clarified in the Gemara (125b). Rabbah bar bar Chanah said in the name of R' Yochanan: Both R' Eliezer and the Sages agree that we may not erect a temporary structure on Yom Tov, and it goes without saying that this is forbidden on the Sabbath. Hence, we may not spread a mat over a frame or over a walled enclosure for shade. By spreading the mat where there was previously no roof, one is making a structure (viz., a roof). Although this roof is a temporary one, all agree that its construction is prohibited.

[However, the prohibition against erecting a temporary structure pertains only to making a *roof*. It is permitted to create a temporary *wall* — for example, by spreading a curtain to afford privacy. The construction of a wall is prohibited only if it is of a permanent nature (*Rashi;* cf. *Tosafos*).]

The Gemara continues, explaining that R' Eliezer and the Sages disagree only as to whether one is permitted to make a temporary *addition* to an existing structure. [For example, if a folded mat was partially covering an enclosure, is one permitted to unfold the mat on the Sabbath or Yom Tov and cover the remaining open space (*Rashi*)?] R' Eliezer says that we may not make even a temporary addition to a building on Yom Tov — and, it goes without saying, on the Sabbath — while the Sages say that we may make a temporary addition to a building even on the Sabbath — and, it goes without saying, on Yom Tov.

[Thus, R' Eliezer forbids unfolding a mat that had been covering part of an area, whereas the Sages permit it. In essence, R' Eliezer holds that it is forbidden Rabbinically to make a temporary *addition* wherever it is prohibited Biblically to make the entire structure. The Sages, however, do not forbid a temporary addition. This very dispute finds expression in our Mishnah, which deals with shuttering a window that is in a permanent wall. Since it would be prohibited to build the wall, R' Eliezer forbids even adding a shutter to it temporarily. He therefore states that one may close a window only with a shutter that is suspended from the wall by a short rope, so that it was previously defined as part of the structure. The Sages, on the other hand, permit shuttering the window in all cases, since this merely constitutes a temporary addition to the structure (*Rashi*).]

A MUSSAR THOUGHT FOR THE DAY

We discussed in *A Torah Thought for the Day* how it was the merit of Nachshon ben Aminadav and his followers, who jumped into the sea with self-sacrifice, that caused the water to split and thereby save all the Jews.

The Gemara in *Sotah* (37a) discusses this very point, based on the verses in *Tehillim* (which we recite as part of *Hallel*) that refer to the time when the Jews were standing at the sea (114:2-3): הָיְתָה יְהוּדָה לְקָדְשׁוֹ יִשְׂרָאֵל מַמְשְׁלוֹתָיו. הַיָּם רָאָה וַיָּנֹס ... *Judah became His sanctuary, Israel His dominions. The sea saw and fled . . .* The Gemara explains that the tribe of Yehudah was singled out to be the family of royalty because they sanctified Hashem's Name at the sea, led by their prince Nachshon ben Aminadav, who was the first to jump into the threatening waters. This whole incident caused the sea to flee.

The Midrash elaborates on this verse, asking: What did the water see that made it flee? There are many answers given in the Midrash. The most well-known is that the sea saw the coffin of Yosef, and this caused it to flee. The Midrash elaborates: When the wife of Potiphar tried to entice Yosef into sinning with her, *he fled and went outside* (*Bereishis* 39:12). Thus, "the sea fled for someone who had fled."

The *Kometz HaMinchah* asks: Isn't it obvious from the verse in *Tehillim* that the water fled because of Yehudah and Nachshon who sanctified Hashem's Name, as mentioned earlier?

It would seem that these two reasons are really one and the same. Nachshon and the tribe of Yehudah jumped into the water with great self-sacrifice, going against a person's instinctive nature, which is to protect one's life at all costs. Yosef in Egypt, too, was all alone without anyone to help him withstand the temptation of sin that was at his doorstep. One can overcome such a test only with supernatural power. *Nefesh HaChaim* states that this power is possessed only by the Jews, and in this they are superior even to the angels.

For the water of the *Yam Suf* to change its nature from flowing freely to suddenly drying up and allowing a nation to pass through, it needed to see a demonstration of this trait, of going against one's nature. It found this in a nation that had a *Shevet Yehudah,* people who sanctified Hashem's Name with self-sacrifice, and in the coffin bearing Yosef, who sanctified Hashem's Name by fighting against his evil inclination and overcoming it.

HALACHAH OF THE DAY

There is an exception to the above-mentioned rule that one is permitted to tie a non-professional knot that will remain in place for less than twenty-four hours. The Sages prohibited the tying of a knot — even where there was specific intent to untie it within twenty-four hours — if one sometimes is in the habit of leaving such a knot tied *permanently.* The reason for this prohibition is as follows: If one were permitted to tie such a knot, he may tie it with the original intent of untying it shortly, and then subsequently change his mind and decide to leave the knot tied permanently. It would then emerge that the tying of this knot was the tying of a truly permanent knot on Shabbos, which is Biblically forbidden! In order to avoid this possibility of a violation of Biblical law on Shabbos, the Sages prohibited the tying of such a knot in all events.

It is important to point out that this prohibition is limited to a knot that one sometimes leaves *permanently.* One may tie a knot to last less than twenty-for hours even if he is *sometimes* in the habit of leaving it for longer than twenty-four hours — but not indefinitely. In this case the Sages felt no need for a decree, because even if the fellow tying the knot changes his mind and leaves the knot for longer than twenty-four hours, he would be in violation of only a Rabbinic decree — not a Biblical law. In general, the Sages do not issue Rabbinic decrees to safeguard against the violation of other Rabbinic decrees (this rule is known as אֵין גּוֹזְרִין גְּזֵירָה לִגְזֵירָה, *we do not issue a decree [as a safeguard] for a decree*).

To summarize what we have learned so far:

One may not tie any of the following types of knots on Shabbos: (1) a tight double knot, regardless of its intended duration; (2) any secure single knot in a single strand of rope, regardless of its intended duration; (3) any sort of secure knot (one that will not simply open by itself) if it will be left intact for more than one day; (4) any knot that people sometimes leave in place permanently.

One *may* tie a non-professional knot (e.g., a single knot-bow combination) for less than twenty-four hours, as long as it is not a type that is at times left permanently.

A CLOSER LOOK AT THE SIDDUR

In the blessing that precedes the *Shemoneh Esrei* of the daily *Shacharis* prayer, we recite: וְיַם סוּף בָּקַעְתָּ, וְזֵדִים טִבַּעְתָּ, וִידִידִים הֶעֱבַרְתָּ . . . וְנָתְנוּ יְדִידִים זְמִרוֹת שִׁירוֹת וְתִשְׁבָּחוֹת . . ., *You split the Sea of Reeds for them, the sinners You drowned, Your dear ones You brought across . . . the dear ones offered hymns, songs, and praises . . .*

In this prayer, we find a new title that was given to the Jewish nation at the time of the Splitting of the Sea — יְדִידִים, *dear ones* or *friends.* What is the meaning of this title, and why did the Jews receive it specifically at this point in time?

Before answering, let us note that the same title is bestowed upon the Jews in the poem *Yom LeYabashah,* customarily recited at a circumcision feast. The final stanza of the poem reads as follows: יְדִידִים רוֹמְמוּךָ, בְּשִׁירָה קִדְּמוּךָ . . . , *The dear ones exalt You, with song they come to greet You,* which also speaks of the day of the Splitting of the Sea, when "the depths turned dry." Again the Jews are given this title of *dear ones* with respect to the time of *Krias Yam Suf.* Additionally, we may ask: Why do we speak of the Splitting of the Sea at a *bris*?

As we explained in *A Mussar Thought for the Day,* the Jews merited to have the sea split before them because of their self-sacrifice and their demonstrating that there was nothing that would hold them back from sanctifying God's Name, even their own lives. This is true יְדִידוּת, *friendship.* The *Maharal* explains: The word יְדִיד is made up of two repetitions of the word יָד, which means *a hand.* Thus, it symbolizes a firm handshake, a symbol of friendship that is fixed in place. The self-sacrifice that the Jews displayed at the *Yam Suf* earned them the title of יְדִידִים, *dear friends* of Hashem.

In one of the blessings recited at a circumcision, we say: אֲשֶׁר קִדֵּשׁ יְדִיד מִבֶּטֶן, *Who sanctified the dear one from the womb.* Who is the *dear one* being referred to here? *Tosafos* to *Menachos* 53a explain that it refers to Yitzchak, who was the first to be born after the commandment of *bris milah,* and the first to have the sign of Hashem's holy covenant sealed upon his flesh at the age of eight days by his father.

This act of holiness performed by a father to his newborn child is also an act of יְדִידוּת, true self-sacrifice for the sake of Hashem. Thus, it is the same characteristic that was portrayed by the Jews at the Sea. This is why we refer to *Krias Yam Suf* at a *bris.* At the *bris,* the newborn — on his level — becomes a יְדִידוּת ה', *a dear friend* to Hashem, because of the act of sacrifice that was performed on him.

A TORAH THOUGHT FOR THE DAY

וַיֹּאמֶר ה׳ אֶל־מֹשֶׁה הִנְנִי מַמְטִיר לָכֶם לֶחֶם מִן־הַשָּׁמָיִם וְיָצָא הָעָם וְלָקְטוּ דְּבַר־יוֹם בְּיוֹמוֹ לְמַעַן אֲנַסֶּנּוּ הֲיֵלֵךְ בְּתוֹרָתִי אִם־לֹא

HASHEM said to Moshe, "Behold — I will rain down for you food from heaven; let the people come out and pick each day's portion on its day, so that I can test them, whether they will follow My teaching or not" (Shemos 16:4).

How did the manna test the Jews, and prove whether or not they would follow the teachings of Hashem? *Rashi* explains that the verse is referring to the two laws that were stated with respect to the manna: the prohibition to save any of it for the next day, and the prohibition to go out to gather it on the Sabbath.

Kli Yakar adds to *Rashi's* comments, noting that the verse states that Hashem was posing a test to see if the Jews would follow תּוֹרָתִי, which can be translated *My Torah.* That is, the test of whether they would follow the two laws that were stated with regard to the manna would shed light on the greater question of whether the Jews would observe all of the Torah. For by not hoarding manna for another day, and not looking for manna when Hashem stated that it would not be there, the Jews would demonstrate their total faith in Hashem.

Since the manna fell daily, the Jewish people literally went to sleep every night during the forty-year period in the Wilderness without the food to feed their families the next morning (this will be discussed further in tomorrow's *Mussar Thought for the Day*). The purpose of this daily test, explain many commentaries (see *Rashbam, Ibn Ezra,* et al.), was to encourage heartfelt prayer and total trust in Hashem.

It is immeasurably difficult to restrain man's natural instinct of survival that would prompt a person do whatever he could to gather as much manna as possible, or save some of what he had for later. A person who followed Hashem's instructions and suppressed this natural inclination demonstrated his understanding that although man may do all that he can to prosper, it is only Hashem Who grants sustenance. The message of the mitzvos given with the manna was that it is pointless to ignore His instructions. Dasan and Aviram indeed tried to collect manna on the Sabbath (see *Shemos* 16:20), only to see it rot. This outlook, concludes *Kli Yakar,* is not limited only to the collecting of manna, but must be applied to how a person balances the often seemingly conflicting obligations of what he must do to earn a living, and the set times for Torah study and other services of Hashem that must be part of his life.

Thus, the issue of whether the Jews would heed the laws governing the gathering of the manna indeed was a test that would show whether they would be able to fulfill the dictates of the Torah.

Ksav Sofer notes a different teaching in the fact that the manna fell every day — it provided the Jews with a gift, a constant feeling of joy and gratitude. A person who receives a large sum of money one time a year to sustain himself will certainly be elated on the day that this gift is given to him, and, in seemingly limitless thanks to his beneficiary, will be moved to do whatever he can to please this person. However, as time goes by, although he still knows that this money was a gift given to him by someone who loves him, the joy will wear off. Since the Jews received the manna on a daily basis, however, receiving this present was always fresh and exciting, evoking in the people a constant state of elation over the care that Hashem took in providing for them every day (indeed, Moshe instituted that *Bircas HaMazon* [Grace After Meals] be recited after the manna was eaten — see *A Taste of Lomdus*). This, in turn, would cause their gratitude to Hashem to be much more heartfelt, and would result in greater devotion to Him and observance of the Torah. This, then, is the sense of the verse; the Jews would pick the manna every day, and the test was whether their correspondingly increased gratitude would spur them to greater heights in *avodas Hashem.*

MISHNAH OF THE DAY: SHABBOS 17:8

The following Mishnah deals with removing and replacing the covers of vessels or utensils that are built into the ground:

כָּל כִּיסּוּי הַכֵּלִים שֶׁיֵּשׁ לָהֶם בֵּית אֲחִיזָה — ***All vessel-covers that have handles***[1] **נִיטָּלִין בְּשַׁבָּת** — ***may be taken on the Sabbath.***[2] **אָמַר רַבִּי יוֹסֵי** — ***R' Yose said:*** **בַּמֶּה דְבָרִים אֲמוּרִים** — ***Regarding what*** type of covers ***was this stated?*** **בְּכִיסּוּי קַרְקָעוֹת** — ***Regarding covers of*** simple holes

NOTES

1. The Gemara (126b) explains that this Mishnah and its rulings refer *only* to vessels and utensils which have been cemented or otherwise connected to the ground.

2. Since its handle makes it evident that it is a lid and not a seal, any cover possessing a handle may be used and moved on the Sabbath. If the lids do not have handles with which to remove and replace them, they appear to be seals that become embedded in the ground, and picking them up and replacing them resembles *building* and *demolishing* respectively (*Rashi; Meiri*).

in *the ground.*[3] אֲבָל בְּכִיסּוּי הַכֵּלִים — *But regarding covers of vessels,*[4] בֵּין כָּךְ וּבֵין כָּךְ נִיטָּלִין בְּשַׁבָּת — *in either case,* i.e., whether they have handles or not, *they may be taken on the Sabbath.*[5]

NOTES

3. I.e., when do we say that unless they have handles the covers may not be moved? Only in cases of coverings over holes in the ground such as wells and cisterns — not in cases of covers of vessels or utensils built into the ground (*Rav* from Gemara 126b).

4. I.e., even lids of utensils that are cemented to the ground (*Rav* from Gemara ibid.).

5. Whether or not they are equipped with handles, they are treated as lids, not as parts of the structure they cover, and therefore they may be moved on the Sabbath (*Rav* from Gemara ibid.).

GEMS FROM THE GEMARA

Some authorities rule that the halachah is in accordance with the Tanna Kamma of our Mishnah, who rules that even the covers of utensils connected to the ground must have handles to be moved (*Rav; Rambam Commentary; Rif*).

This decision is difficult, however, for it is seemingly contradicted by the Gemara (125a) that rules in accordance with the statement of R' Eliezer ben Yaakov that it is permitted to move an oven lid on the Sabbath. Since the ovens of that time were cemented to the ground (see *Rashi* to 126b, who cites ovens as an example of utensils cemented to the ground), and since the lids of the ovens discussed did not have handles (*Rashi* to 125a), it would seem that the opinions of R' Eliezer ben Yaakov and R' Yose are identical. Thus, by ruling that oven lids may be moved, the Gemara is, in effect, ruling in accordance with R' Yose, too. *Rosh,* therefore, rules that the halachah is, indeed, in accordance with R' Yose, who permits removing the lids of utensils connected to the ground even if they are not equipped with handles.

In defense of the view of *Rav* and *Rambam, Ran* explains (see also *Maggid Mishneh, Hil. Shabbos* 25:13) that our Mishnah and R' Eliezer ben Yaakov are speaking of two different cases. In the Mishnah, when it speaks of utensils connected to the ground, it is referring only to utensils that are *completely buried* in the ground. Since these utensils are almost identical in appearance to cisterns, it is prohibited to move their covers according to the Tanna Kamma. In this, the halachah follows the Tanna Kamma. R' Eliezer ben Yaakov, however, refers to ovens that are completely above-ground. Since these are not so readily confused with cisterns, despite their being connected to the ground, even the Tanna Kamma agrees that their lids need not have handles for them to be moved on the Sabbath. Thus, it is possible to side with the Tanna Kamma with regard to the case of the Mishnah, and still rule in accordance with R' Eliezer ben Yaakov.

A MUSSAR THOUGHT FOR THE DAY

We explained in *A Torah Thought for the Day* that since a human being quickly loses the excitement he feels when something is new to him, Hashem sent the manna every day, so that the Jews would always live with the joy of receiving a gift. Moreover, since the strong feeling of gratitude to the beneficiary that is found only while one is in this state of joy would always be present, the Jews would be able to use this feeling to better thank and serve Hashem. We, who are not blessed with daily inspiration of open miracles, often find it much more difficult to garner the necessary enthusiasm to properly serve Hashem.

R' Shlomo Wolbe, in his *Maamarei Yemei HaRatzon* (p. 23), observes that since an inherent part of man is his need for constant newness, a person who sees nothing that naturally inspires him to serve Hashem will quickly grow uninterested in what he is doing, and turn elsewhere to bring excitement and challenge into his life. What can we do to maintain our inspiration when performing mitzvos, and not spend our lives merely "serving" Hashem by rote and deriving our true satisfaction from other endeavors?

R' Wolbe answers this question by quoting the Gemara in *Chagigah* (27a) that observes that even Jewish sinners are "filled with mitzvos like a pomegranate is filled with seeds." Even Jews who are regrettably far from the proper level of observance nevertheless perform many mitzvos. If this is true, asks R' Wolbe, and the lives of both of a Jewish sinner and a righteous person are in fact filled with mitzvos, what is the difference between these two people?

The answer must be, he concludes, that the difference is not in the amount of mitzvos that they perform, but in the quality of their mitzvos. The mitzvos of a Jewish sinner, while numerous, are those that are easy for the person to perform. Every person has his or her own areas of strength, and will naturally perform the mitzvos appropriate to this area. For example, a naturally generous person will find it easy to distribute *tzedakah,* and one who is inherently compassionate will gravitate toward helping others with their problems. While it is true that some reward is given for *every* mitzvah performed, true service of Hashem is achieved when a person does something that he would rather *not* do, and, ignoring his innate inclination, does so because Hashem commanded that this action be carried out. In short, the only way for a person to grow and change himself into a righteous person is by performing mitzvos that are a challenge to him.

Performing mitzvos that are difficult for us, continues R' Wolbe, also has another benefit; since carrying out such a mitzvah — which one in truth would rather not do — is foreign to this person, successfully doing so gives him a fresh sense of accomplishment. Thus, a person looking for fulfillment in his service of Hashem should, one small step at a time, undertake commitments to fulfill mitzvos that are difficult for him to perform. For some people, this means refraining from *lashon hara* for one hour every day; for others, spending 15 minutes on uninterrupted Torah study. When a person, instead of doing mitzvos by rote, pushes himself to perform those mitzvos that are difficult for him, he will find constant freshness and a sense of accomplishment in his daily service of Hashem.

HALACHAH OF THE DAY

Up to this point, we have focused our discussion on knots — professional or non-professional, permanent or temporary. We will now turn our attention to various other methods of tying that are permitted. Some of these methods are permitted because they do not involve the use of knots at all, and may therefore be employed even to fasten something permanently. Others involve the use of non-professional knots, and may therefore be employed for temporary fastening only.

A single knot created with two strands of string, such as the first knot commonly tied when tying shoelaces, is not halachically deemed a knot at all, since such a knot tends to become undone by itself under the slightest pressure. For this reason, it is permissible to tie this type of knot on Shabbos, even if the knot is drawn tightly. This remains true even if one has intent to leave the knot tied indefinitely.

A bow that is tied without an underlying knot also does not have the status of a knot, because such a bow will also open under even slight pressure. One may therefore tie a bow even if he draws it tight with intention to leave it intact indefinitely. Furthermore, one may make one bow on top of another bow and leave them tied permanently. Since a bow will open with the pull of one end of its string, even a double bow is not considered to be a knot.

A slipknot is not considered a knot. Once again, since a slipknot will come apart with the tug of one end of its string, halachah does not consider it to be a knot.

While a single knot alone or a single bow alone are not considered knots individually, a single knot with a bow tied *on top of it* is considered to be a knot. Since the bow holds the underlying knot in place, it will not open completely with one pull. However, the halachah does not view such a tie as a professional knot. Therefore, one may tie such a knot for temporary (less than twenty-four hour) use.

Although we have said that a single knot is not halachically considered to be a knot, if one ties a single knot and then wraps the ends of the string beneath itself, it does receive the status of a knot. This is because a knot tied in this manner will not open without manipulation. It is, however, only a non-professional knot; thus it may be used for temporary purposes.

One may wrap a string around an item and tuck the ends under the string itself so that it stays in place. Since no knot is being employed at all, this may be done even with the intent to leave it there permanently.

A double knot that is *tied loosely* is considered to be a non-professional knot, and thus may be tied for less than twenty-four hours. For example, one may tie the belt of his coat — obviously, he will be untying it within twenty-four hours — with a *loose* double knot on Shabbos.

A CLOSER LOOK AT THE SIDDUR

We explained in *A Torah Thought for the Day* that one of the reasons the manna fell daily was so the Jews would appreciate the fact that Hashem was providing for them on a daily basis. *Ksav Sofer* points out that we ask Hashem for this ongoing satisfaction in a *tefillah* recited on Shabbos morning: שַׂבְּעֵנוּ בַבֹּקֶר חַסְדֶּךָ וּנְרַנְּנָה וְנִשְׂמְחָה בְּכָל־יָמֵינוּ, *Satisfy us in the morning with Your kindness, then we shall sing out and rejoice throughout our days* (*Tehillim* 90:14). *Metzudas David,* in his comments to *Tehillim,* explains that the request *satisfy us* ***in the morning*** *with Your kindness* refers to each and every morning. It is only when we feel Hashem's kindness on a daily basis, concludes *Ksav Sofer,* that *we shall sing out and rejoice throughout our days.*

The Alter of Slabodka, in his *Ohr HaTzafun* (vol. 3, p. 84), explains that Hashem created the world because of His great desire to perform *chesed* with man; and it is His wish that, as much as is possible, man should *enjoy* everything that he does over the course of his days and his life, rather than just go through the motions without enjoying what he is doing. This is because besides the gifts of food, clothing and life itself — to name a few — the gift of happiness is also a form of *chesed* from Hashem. This happiness is possible, though, only when a person consciously appreciates what Hashem is giving him. And the more a person appreciates what Hashem has given him, the happier he will be.

The daily miracle of the manna made it easier for the Jewish people living in the Wilderness — who constantly sensed Hashem's kindness to them — to be happy. However, we too can feel a constant joy in every one of Hashem's kindnesses every single day of our lives. In order to help us attain this level of realization, the Sages instituted *birchos hashachar,* the morning blessings. Imagine the elation, remarks the Alter, that parents feel as they watch their child take his first steps. Several months later, when the child begins to speak, they are once again overjoyed at this wondrous accomplishment. A few short years later, the parents look on with delight as the child goes to school, learns to read and write, and slowly begins to become his own person. Indeed, parents react with unconcealed joy at every new stage in life that their child reaches. Why, asks the Alter, does the feeling of happiness at a new accomplishment subside after the child has been doing this action for a few days or weeks? If the parents are so happy that the child is able to walk, why do they not smile with delight every time he walks across the room as an older child or teenager? After all, the child is doing the same thing that brought them so much joy many years ago; what has changed?

The answer to this question, of course, is that although the parents are certainly happy that their 15-year-old child is able to walk, they have gotten used to his being able to do so. Although a visit to a hospital will make us realize that an adult who can walk is in truth no smaller miracle than a baby taking his first steps, we, used to the "natural world," forget that in truth, each and every step is a great kindness of Hashem. Since the parents have thankfully seen their child walk for years, they, like most people, no longer feel the great joy that they should when seeing every step, hearing every word that is spoken, or appreciating any of the countless acts of kindness that Hashem allows man on a daily basis.

Recognizing these kindnesses, explains the Alter, is the purpose of the *berachos* that we say to begin the *Shacharis* prayers. Instead of taking the gift of being able to walk for granted, we thank Hashem as הַמֵּכִין מִצְעֲדֵי גָבֶר, *hameichin mitzadei gaver,* "He Who firms the footsteps of man," and, appreciating the simple ability to see, we praise Him for being פּוֹקֵחַ עִוְרִים, *pokei'ach ivrim,* "He Who opens the eyes of the blind." Saying and thinking about these *berachos* help us recognize Hashem's great kindnesses on a daily basis.

A TASTE OF LOMDUS

The Gemara in *Berachos* (51b) rules that *Bircas HaMazon* [Grace After Meals] may be recited after eating as long as the person still feels full from his meal. *Chazon Ish* (*Orach Chaim* 28:4) asks: If it is true that satiation is needed in order to recite *Bircas HaMazon,* how can the Gemara (*Berachos* 48b) tell us that Moshe instituted that the Bnei Yisrael recite *Bircas HaMazon* after eating the manna? The Gemara states in *Yoma* (75b) that the manna was called *lechem abirim,* angelic food, because it was not digested by the body; the person eating it enjoyed the taste, and his body miraculously received nourishment without his stomach actually becoming full and needing to break down the food and excrete wastes. Thus, the manna did not "satiate" in the literal, gastronomical sense. How, then, were the Jewish people able to recite *Bircas HaMazon* to thank Hashem for their satiation?

Chazon Ish proves, on the basis of this question, that the logic behind the permission for one to recite *Bircas HaMazon* only within the time that he still feels full is not based on a person thanking Hashem for his state of being satiated. Rather, the requirement that the person must still feel full in order to recite *Bircas HaMazon* is based on another rule in the laws of *berachos* — the need to avoid *hefsek* (interruption) between reciting a blessing and the action to which the blessing is connected. Since *berachos* are always made for a purpose, such as eating or performing a mitzvah, the *berachah* can be recited only while this need is actually taking place. It is for this reason that a *berachah* should always be recited immediately prior to beginning an action.

This being so, the laws of *hefsek* should ostensibly dictate that *Bircas HaMazon,* which is said to thank Hashem after a meal, should be recited immediately upon completing a meal (just as a person, after being called to the Torah, makes the second *berachah* as soon as the Torah reading is finished). However, this is not the case, for, as we said above,

a person may recite *Bircas HaMazon* as long as he is still full from the meal, even if some time has elapsed. The reason why there is no problem of *hefsek* with this wait, explains *Chazon Ish,* is because as long as a person is still satiated from the food that he ate, he is still considered involved with his meal, and his *berachah* is still deemed to be connected with the food that he has eaten.

This is also true in regard to the manna, *Chazon Ish* concludes. Even though the manna did not physically satiate the Bnei Yisrael, they enjoyed this food like they did any other, and as such, were commanded by Moshe to thank Hashem for this pleasure.

The commentaries discuss many practical ramifications of this explanation. *R' Akiva Eiger (Gilyon Shulchan Aruch, Orach Chaim* 186:1) analyzes the case of a child who eats a meal just before reaching maturity, and is still full once he assumes adult status. Must he recite *Bircas HaMazon*? If the purpose of *Bircas HaMazon* is to thank Hashem for being satiated, then this young person, who is still feeling full as an adult, must recite *Bircas HaMazon.* If, however, the need to be full only serves to continue the person's connection to his meal, this meal, eaten while the person was still a minor, cannot prompt an adult-level obligation to recite *Bircas HaMazon.*

QUESTION OF THE DAY:

How did the manna distinguish between the righteous and the wicked?

For the answer, see page 220.

A TORAH THOUGHT FOR THE DAY

וַיִּקְרְאוּ בֵית־יִשְׂרָאֵל אֶת־שְׁמוֹ מָן וְהוּא
כְּזֶרַע גַּד לָבָן וְטַעְמוֹ כְּצַפִּיחִת בִּדְבָשׁ

*And the House of Israel called it manna;
and it was like coriander seed, white, and it tasted
like a wafer fried in honey* (*Shemos* 16:31).

There is a major discussion in the commentaries as to which blessing was recited on the manna. Generally, on foods that are called לֶחֶם, *bread,* we recite הַמּוֹצִיא לֶחֶם מִן הָאָרֶץ, *Who brings out bread from the ground.* However, this "bread" descended from Heaven, so would it be proper to alter the words of the blessing and say: הַמּוֹצִיא לֶחֶם מִן הַשָּׁמַיִם, *who brings out bread from Heaven*? Or perhaps on such heavenly bread no blessing should be recited at all?

[As far as *Bircas HaMazon,* which is recited after eating, it is clear that they did recite the regular Grace After Meals. In fact, the Gemara states (see yesterday's *A Taste of Lomdus*) that Moshe Rabbeinu composed *Bircas HaMazon* for the Jews to recite after eating the manna.]

Rav Yehudah HaChassid and *Rama Mipano* claim that the Jews recited the blessing "*Who brings out bread from Heaven*" before eating the manna. The same will be true, they say, at the סְעוּדַת לִוְיָתָן, the festive meal that will be served when Mashiach arrives. The Midrash states that manna will be taken out from storage (see verse 33, where it is stated that manna was stored away) and served; and at that time, too, they will recite this blessing.

The *Bircas Aharon* to *Berachos* (51b) explains the rationale behind the opinion that no blessing was recited upon the manna. As the Talmud states elsewhere (ibid. 35a), we know that there is an obligation to recite a blessing prior to eating because it is forbidden to enjoy anything from this world without a blessing, and doing so constitutes stealing. Now, it can be inferred from the wording of this Gemara that this obligation applies only to things that come *from this world.* The manna, however, came from *Olam Haba,* the World to Come, as *Maharsha* states; it therefore did not require a blessing.

Bircas Aharon uses this idea to explain another verse in our passage. The Torah states (16:15): וַיִּרְאוּ בְנֵי־יִשְׂרָאֵל וַיֹּאמְרוּ אִישׁ אֶל־אָחִיו מָן הוּא כִּי לֹא יָדְעוּ מַה־הוּא וַיֹּאמֶר מֹשֶׁה אֲלֵהֶם הוּא הַלֶּחֶם אֲשֶׁר נָתַן ה׳ לָכֶם לְאָכְלָה, *And the Children of Israel saw it and said to one another, "It is manna!" — for they did not know what it was. Moshe said to them, "This is the food that* HASHEM *has given you to eat."* He explains that the Children of Israel saw

the manna and did not know what blessing to recite over it. Thus, they said, מָן הוּא, which literally translates as, *What is it?* That is, how should we classify it with respect to *berachos?* Moshe answered them, *This is the food that HASHEM has given you to eat,* meaning, the manna is not from this world and is therefore exempt from a blessing.

Mirkeves HaMishneh writes that since the manna tasted like whatever the eater wanted, it did not have a set blessing. Rather, the person recited the blessing appropriate to the food he wished to be tasting. [Possibly, this dispute would hinge on the Talmudic debate as to whether the manna assumed the taste *and* texture wished by the taster (in which case the *berachah* would indeed change to the *berachah* of the food wished for) or only its taste (in which case the *berachah* would not change).]

MISHNAH OF THE DAY: SHABBOS 18:1

The Rabbis prohibited certain activities on the Sabbath because they involve excessive exertion. However, they relaxed this prohibition (subject to certain conditions) where the exertion is needed for the performance of a mitzvah, the care of animals or the care of the ill (*Meiri*). These exemptions are discussed in the Mishnahs of this chapter:

מְפַנִּין— *We may clear away* on the Sabbath,[1] **אֲפִילוּ אַרְבַּע וְחָמֵשׁ — *even four or five***[2] **קוּפּוֹת שֶׁל תֶּבֶן וְשֶׁל תְּבוּאָה — *boxes of straw or of grain,***[3]

NOTES

1. I.e., if their place is needed, the objects mentioned below may be cleared away on the Sabbath, although this involves excessive toil. As we saw in the prefatory remarks to this Mishnah, this is permissible only to facilitate the performance of a mitzvah (*Rav*).

2. There is a difference of opinion in the Gemara (126b) between Shmuel and Rav Chisda as to whether the numbers "four or five" are to be taken literally or not. We will explain the Mishnah according to Shmuel's opinion that they are not meant literally, since this is the explanation adopted by *Rav* in his commentary. We will explain Rav Chisda's view, which takes them literally, in *Gems from the Gemara.*

3. These were large containers, each of which held three *se'ah* — a measure of volume equal to the displacement of 144 average-size hen's eggs (*Tos. Yom Tov, Tiferes Yisrael* from *Tosafos*). In reality, however, one may clear away any number of boxes (*Rav* from Gemara 127a). The Tanna avails himself of a common idiom to indicate that there is no fixed limit as to how many he may clear if he needs the extra space (*Rashi* to Gemara ibid.).

מִפְּנֵי הָאוֹרְחִים — ***because of guests,***[4] **וּמִפְּנֵי בִּטּוּל בֵּית הַמִּדְרָשׁ** — ***or because of curtailment of*** attendance at ***the study hall.***[5] **אֲבָל לֹא אֶת הָאוֹצָר** — ***But*** we may ***not*** remove ***an*** entire ***storehouse*** of straw or grain.[6]

The Mishnah discusses what halachic categories of grains may be cleared away. The list includes only grains that we might have thought would be forbidden to move for some reason, but in fact may be moved under the circumstances described by the Mishnah above:

מְפַנִּין תְּרוּמָה טְהוֹרָה — ***We may clear away terumah that is tahor,***[7] **וּדְמַאי** — ***and demai.***[8]

We will conclude our elucidation of this Mishnah tomorrow.

NOTES

4. The definition of a "guest" in the context of our Mishnah is limited to those who need a place to stay or eat. However, inviting a friend who could just as easily eat in his own house to join him for a meal is not considered a mitzvah, and the leniency of the Mishnah does not apply to such a case (*Rama, Orach Chaim* 333:1 from *Terumas HaDeshen* §72).

5. I.e., to make room for pupils who wish to attend a Torah lecture (*Rav; Rashi*).

6. I.e., we may clear away many baskets, but only as long as we do not thereby clear away the entire storehouse. The Rabbis prohibited this because they were concerned that once the floor would be uncovered, one might discover that the earthen floor of the storehouse was uneven and, in a moment of forgetfulness, smooth out the floor, thus performing a derivative of the forbidden *melachah* of *building* (*Rav* from Gemara 127a).

7. After harvesting his crop, a farmer separates its *terumah* (also called *terumah gedolah;* generally, the *terumah* is 1/50 of the crop) and gives it to the Kohen. *Terumah* may not be eaten by a non-Kohen, but only by a Kohen, the members of his household and his animals. The Mishnah here teaches that the general rule — that we may clear away only food fit for consumption on the Sabbath — does not extend only to ordinary produce, which all may eat, but even to *terumah,* which only a Kohen may eat. Since it is fit for a Kohen, it is considered fit for consumption, and is not *muktzeh* (*Rav; Rashi* from Gemara 127b).

This ruling applies only to *terumah* that is *tahor.* As we learned above (2:1), *terumah* that has become *tamei* may not be eaten, even by a Kohen. It must be destroyed — either by being burned, or by being fed to a Kohen's livestock. As we explained there, there is a prohibition against destroying *terumah* on either the Sabbath or Yom Tov. Consequently, contaminated *terumah* has no permitted use on the Sabbath. This renders it *muktzeh,* and it may not be handled even to make room for the performance of a mitzvah (*Rashi*).

8. As we have learned (above, 2:7), *demai* is produce belonging to, or purchased from, עַמֵּי הָאָרֶץ [*amei haaretz*], *unlearned people.* When the Rabbis discovered that many of them were lax in their observance of the laws of tithes, they decreed that any produce purchased from unlearned people must be tithed to remove all doubt that it might be *tevel,* untithed produce. However, since the majority of even unlearned people did

NOTES

faithfully observe the tithe laws, there is no *Biblical* requirement to retithe *demai.* Consequently, when enacting this law, the Rabbis could be lenient in its application. They therefore chose not to impose this requirement on the poor. As a result, a poor man may purchase produce from an *am haaretz* and eat it without tithing.

It is Rabbinically forbidden to tithe produce on either the Sabbath or Yom Tov (above, 2:7; *Beitzah* 1:6). Since *demai* must be tithed before being used, it should seemingly be unusable on the Sabbath and therefore *muktzeh* (as is any unusable item). However, since one has the right to renounce his property, thereby rendering himself impoverished, it is regarded as at least *possible* for anyone to be able to eat *demai.* Therefore, it is not *muktzeh* (*Rav* from Gemara 127b).

GEMS FROM THE GEMARA

We explained the Mishnah according to Shmuel. The Gemara (127a) states that Shmuel interprets the Mishnah in line with the view of the Tanna R' Shimon, who defines *muktzeh* narrowly (Gemara 45a; *Tosafos* to *Beitzah* 2a). According to Shmuel, in accordance with R' Shimon, straw placed in storage before the Sabbath is not considered *muktzeh,* despite the fact that one did not intend to use it on the Sabbath. Shmuel therefore rules that although the storehouse was not even partially cleared before the Sabbath, and one had no intention of using the baskets, he may, nonetheless, clear them away in order to facilitate a mitzvah. Since no prohibition is involved here other than that of excessive toil or weekday activities, he may clear away as many baskets as necessary, provided he does not clear out the storehouse completely.

Rav Chisda, however, interprets the Mishnah as following the view of the Tanna R' Yehudah, who defines *muktzeh* more broadly and considers any item placed in long-term storage as *muktzeh.* [This is because the person indicates his intention *not* to use it on the Sabbath by placing it into storage.] Consequently, clearing any part of a storehouse should be prohibited because the stored items are *muktzeh.* He therefore explains that the Mishnah is speaking of a storehouse from which one had already begun using the straw before the Sabbath, thereby indicating his intention to use the straw rather than store it. Consequently, it is no longer *muktzeh.* According to Rav Chisda, one may not clear away baskets in a storehouse when none have been previously cleared, even to facilitate a mitzvah.

Rav Chisda explains the Mishnah as follows: *We may clear away four baskets* [in a small storehouse from which we have already begun to clear, that contained five baskets], *or* [a maximum of] *five baskets of straw or produce* [in a larger storehouse. Clearing away more than five baskets is prohibited, either due to excessive toil or because it is a weekday activity]. *But* [he may] *not* [clear away] *a storehouse* [that he has not yet begun to clear].

[Rav Chisda understands the numbers *four or five* to be literal. It is for this reason that he is forced to explain the Mishnah according to R' Yehudah. Since one is normally permitted to clear five baskets, the only time that there can be a limit of four is where there are only five baskets to start off with (and one was already cleared). Therefore, it is clear from the beginning of the Mishnah that there is a prohibition to completely clear a storehouse. The phrase *but not a storehouse* is then redundant; thus, we are forced to explain it as meaning that we may not clear a storehouse that one has not yet begun to clear. This accords with the view of R' Yehudah, who holds that items in a storehouse that one did not begin to clear before the Sabbath are *muktzeh* (Gemara 126b).]

A MUSSAR THOUGHT FOR THE DAY

Rashi (to *Shemos* 16:32) writes that when the Torah states that an *omer* of manna (one daily ration) was put away for safekeeping for "generations," it is referring to its intended use in the days of Yirmiyahu. When Yirmiyahu rebuked the Bnei Yisrael for not engaging in Torah study, they responded, "If we were to lay aside our work and engage in Torah study, from where would we derive our livelihood?" He then brought out the jar of manna and said to them, "You *see* the word of Hashem!" The verse (*Yirmiyahu* 2:31) does not say *hear,* but rather *see,* indicating that Yirmiyahu actually showed them the jar of manna. Yirmiyahu then told them, "With this manna your ancestors sustained themselves. The Omnipresent has many emissaries to prepare nourishment for those who fear Him!"

We see from here that the lesson from the manna was a prerequisite to receiving the Torah. Indeed, our Sages teach us: לֹא נִיתְּנָה תּוֹרָה אֶלָּא לְאוֹכְלֵי הַמָּן, *the Torah was given only to the generation that ate manna.* As we discussed in yesterday's studies, only someone who is able to live with pure אֱמוּנָה, *trust* in Hashem that He will sustain us, is ready to dedicate his life to Torah study without any distraction based on the fear of not being able to earn a livelihood.

The Talmud (*Yoma* 76a) illustrates how this lesson was taught by the manna. The students of R' Shimon ben Yochai asked their rebbi: Why did

the manna fall every day, and not once a year? He answered with a parable: A father had one son, whom he supported by giving him one large sum for the entire year. The son took to visiting his father only once a year, on the day he would receive his stipend. Seeing this, the father started giving him small rations every day, and the son started greeting his father every day. Here, too, said R' Shimon ben Yochai, a father with several children would go to sleep every night with the fear that perhaps tomorrow there would be no manna, and his children would perish. This resulted in all of Bnei Yisrael thinking of and relying on Hashem. Their trust in Hashem sustained them and became part of their way of life, reinforcing their bond with Hashem daily.

The Talmud states in *Sotah* (48b) that after the destruction of the Temple, there ceased to be אַנְשֵׁי אֲמָנָה, *people of trust.* The Gemara asks: Who is considered to be lacking in trust? Someone who has food for today yet worries about what he will eat tomorrow and puts away some bread from his night meal so he will have food for the next morning.

Rav Chatzkel Levenstein used to say, "If the greatest of generations who saw Hashem and heard his words by Sinai needed this daily reminder to bolster their trust in Hashem, how much more so in exile, when Hashem's full power is hidden from us, must we work to strengthen our trust in Hashem every day!"

HALACHAH OF THE DAY

There are some exceptions to the restrictions of tying that we have outlined above. These exceptions apply in cases of necessity, as well as in cases where the proper performance of a mitzvah requires the tying of a knot.

Although we stated above that a tight double knot is regarded as a professional knot, there are *poskim* who maintain that if the knot was intended to be tied for less than twenty-four hours, it cannot be considered a professional knot. According to this opinion, one may tie a tight double knot with intent to untie it within twenty-four hours. This opinion may be relied upon in cases of necessity.

For example, if a child's shoelaces become repeatedly untied, so that a parent must constantly retie them again and again, it is permissible to tie them with a tight double knot so that they should remain tied. *This is permissible only if the laces will be untied during that day.*

Another rule mentioned above is that any knot tied with the intent that it remain in place for more than twenty-four hours is considered

somewhat permanent, and may not be tied on Shabbos. However, there are *poskim* who hold that only a knot intended to last for longer than *seven* days is considered semi-permanent, and one may therefore tie a non-professional knot that will remain tied for up to seven days. This opinion may also be relied upon in cases of necessity.

According to some *poskim,* it is permitted to tie a knot that is ordinarily Rabbinically forbidden (i.e., a non-professional knot that will remain in place longer than twenty-four hours but not indefinitely) for the purpose of performing a mitzvah. *This applies only if the mitzvah cannot be accomplished without the tying of the knot.*

This rule has a very common application in the course of Shabbos davening. The Sefer Torah is closed upon the completion of the Torah reading at *Minchah* of Shabbos. In some congregations, the Torah is tied closed with a sash. In most cases, the Sefer Torah will not be used again for several days (until Monday morning). Thus, one may certainly not use a double knot when tying the sash. However, it would seem that the use of a single knot with a bow should also be prohibited, since the knot will remain in place for more than twenty-four hours. Nevertheless, this is permissible for the following two reasons: One, the knot is necessary for the proper observance of the custom of *gelilah* (the tying of the Sefer Torah). Second, this is considered a case of necessity — we may therefore rely on the opinion that permits the tying of an ordinary knot that will last up to seven days.

This concludes our discussion of the *melachah* of *tying.*

A CLOSER LOOK AT THE SIDDUR

This week, we will discuss the eleventh of the Thirteen Fundamental Principles (י״ג עיקרים) enumerated by *Rambam,* which states:

> אֲנִי מַאֲמִין בֶּאֱמוּנָה שְׁלֵמָה שֶׁהַבּוֹרֵא יִתְבָּרַךְ שְׁמוֹ גּוֹמֵל טוֹב לְשׁוֹמְרֵי מִצְוֹתָיו וּמַעֲנִישׁ לְעוֹבְרֵי מִצְוֹתָיו.
>
> *I believe with complete faith that the Creator, Blessed be His Name, rewards with good those who observe His commandments, and punishes those who violate His commandments.*

This principle underscores the requirement to believe in the system of שָׂכָר וָעוֹנֶשׁ, *reward and punishment.* We as Jews do not believe that the world is a place of anarchy and lawlessness, a jungle where people may choose to do as they wish without fear of reprisal. For every action there

is a reckoning; good deeds do not go unrewarded, and evil does not go unpunished. This realization holds a person back from sinning, as the Mishnah in *Avos* (3:1) states: הִסְתַּכֵּל בִּשְׁלֹשָׁה דְבָרִים וְאֵין אַתָּה בָא לִידֵי עֲבֵרָה ... וְלִפְנֵי מִי אַתָּה עָתִיד לִתֵּן דִּין וְחֶשְׁבּוֹן – לִפְנֵי מֶלֶךְ מַלְכֵי הַמְּלָכִים, הַקָּדוֹשׁ בָּרוּךְ הוּא, *Consider three things and you will not come into the hands of sin . . . And before Whom are you destined to give an accounting? Before the King of kings, the Holy One, Blessed is He.*

Moreover, this principle stresses that the system of reward and punishment is not simply a table of values assigned to each good deed and sin, for a person to evaluate and then obey or disregard as per his will. The life that we are to live is the one that is *commanded* of us. A person cannot say: I am willing to pay the penalty or undergo a punishment in order to obtain the pleasure of a certain sin. The Torah forbids certain acts, and they may not be performed even if the person is willing to suffer a punishment.

Sefer HaChinuch notes that there is a general rule that for every prohibition that carries a penalty of *kares* (Divinely imposed premature death) or court-ordered execution, there are *two* verses in the Torah forbidding it — one that is called the *azharah,* the "warning," and the other that is called the *onesh,* the verse that describes the "punishment" that one receives for violation of the prohibition. He explains that two verses are necessary so that a person does not make the mistake of thinking that Hashem gives him the permit to perform the forbidden act as long as he is willing to pay the price. This is not so, for the Torah's prohibitions are absolute. The sin is forbidden because Hashem wills it so. In addition, one who violates the laws of the Torah is punished.

The same is true of positive acts. When Hashem commands us to do good, one should not believe that if he is willing to forgo reward it is not incumbent upon him to perform good works. This is untrue! Hashem requires us to live according to His commandments because that is the proper way to act and live. While it is certain that the reward will come in the end — indeed, we are *required* to believe this — reward is not, and should not be, the reason for our service to Him.

We will continue with our discussion of this principle next week.

QUESTION OF THE DAY:

What tastes could the manna not assume, and why?

For the answer, see page 220.

A TORAH THOUGHT FOR THE DAY

וְהָיָה כַּאֲשֶׁר יָרִים מֹשֶׁה יָדוֹ וְגָבַר יִשְׂרָאֵל
וְכַאֲשֶׁר יָנִיחַ יָדוֹ וְגָבַר עֲמָלֵק

And it happened that when Moshe would raise his hand, the Jews would be stronger, and when he lowered his hand, Amalek was stronger (*Shemos* 17:11).

Rashi cites the Mishnah in *Rosh Hashanah* (29a) that asks the question: Was it the hands of Moshe that determined whether the war would be won or lost? We may explain the question further: If the tide of the war was dependent on Moshe's hands, is it not obvious that he never would have lowered them? Furthermore, the verse (v. 9) states specifically that Moshe commanded Yehoshua to pick men to fight with Amalek, and *Rashi* explains that he was instructed to pick certain men who would be especially suited for this battle (see there). If all Moshe had to do was to keep his hands raised, why was there any need for such preparation?

The Mishnah answers that indeed, it was not the position of Moshe's *hands* that determined whether the battle would be won; it was the sentiment in the *hearts* of the Jews. As the Mishnah states: "As long as the Jews looked heavenward and subjugated their hearts to their Father in Heaven, they would prevail; but when they did not, they would falter." This, of course, is much easier to understand. It was the faith that the Jews showed in Hashem as their Savior that gave them the ability to triumph, for ה׳ אִישׁ מִלְחָמָה, *HASHEM is the Master of war* (*Shemos* 15:3). Chasam Sofer explains that by the very act of looking heavenward during battle the Jews would express their faith in Hashem, for in war the first rule of combat is never to take your attention away from your adversary. By ignoring this cardinal precept, the Jews demonstrated that they knew Who was really fighting the war.

However, we must still explain: Why does the verse express the idea of the Jews' faith in terms of the hands of Moshe? *Tiferes Yisrael* (to *Rosh Hashanah* ibid.) suggests that Moshe raised his arms as a signal, to remind the Jews to raise their eyes and hearts to Hashem. However, this leaves us with the difficulty: Why would Moshe lower his arms? *Yom Teruah* proposes a novel idea: He suggests that Moshe was the barometer of the Jews' faith. When the Jews directed their hearts toward Hashem properly, Moshe had the strength to raise his hands to Hashem; but when they faltered, so did Moshe's hands. [However, it must be

noted that the following verse seems to indicate that Moshe was assisted in holding his hands aloft when they faltered; according to *Yom Teruah,* it is difficult to understand what this would accomplish, while according to *Tiferes Yisrael,* the reason for such action would be clear.]

MISHNAH OF THE DAY: SHABBOS 18:1

The Mishnah continues to discuss which halachic categories of grains may be cleared away on the Sabbath. As we learned yesterday, the list includes only grains that we might have thought we would be forbidden to move for some reason, but in fact may be moved under the circumstances described by the Mishnah above:

וּמַעֲשֵׂר רִאשׁוֹן שֶׁנִּיטְּלָה תְּרוּמָתוֹ — We may ***also*** clear away ***maaser rishon whose terumah has been taken;***[1] **וּמַעֲשֵׂר שֵׁנִי וְהֶקְדֵּשׁ שֶׁנִּפְדּוּ** — ***and maaser sheni or consecrated produce that was redeemed;***[2]

NOTES

1. If this statement were taken literally, it would be obvious; since *terumah* was separated, one may eat the grain. The Gemara (127b), therefore, states that the Mishnah speaks of a situation in which the *maaser rishon* in question had *its own terumah* (i.e., *terumas maaser,* which is the "tithe of the tithe" that the Levi must give the Kohen from any *maaser* he receives) separated from it, but the regular *terumah* (תְּרוּמָה גְּדוֹלָה) was *not* separated from it by the owner before giving the *maaser* to the Levi. [Normally, the owner separates *terumah* for the Kohen from his crop *before* separating *maaser* for the Levi, so that the Levi receives grain from which *terumah gedolah* has already been taken. Here, however, this was not done.]

In most cases, the fact that *terumah gedolah* was not taken from the *maaser* would render it *tevel* (untithed) and prohibited, and it would be forbidden to clear it away on the Sabbath. However, the Gemara explains that the Mishnah refers to a case in which the owner separated the *maaser* and gave it to the Levi before the grain was threshed, at which point the obligation to separate *terumah* and the other tithes was not yet in effect. Under such circumstances, the Levi who received the *maaser* is obligated to give the Kohen only the *terumas maaser;* the grain is completely exempt from *terumah gedolah* (*Rav*). Thus, such *maaser* is not forbidden for use on the Sabbath, and may be cleared away.

2. In the first, second, fourth and fifth years of the seven-year *shemittah* cycle, the farmer separates *maaser sheni* (the second tithe) from the remainder of his crop (after the *terumah* and *maaser rishon* have been removed). The farmer brings this second tithe to Jerusalem and eats it there, or he may redeem the *maaser sheni* with money, which he brings to Jerusalem to buy food to be eaten there (see *Devarim* 14:22-26).

One may redeem his *maaser sheni* or consecrated objects (הֶקְדֵּשׁ) with money. The redeemed produce loses its sacred status and may be consumed as ordinary,

וְהַתּוּרְמוּס הַיָּבֵשׁ — ***and dried lupin,*** מִפְּנֵי שֶׁהוּא מַאֲכָל לָעֲנִיִּים — ***because it is food for the poor.***[3]

The Mishnah now lists the halachic categories of grains that may *not* be cleared away — even under the circumstances described by the Mishnah above:

אֲבָל לֹא אֶת הַטֶּבֶל — ***However,*** we may ***not*** clear away ***tevel;***[4] וְלֹא אֶת מַעֲשֵׂר [רִאשׁוֹן] שֶׁלֹּא נִטְּלָה תְּרוּמָתוֹ — ***nor maaser rishon whose terumah has not been taken;***[5] וְלֹא אֶת מַעֲשֵׂר שֵׁנִי וְהֶקְדֵּשׁ שֶׁלֹּא נִפְדּוּ — ***nor maaser sheni or consecrated produce that was not redeemed;***[6] וְלֹא אֶת הַלּוּף — ***nor luf;***[7] וְלֹא אֶת הַחַרְדָּל — ***nor mustard.***[8] רַבָּן שִׁמְעוֹן בֶּן גַּמְלִיאֵל מַתִּיר בְּלוּף — ***Rabban Shimon***

NOTES

non-sanctified food. The redemption money assumes, in turn, the sacred status of the second tithe or consecrated substance. If the redeemer is the original owner, he must add a fifth to the value of the item being redeemed.

Since redeemed produce is considered ordinary food, it would seem obvious that it may be handled on the Sabbath. The Gemara explains that the Mishnah speaks of a situation in which the fifth was not added, and teaches us that although adding the fifth is an obligation, failure to do so does not invalidate the redemption. Therefore, one may handle this produce on the Sabbath (*Rav* from Gemara 127b).

3. Dried lupins are so bitter that ordinary people would not eat them until they were cooked seven times (see *R' Chananel* to *Beitzah* 25b). Poor people, however, would eat them even raw.

4. Ordinary טֶבֶל [*tevel*], *untithed produce,* may not be eaten (see Mishnah 2:7), and therefore it is obviously *muktzeh.* Our Mishnah means to include even Rabbinically forbidden *tevel* — e.g., grain grown in an unperforated flowerpot — in the category of *muktzeh* (see Mishnah 10:6). By Biblical law, such grain is not considered produce of the earth and need not be tithed, but the Sages imposed the tithe obligation on it (*Rav* from Gemara 128a).

5. The Gemara explains that in this case as well, the owner reversed the regular sequence and gave the *maaser rishon* to the Levi before separating the *terumah gedolah.* However, he did so *after* the grain was threshed. Because the *maaser rishon* was taken off after threshing, when the obligation to separate the regular *terumah* had already taken effect, the Levi *is* obligated to separate both the *terumah gedolah* and the *terumas maaser* (as opposed to the instance discussed above, in note 1). If he did not do so before the Sabbath, the grain is *muktzeh* and may not be moved (Gemara 128a).

6. Even if they were redeemed, but that redemption was not performed properly — e.g., *maaser sheni* was redeemed with unminted slugs of metal, or consecrated produce was redeemed with land (ibid.).

7. *Luf* is a type of legume that is inedible when raw even for livestock and domestic fowl (*Rav; Rashi*). Since one may not cook on the Sabbath, the raw *luf* is *muktzeh.*

8. This refers to green mustard, fit only for doves. The Mishnah deals with a place where doves are not common. The mustard, therefore, is of no use and is consequently *muktzeh* (*Tiferes Yisrael* based on *Ran*).

ben Gamliel permits clearing away *luf,* מִפְּנֵי שֶׁהוּא מַאֲכַל עוֹרְבִין — *because it is food for ravens.* [9]

NOTES

9. Although only the wealthy raise ravens for pets, Rabban Shimon ben Gamliel rules that since all Israel are considered royal children, anything considered fit for royalty is considered fit for them, too. In this, his opinion is similar to R' Shimon's in Mishnah 14:4 (*Tos. R' Akiva Eiger* from Gemara 128a).

The Mishnah refers to places where ravens are uncommon. Where ravens are common, even the Tanna Kamma concurs that we may move *luf,* since it is food for ravens, even though one does not own any (*Tiferes Yisrael* from *Shulchan Aruch* 308:29).

GEMS FROM THE GEMARA

Our Mishnah considers measures that may be taken in order to receive guests. R' Yochanan (Gemara 127a) includes this mitzvah in the broader category of גְּמִילוּת חֲסָדִים, *performing acts of kindness.* R' Yochanan then enumerates several other virtuous traits that one should practice. One of the precepts enumerated by R' Yochanan is "judging one's fellow man favorably [הֱוֵי דָן אֶת כָּל הָאָדָם לְכַף זְכוּת]." The Gemara (127b) cites several incidents that exemplify this virtue. This is the first incident:

The Rabbis taught in a Baraisa: One who judges his fellow man favorably is himself judged favorably [by God]. And there was the incident involving a certain man who went down from Upper Galilee and entered the employ of a certain homeowner in the south for three years. On the eve of Yom Kippur [following his three years of work], the worker said to the homeowner, "Give me my wages, and I will go and provide for my wife and children." The homeowner replied to him, "I have no money." Said the worker to him, "Then give me [my wages in the form of] produce." He said to the worker, "I have none." Said the worker, "Then give me land." Replied his employer, "I have none." Said the worker, "Then give me livestock." Replied the employer, "I have none." Said the worker, "Then give me pillows and cushions." Replied the employer, "I have none."

Unable to obtain any of the wages due him, the worker slung his belongings over his back and returned home dejectedly. After the festival, the homeowner took the [worker's] wages in his hand along with three laden donkeys — one carrying food, one carrying drink and one carrying various sweet delicacies — and traveled to his [former worker's] house. After they had eaten and drunk, he paid the worker his wages. He then said to the worker, "When you said to me, 'Give me my wages,' and I said, 'I have no money,' of what did you suspect me?" The worker replied, "I said perhaps underpriced merchandise came your way and you bought it with the money that you would have otherwise used to pay my wages." The employer pressed on, "And when you said to me, 'Give me livestock,' and I said, 'I have no livestock,' of what did you suspect me?" The worker replied, "I said perhaps they were leased to others." Continued the employer, "And when you said to me, 'Give me land,' and I said, 'I have no land,' of what did you suspect me?" The worker replied, "I said perhaps it was leased to others." The employer asked further, "And when I said to you, 'I have no produce,' of what did you suspect me?" The worker answered, "I said perhaps it was not tithed." The employer continued, "And when I said to you, 'I have no pillows or cushions,' of what did you suspect me?" The worker replied, "I said perhaps my employer has consecrated all his possessions to Heaven." Whereupon the employer exclaimed to him, "By the Divine service! [This is a form of oath.] So it was! I had vowed all my possessions to Heaven because of my son Horkenos who did not occupy himself in Torah study, so I did not wish him to benefit from them. And when I came to my colleagues in the South, they annulled for me all my vows. And as for you — just as you have judged me favorably, may the Omnipresent judge you favorably!"

A MUSSAR THOUGHT FOR THE DAY

With regard to Amalek, we find that the Torah states: כִּי־יָד עַל־כֵּס יָהּ מִלְחָמָה לַה׳ בַּעֲמָלֵק מִדֹּר דֹּר, *For there is a hand on the throne of HASHEM; HASHEM maintains a war against Amalek, from generation to generation* (*Shemos* 17:16). According to *Rashi,* the verse's reference to a hand refers to the hand of Hashem (so to speak); Hashem raises His hand to swear by His throne that He will always be at war with Amalek. Other commentators (see *Ramban* et al.) understand this to be limiting the verse's command to eradicate Amalek to a time when there is a king on the throne of Israel; and yet others (see *Daas Zekeinim*) understand the hand to be the hand of Amalek that is stretched against Hashem.

Rashi continues, stating that the word for *throne* (כֵּס) and the word for Hashem's Name (י־ה) are both spelled deficiently in this verse (the longer versions would be כִּסֵּא and the Four-Letter Name of Hashem — י־ה־ו־ה). He explains that these words are shortened to teach us that neither the throne nor the Name of Hashem are considered to be complete while Amalek survives.

R' Moshe Feinstein derived a powerful lesson from this *Rashi,* one that he would often relate to a *chassan* and *kallah* at a *Sheva Berachos.* The Gemara tells us in *Sotah* (17a) that Hashem blessed the union of man and wife with His Holy Name — for the word אִישׁ (man) contains a *yud,* and the word אִשָּׁה (woman) contains a *hei,* which combine to form Hashem's Name. If the union is harmonious, the Divine Presence (*Shechinah*) rests with them; if not, God forbid, it departs, and nothing is left but אֵשׁ (the fire of discord).

R' Moshe would ask: From this *Rashi* we see that the Name of Hashem that contains only two letters is considered an incomplete Name. Why did Hashem bless the union of man and wife with a less-than-perfect Name? And he would answer: Hashem does not provide all of the ingredients that make the union of man and his wife into a perfect home. Rather, He gives the process a good beginning and a solid foundation, by allowing His Two-letter Name to grace the union. But that beginning will blossom into a full realization of a *bayis neeman* — a house faithful to Torah and its values — only if the *chassan* and *kallah* are cognizant of their responsibilities, and are ready to work to achieve their goals.

This lesson has application to all aspects of the service of Hashem as well. We serve Hashem with the knowledge that without *siyata d'Shmaya,* Divine assistance, we cannot hope to succeed. But we are never permitted to rely on Hashem to do all the work. We must strive with all of our effort to do Hashem's will, and only then can we ask for, and trust to receive, His assistance.

HALACHAH OF THE DAY

Untying a knot is one of the thirty-nine categories of *melachah* forbidden on Shabbos. As we explained in our discussion regarding the *melachah* of *tying,* one of the ways that knots were used in the Mishkan was for adjusting the nets used to catch the *chilazon.* These same knots had to be untied at times, in order to readjust the nets. Thus, *untying* is also considered a *melachah.*

The *melachah* of *untying* applies to the opening of knots in any pliable material, such as rope, thread, ribbon, or soft plastic.

Generally, a destructive activity is not Biblically prohibited unless it is being done for a constructive purpose. In its essence, the act of untying is a destructive act; when untying, one destroys a knot that has been previously tied. For this reason, untying is not Biblically prohibited

unless it is a part of an act that is ultimately constructive. One such purpose would be untying a knot in order to retie it more effectively. A case in point would be the above-mentioned readjustment of the nets that took place in the Mishkan — the knots were untied in order to retie them properly. Another example of a constructive purpose would be to untie a knot in string in order to use the string for some other purpose.

Untying a knot simply to remove the obstacle it presents is prohibited only Rabbinically.

The *melachah* of *untying* is closely related to the *melachah* of *tying.* Any knot that one is forbidden to tie under Biblical law, one is likewise forbidden to untie under Biblical law. Similarly, any knot one is forbidden to tie under Rabbinic law, one is also forbidden to untie under Rabbinic law. Furthermore, any knot that one is permitted to tie on Shabbos, one may also untie on Shabbos.

When presenting the *melachah* of *tying,* we discussed which knots fall into each category. We will now briefly review these categories.

It is forbidden under Biblical law to tie or untie any permanent knot. A permanent knot is one that is intended to stay in place indefinitely.

It is forbidden under Rabbinic law to tie or untie any professional knot. Examples of a professional knot include a tight double knot, or a tight single knot in a single strand of rope.

It is also forbidden under Rabbinic law to tie or untie a non-professional knot that is intended to remain in place for twenty-four hours or more. This includes a loose double knot, a single knot with a bow and a single knot with the ends tucked in.

In cases of necessity it is permitted to tie or untie a nonprofessional knot that is intended to remain in place for less than seven days.

A single knot in two strands and a single or double bow without an underlying knot are halachically not considered knots at all. Hence, one is permitted to tie and untie them, even if they are intended to remain in place permanently.

QUESTION OF THE DAY:

Where else do we find a similar phenomenon, where a seemingly powerful item in truth had no power of its own, but served only to focus the Jews' thoughts toward Hashem?

For the answer, see page 220.

A CLOSER LOOK AT THE SIDDUR

In earlier studies, we noted that the closing phrase of the central *berachah* of the Shabbos *Shemoneh Esrei* — וְיָנוּחוּ בָהּ יִשְׂרָאֵל מְקַדְּשֵׁי שְׁמֶךָ, *and may Israel, the sanctifiers of Your Name, rest upon it* — varies slightly from *tefillah* to *tefillah.* On Friday evening we say וְיָנוּחוּ בָהּ, using the feminine form; on Sabbath morning we say וְיָנוּחוּ בוֹ, using the masculine form; and at *Minchah* we say וְיָנוּחוּ בָם, in the plural. We noted (see *A Closer Look at the Siddur,* Friday of *Parashas Bereishis*) that these differing phrases allude to the different Sabbaths about which the three prayers speak. *Nesiv Binah* cites another allusion found in these three expressions, from the *sefer Mekorei HaMinhagim:* He notes that the numerical value of the three words: בוֹ ,בָהּ and בָם add up to 57 which is also the numerical value of the word זָן, which means *to nourish.* He relates this to the statement of the Gemara in *Shabbos* (117b-118a): Whoever delights in the Sabbath is granted a heritage without boundaries — that is to say, he is granted sustenance in abundance. Thus, the words of the prayers hint that one who embodies the message of Sabbath throughout the day — from *Maariv* on Friday night through *Minchah* on Shabbos afternoon, will merit that Hashem will *nourish* him in a bountiful way.

It is also noteworthy that we close this blessing with the mention of the Jews as *the sanctifiers of Your Name. Shiras David* mentions the contrast between Jews and idolaters in this respect, citing the Gemara in *Megillah* (12b). The verse (*Esther* 1:10) states: בַּיּוֹם הַשְּׁבִיעִי כְּטוֹב לֵב־הַמֶּלֶךְ בַּיָּיִן, *On the seventh day* (of the feast of Achashveirosh), *when the king's heart was merry with wine.* The Gemara asks: Was his heart not merry with wine before the seventh day? And it answers: That day was the Sabbath, and it was the day upon which the difference between Jews and idolaters becomes clear to all. For when Jews eat and drink, they discuss words of Torah and praise Hashem. But when idolaters feast, they begin discussing matters of lewdness (as was the case with Achashveirosh and his courtiers).

As we close our blessing, in which we ask Hashem to bestow upon us the blessings of the Sabbath, we beseech Him to take into account that we use the feasting of Sabbath as an opportunity to *sanctify* His Name, and not as an excuse for excess or gluttony. In this merit, we hope that our prayers will be favorably received.

A TORAH THOUGHT FOR THE DAY

וַיֹּאמֶר ה׳ אֶל־מֹשֶׁה כְּתֹב זֹאת זִכָּרוֹן בַּסֵּפֶר וְשִׂים בְּאָזְנֵי יְהוֹשֻׁעַ כִּי־מָחֹה אֶמְחֶה אֶת־זֵכֶר עֲמָלֵק מִתַּחַת הַשָּׁמָיִם

HASHEM said to Moshe, "Write this as a remembrance in the Book and recite it in the ears of Yehoshua, that I shall surely erase the memory of Amalek from under the heavens" (*Shemos* 17:14).

R' *Chaim Volozhiner* asks: Once Hashem commanded Moshe to record this mitzvah of wiping out Amalek, what was the point of commanding him to tell it to Yehoshua verbally? Why could Yehoshua not read about it in the Torah, like all the other mitzvos?

The answer he gives is brilliant in its simplicity. The Talmud in *Bava Basra* (21a) tells us of the major mistake that Yoav ben Tzeruyah committed when he was sent by King David to kill all the Amalekim, and he killed only the males. David questioned him about this, asking why he had not fulfilled the directive of תִּמְחֶה אֶת־זֵכֶר עֲמָלֵק, *wipe out the memory of Amalek* (*Devarim* 25:19), which includes females. Yoav replied that his teacher had erroneously taught him that the verse reads תִּמְחֶה אֶת־זָכָר עֲמָלֵק, meaning to wipe out only the male Amalekim.

We see from here that with respect to this mitzvah, just reading the words in the Torah (which is written without *nikud*) can cause a misinterpretation and yield dangerous results. For this reason, when Hashem told Moshe to record this mitzvah in the Torah, He also told him to dictate the words to Yehoshua "in his ears" — that is, to ensure that Yehoshua knew the proper pronunciation of this word — זֵכֶר, meaning *memory,* and not זָכָר, meaning *males.*

Gra, however, understands that this command to Moshe to *recite it in the ears of Yehoshua* was not unique to this mitzvah, for he maintains that *all* of the Torah was taught verbally by Moshe to Yehoshua. He notes that the Torah is divided into two parts: the written portion (תּוֹרָה שֶׁבִּכְתָב) and the oral portion (תּוֹרָה שֶׁבְּעַל פֶּה), which must be transmitted verbally. Yehoshua, who, as we know, was the one who received the entire Torah that was to be given over to the next generation (see *Avos* 1:1), received both the oral and written portions of the Torah from Moshe.

It is interesting to note that *Megillas Esther,* which is one of the twenty-four books of the Written Torah, would not have attained this status if not for Esther's special request from the Sages. As the Gemara states in *Megillah* (7a), Esther asked the Sages to write her story (the *Megillah*) as part of the כְּתוּבִים. They were not amenable to this request until they

found a hint to do so in our verse — כְּתֹב זֹאת זִכָּרוֹן בַּסֵּפֶר. This gave the *Megillah* the status of the Written Torah. [This special status was not given to other Rabbinic Yamim Tovim, such as Chanukah, about which there is no *megillah* in the Written Torah, nor tractate in the Oral Torah.]

MISHNAH OF THE DAY: SHABBOS 18:2

The following Mishnah expands the discussion of what items may and may not be moved on the Sabbath:

חֲבִילֵי קַשׁ וַחֲבִילֵי עֵצִים — ***Bundles of straw, and bundles of twigs,***[1] וַחֲבִילֵי זְרָדִים — ***and bundles of tender branches,***[2] אִם הִתְקִינָן לְמַאֲכַל בְּהֵמָה מְטַלְטְלִין אוֹתָן — ***if one prepared them for*** use as ***animal feed*** before the Sabbath, ***we may move them;*** וְאִם לַאו אֵין מְטַלְטְלִין אוֹתָן — ***but if*** one has ***not*** set them aside for use as animal fodder, ***we may not move them.***[3]

כּוֹפִין אֶת הַסַּל לִפְנֵי הָאֶפְרוֹחִים — ***We may invert a basket in front of chicks,***[4] כְּדֵי שֶׁיַּעֲלוּ וְיֵרְדוּ — ***so that they may*** use it as a ladder to ***climb up and down*** to get to their coop.

תַּרְנְגֹלֶת שֶׁבָּרְחָה — ***A hen that has run away*** from the house, דּוֹחִין אוֹתָהּ עַד שֶׁתִּכָּנֵס — ***we may push her until she enters.***[5] מְדַדִּין עֲגָלִין

NOTES

1. I.e., bundles of tender twigs that can be used as animal fodder (*Mishnah Berurah* 308:117).

2. I.e., bundles of moist branches that were pruned from a tree to be used as fodder (*Rav;* see *Rashi*).

3. Since they are generally used as kindling, these bundles are *muktzeh* unless they were expressly designated as animal feed before the onset of the Sabbath (*Mishnah Berurah* 308:118).

4. The chicks themselves may not be moved on the Sabbath. Nevertheless, a basket may be moved for their benefit. Although we have learned (above, 3:6) that one may not nullify the usability of a utensil by causing it to become *muktzeh* — viz., by rendering it a *base to a prohibited article* — in this case, since the chicks do not stay on the basket (rather, they merely use it as a step up to their coop), the basket does not become a *base to muktzeh* for the entire Sabbath. Consequently, one has not made it unusable (*Rav; Tiferes Yisrael* from *Ri* in *Tosafos*). [The rule that something which became *muktzeh* as a *base* remains *muktzeh* even after the object resting on it has been removed applies only to something which was a *base to muktzeh* at the *onset* of the Sabbath.]

5. I.e., we may push the hen from behind (*Tiferes Yisrael*) even with our hands, until it re-enters the house. [We may not, however, help her walk by holding her wings,

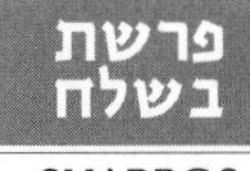

וְסַיָּחִין — *We may make calves and foals walk*[6] בִּרְשׁוּת הָרַבִּים — *in a public domain.*[7] אִשָּׁה מְדַדָּה אֶת בְּנָהּ — *A woman may make her child walk.*[8] אָמַר רַבִּי יְהוּדָה אֵימָתַי — *Said R' Yehudah: When?*[9] בִּזְמַן שֶׁהוּא נוֹטֵל אַחַת וּמַנִּיחַ אַחַת — *At at a time when he raises one foot and puts down the other;*[10] אֲבָל אִם הָיָה גּוֹרֵר אָסוּר — *but if he drags* his feet, *it is prohibited.*[11]

NOTES

since chickens have a tendency to jump and one will then find himself in the position of carrying the chicken, which is *muktzeh* (see Gemara 128b).] Other birds, such as geese, may be helped along, since they do not exhibit this tendency (*Rav* from Gemara ibid.).

6. I.e., we may hold them by their necks and sides, and move their legs (*Rav; Rashi*).

7. In the Mishnah printed with the Gemara, these words are missing. Indeed, the Gemara seems to indicate that animals may not be made to walk in a public domain (out of concern that one will pick them up and carry them). [Since the principle of *a living creature carries itself* applies only to human beings, not to animals, if one carries a living animal in a public domain, he is liable to a *chatas.* See above, 10:5 (*Tiferes Yisrael;* see also next note).]

8. I.e., she may walk in a public domain holding his arms from behind him, so that he will walk (*Rav; Rashi* from Gemara 128b). In this case, we need not be concerned that she may come to carry him, since even if she does, she is not liable to a *chatas.* As mentioned above, in the case of human beings the principle of *a living creature carries itself* does apply, so she does not violate a Biblical prohibition (*Tiferes Yisrael*).

9. I.e., in what case did the Tanna Kamma permit a woman to make her child walk in a public domain? (*Rav; Rosh*).

10. I.e., when the child is old enough that he will move his feet one at a time, picking up one foot and putting down the other. In this manner, he is considered to be walking, albeit with help.

11. I.e., if he cannot yet move his own feet, even if his mother holds his hand and drags him, it is tantamount to her carrying him (*Rav; Rashi*). Since the child is so young that he cannot walk without dragging his feet, the principle of *a living creature carries itself* does not apply to him (*Ran*). Moreover, although the wording used here (אָסוּר, *prohibited,* as opposed to חַיָּיב, *liable*) generally indicates a violation of a Rabbinic decree, in this specific case, where the mother is, in effect, carrying a child who cannot walk in a public domain, she is in violation of the Biblically forbidden *melachah* of carrying in a public domain (*Tos. Yom Tov*).

QUESTION OF THE DAY:

Why does the verse stress that Hashem Himself is at war with Amalek?

For the answer, see page 220.

GEMS FROM THE GEMARA

Apropos of our Mishnah, the Gemara (128a) discusses the *muktzeh* status of certain types of meat. Everyone is in agreement that raw, salted meat may be moved on the Sabbath, since salted meat, though uncooked, is edible as is. On the other hand, raw meat that is unsalted is the topic of a disagreement: Rav Huna says it is permitted to move it, whereas Rav Chisda says that it is forbidden to move it.

The Gemara questions the assertion that Rav Huna considers raw, unsalted meat to be non-*muktzeh.* Was not Rav Huna a disciple of Rav, who held in accordance with the view of R' Yehudah, who in turn held of a broad interpretation of *muktzeh* and who certainly considered raw, unsalted meat *muktzeh* (because it is set aside for human consumption, and it is unfit for that purpose in its present state)? How, then, can Rav Huna maintain that one is permitted to move it?

The Gemara answers that it is only in regard to eating *muktzeh* that Rav holds in accordance with the view of R' Yehudah — i.e., that it is forbidden to eat *muktzeh.* But concerning the *moving* of *muktzeh,* Rav holds in accordance with the view of R' Shimon, that it is permitted to move *muktzeh.*

The Gemara then questions the assertion that Rav Chisda forbids one to move raw, unsalted meat on the Sabbath: Can it be that Rav Chisda says with regard to raw, unsalted meat that it is forbidden to move it? Did not Rav Yitzchak bar Ami visit the home of Rav Chisda on the Sabbath, and see a certain slaughtered duck (which was unsalted and uncooked) that the servants were carrying from the sun to the shade, with Rav Chisda's permission? [Rav Chisda had said to them, upon observing the raw meat lying in the sun, "We see here a financial loss (should the meat remain in the sun)."] Thus we see that Rav Chisda permits the movement of raw, unsalted meat on the Sabbath. How is that to be reconciled with the view attributed to him above?

The Gemara answers that the raw meat of a duck is different from other raw meats (whose movement Rav Chisda *does* prohibit), for it is tender, and therefore fit to be eaten raw. Hence, it is not *muktzeh,* and may be moved in case of necessity.

A MUSSAR THOUGHT FOR THE DAY

From among all the enemies of the Jewish nation (and there have, sadly, been all too many over the ages), there seems to be an abundance of anger and animosity toward Amalek, to the point where we are commanded not to leave even a trace of them in this world. The question arises: Although their actions, as described in the Torah, were very evil, isn't it the way of the Torah not to hold onto anger, and certainly not to take revenge? Why, here, do we find such a blatant exception to this?

Ramban in *Sefer HaMitzvos* discusses this matter. In his comments on *Rambam's* listing of the mitzvos (§7), he explains that part of the mitzvah of remembering what Amalek did to us is to fully understand why Hashem commanded us to wipe out a whole nation such as Amalek. It was because of Hashem's compassion and love for Bnei Yisrael; Amalek had to be punished for what they stole from us when we left Egypt.

Sefer HaChinuch (in Mitzvah §603) elaborates on this point. He states that the Amalekim antagonized the Bnei Yisrael even before they were an established nation. When the Jews left Egypt, all the nations of the world were in awe of Hashem and the nation that He had chosen to bring glory to His Name, through all the miracles that had occurred in Egypt for the sake of Bnei Yisrael. This admiration and reverence that all nations had for the Jewish people dissipated after the Amalekim attacked them.

It would seem from these Rishonim that this encounter caused long-term damage to the image of the Bnei Yisrael. The *Ramban* called the attack of Amalek חָמָס, *thievery*. They did not attack to achieve some goal, such as possession of land or treasure. It was a battle for no other reason than to tarnish the status of the Bnei Yisrael in the eyes of the nations. And they succeeded in causing irreparable harm.

As *Rashi* says in *Parashas Ki Seitzei,* where Amalek's actions are described as אֲשֶׁר קָרְךָ בַּדֶּרֶךְ, which literally means *that they cooled you on the way* (*Devarim* 25:18): Amalek chilled you, and cooled you off from your boiling heat. For the nations were afraid to do battle with you, and Amalek came and began to do battle, and created a possibility in the minds of others. This can be compared to a boiling hot bath into which no person could descend. One scoundrel came and jumped into it; although he was scalded, he cooled it off for others (*Tanchuma* §9).

For merely *attacking* the Jewish nation, it is possible that forgiveness could have been achieved. But for permanently undermining the status of Bnei Yisrael, and thus minimizing the glory of Hashem, there is never forgiveness. Thus, the only end for Amalek can be total eradication.

פרשת בשלח

SHABBOS

PARASHAS BESHALACH

HALACHAH OF THE DAY

A knot that was tied unintentionally may be untied on Shabbos. This is due to the fact that the halachah defines a knot as an intertwinement made specifically for the *purpose* of holding something together. Since the knot was made inadvertently, it is not considered to be a knot at all according to halachah, and may be untied. Therefore, if one inadvertently tied a double knot on his shoes on Shabbos, he is permitted to undo it. Similarly, if while undoing a permissible knot, such as a bow, the string becomes tangled and turns into a forbidden knot, one is permitted to undo the knot.

While it forbidden to undo a knot, it is permissible to cut open a knotted rope, as long as it is cut in a destructive manner.

There are cases in which certain types of knots that normally may not be untied due to Rabbinic decree may be untied, depending on the circumstances. If one's inability to untie a knot causes one physical discomfort, he may open any type of Rabbinically prohibited knot. This includes a non-permanent double knot, a non-permanent single knot in a single strand of rope, and a knot and bow that were intended to remain in place for more than twenty-four hours. For example, if one's shoelaces are tied in a double knot and he wants to go to sleep, he may undo the knot in order to be able to remove the shoes. The Sages provided this dispensation in order to enable a person to alleviate his discomfort. However, this dispensation does not extend to knots that are prohibited Biblically, such as permanent knots.

Another case where the Sages allowed a Rabbinically prohibited knot to be untied is when the existence of the knot precludes one from performing a mitzvah. As an example, if a Sefer Torah that is necessary for the Torah reading had been tied up with a double knot, it is permitted to undo the knot so that the Torah may be read. However, even when a knot stands in the way of one's performing a mitzvah, one should not untie it if the difficulty can be circumvented in another way. For instance, if the *challah* that one needs for his Shabbos meal is in a bag that is tied up in a Rabbinically prohibited knot, one should not undo the knot. Rather, he should tear open the plastic bag in a destructive manner. [One should be careful not to tear any words or pictures on the bag when doing this.]

A CLOSER LOOK AT THE SIDDUR

In the prayer of *Emes VeYatziv,* which we recite after *Krias Shema* of *Shacharis,* we say: לְדֹר וָדֹר הוּא קַיָּם וּשְׁמוֹ קַיָּם וְכִסְאוֹ נָכוֹן וּמַלְכוּתוֹ וֶאֱמוּנָתוֹ לָעַד קַיָּמֶת, *From generation to generation He endures and His Name endures and His throne is well established; His sovereignty and faithfulness endure forever.*

At first glance, there seems to be no connection between the thoughts mentioned here. How does the fact that Hashem endures from generation to generation cause His Name to endure? What is the connection between the endurance of His Name and the establishment of His throne? And what is added by the final statement that *His sovereignty will endure forever*? *Bircas Yaakov* explains that this prayer is referring to the generations when Hashem's kingdom will be recognized universally, and He will be given His proper glory. That time will arrive only when the Bnei Yisrael are able to fulfill the command to eradicate all the offspring of Amalek. This will cause a completion of both Hashem's Name and His throne, for the verse states: כִּי־יָד עַל־כֵּס יָהּ מִלְחָמָה לַה׳ בַּעֲמָלֵק מִדֹּר דֹּר, *For there is a hand on the throne of* HASHEM; HASHEM *maintains a war against Amalek, from generation to generation* (*Shemos* 17:16). As we discussed in yesterday's *Mussar Thought for the Day, Rashi* explains that Hashem swore by His throne that His Name would not be complete and His throne would not be complete until the Amalekim were totally wiped out. Their very presence in the world is a continuing deterrent for the full establishment of the glory of Hashem.

When Mashiach comes, and Amalek is finally removed, then Hashem's Name will be complete. He will be referred to and recognized by His full Four-letter Name, and His throne will also be fully established.

This is the meaning of our prayer. We say that *From generation to generation,* meaning, when the generation that will be able to eradicate Amalek arrives, His Name and His throne will be fully established. Once this occurs, *His sovereignty will endure forever.* While Amalek survives, the nations do not realize the full majesty of Hashem (as we discussed in *A Mussar Thought for the Day*). But once Amalek is no more, His sovereignty and faithfulness will be established for everyone to recognize.

ANSWERS TO QUESTIONS OF THE DAY

Sunday:

According to one view cited in *Ramban,* this is to be understood as a *command,* never to return to Egypt (see *Devarim* 17:16).

Monday:

The Gemara in *Shabbos* (88a; see *Rashi* to *Bereishis* 1:31) tells us that Hashem stipulated with all of Creation that it would endure only if the Jews would accept upon themselves the Five Books of the Torah.

Tuesday:

Sforno and *Ibn Ezra* state that this verse teaches us that, miraculously, the Egyptians were drowning on the near side of the sea even before the Jews finished crossing to the far side.

Wednesday:

The Gemara in *Yoma* (75a) states that the righteous would find the manna each morning right outside their doors, while the wicked would have to search for their portions. Also, the manna of the righteous was ready to eat, while that of the wicked had to be ground and/or baked.

Thursday:

According to one opinion in the Gemara (*Yoma* ibid.), the manna could not assume the taste of cucumbers, melons, leeks, onions or garlic (see *Rashi* and *Iyun Yaakov* there for reasons).

Friday:

We find it in *Numbers* 21:8, where Hashem instructed Moshe to place a copper serpent on a pole so those who had been bitten by the fiery serpents would see it, direct their hearts to Hashem in prayer, and be saved (see Mishnah, *Rosh Hashanah* 29a).

Shabbos:

Likkutei Anshei Shem writes that Amalek is treated more harshly than Egypt and other nations, who sought only to oppress the Jews, while Amalek's target was not the Jews, but Hashem Himself.

This volume is part of
THE ARTSCROLL SERIES®
an ongoing project of
translations, commentaries and expositions
on Scripture, Mishnah, Talmud, Halachah,
liturgy, history, the classic Rabbinic writings,
biographies and thought.

For a brochure of current publications
visit your local Hebrew bookseller
or contact the publisher:

Mesorah Publications, ltd

4401 Second Avenue
Brooklyn, New York 11232
(718) 921-9000
www.artscroll.com